Finding
What You
Didn't Lose

Finding What You Didn't Lose

Expressing Your Truth and Creativity Through Poem-Making

John Fox, CPT

A Jeremy P. Tarcher / Putnam Book
Published by G. P. Putnam's Sons
New York

the trick of finding what you didn't lose
(existing's tricky: but to live's a gift)
the teachable imposture of always
arriving at the place you never left . . .
            —*e. e. cummings*

For permissions and copyright, see page 285
A Jeremy P. Tarcher/Putnam Book
Published by G. P. Putnam's Sons
Publishers Since 1838
200 Madison Avenue
New York, NY 10016

Library of Congress Cataloging-in-Publication Data
Fox, John, date.
Finding what you didn't lose : expressing your truth
and creativity through poem-making / John Fox.
p.   cm.
"A Jeremy P. Tarcher/Putnam book."
Includes bibliographical references and index.
ISBN 0-87477-809-3 (alk. paper)
1. Poetry—Authorship.   2. Poetry—Psychological aspects.
I. Title.
PN 1059.A9F68   1995   95-14638 CIP
808.1—dc20

Design by Chris Welch
Cover design by Susan Shankin
Front cover illustration by Ruta Daugavietis

Printed in the United States of America

1   3   5   7   9   10   8   6   4   2

This book is printed on acid-free paper. ♾

*Dedicated to
the voice of poetry
within us all*

Acknowledgments

Jim Fadiman, who got this started and then offered humor and wise counsel.

Terry Attwood, Beth Ferris, David Frawley, John Freeman, Adrian Griffin, Jeanie Lawrence, Katrina Middleton, Susan Livingstone Montana, Loraine Ballard-Morrill, Anjani O'Connell, John and Lynett Petrula, Alfred Robinson, Jacqueline Snitkin, and Jack Winkle—they listened, made suggestions, and asked for clarifications.

Susan Thompson, Dorothy Fadiman, Kai Totamotum, and Hans Liband taught me the blessings of sacred silence and words.

Dedicated poets in the California Poets in the Schools Program: especially Kimberley Nelson, friend, creative radical, and teaching collaborator.

Colleagues and friends in the National Association for Poetry Therapy: Joy Shieman helped me find what I hadn't lost, with originality and grace. Kathleen Adams offered her journal expertise and demonstrated to me every time we talked an ability to combine brainstorming, spirituality, and making plain sense. Sherry Reiter made important suggestions and told marvelous stories. Peggy Osna Heller by her example fueled my passion for poetry as healer.

To those in the Graduate School of Psychology at John F. Kennedy University in Orinda, California, who believe in the healing value of the creative arts: Dean Ron Levinson and Assistant Dean Ellyn Herb; Rhonda James, the director of the Expressive Arts program; Sterling O'Grady, administrative director; Jodie Senkyrick and Nancy Ghanim, faculty coordinators.

Gar Aikens, George Starbuck, Robert Kelly, Odysseus Elytis, and Mary TallMountain—teachers and poets who taught me about writing and life.

Mary Elizabeth Carmack (Beth) helped me to explore possibilities.

Caryl Kruse and Judith Butler did the meticulous gathering of permissions with great patience.

Mr. G. reminded me that humans aren't the only beings with poetic enthusiasm—and of the importance of long walks!

My parents, Jim and Eleanor Fox, gave their love and support.

Laurie La Berge offered her talent and time to many aspects of this book—and perhaps most of all, gave me greater faith in this project.

The fine people at Jeremy P. Tarcher, Inc., who make everything flow:

Susan Shankin designed a superb cover with the marvelous artwork of Ruta Daugavietis.

Lisa Chadwick, Allen Mikaelian, and Joyce Newill.

Laura Golden Bellotti, my editor, put unwavering attention and care into the making of this book. Her gift for seeing the essential helped me to say it well.

Jeremy P. Tarcher, who combines courage, vision, and common sense to make excellent things happen.

And most of all, for the poets and contributors to this book: the well-known, graduate students, workshop participants, school children, lovers of truth and creativity across the country—to all those who share the gift of themselves through poems and life stories . . . and to everyone above, I give my deep gratitude.

Contents

Introduction

Poetry does not consist in saying everything but in making one's dream everything.

—*Charles-Augustin Sainte-Beuve*

I want to tell you a story. Elements of this story apply to many of us who start out in life with a creative spark and even a delight in poetry, but have that delight snuffed out by adults "teaching" us about poetry. (And, usually, at the same time, insisting we get "realistic" about our lives.)

Sitting in a local diner with a group of friends, Edith told me about her son; Jeremy was just about to graduate from Brown University with a degree in science, but he had also written poetry since he was fifteen.

I was interested to hear about Jeremy because he represents the natural combination and new paradigm of scientist and poet—a balance that is deeply needed in our culture. I asked her if Jeremy had taken any creative writing courses while at Brown. Apparently, he had submitted some of his work, but there was great competition for a few class spaces, and he had not been accepted.

I told her that Jeremy's not getting into that class might not

Truth is such a rare thing, it is delightful to tell it.

—*Emily Dickinson*

have been such a bad thing after all. Maybe this way he might remain a poet much longer! Agreeing with me, Edith related the following story:

In some ways, I felt glad that Jeremy wasn't accepted into the poetry workshop at Brown University, not because I don't appreciate the fact that writing good poetry takes a lot of work, but because I think it is so easy to lose the spontaneous joy of creation when one is overly instructed. I remember an earlier time in Jeremy's life.

We had a walnut tree with a small treehouse in our back yard. When Jeremy was about five, he set up a little laboratory in his treehouse. He filled lots of jars with food coloring, vinegar, and baking soda—among other things—and mixed them together in many ways. "Potions" was the word he used to describe his concoctions. He had such a great time making his potions! Jeremy's experiments became something that his friends wanted to be involved with and they would all do experiments for entire afternoons. It was a fascinating type of play for Jeremy and his friends.

Finally the end of the year came and it was Christmas. My sister knew that Jeremy was interested in "potions" and she thought the logical next step was to buy him a chemistry set. Her reasoning was that it was time for him to move beyond food coloring, vinegar, and baking soda. Initially, Jeremy was happy to get the chemistry set, but soon he realized there were so many rules and dangers that required adult supervision that his joy in the process left him. That was the end of the potion era in our household. I think it came to a premature end because an experience that had initially been happily unfettered and free came up against all of these well-intentioned rules that left him with the fear of being wrong.

I see Jeremy's potions as a metaphor for his absolute happiness in messing around with whatever the creative process is. When he began to both play the guitar and write poetry at about fifteen, it felt very much like a return to the era of potions. The writing began when Jeremy had a serious ski accident and tore all the ligaments in his left knee. He had three operations in the next three years to repair that knee. Poetry and songs started to flow out of him and it wasn't because of an English class—he wasn't writing sonnets, rhymes, iambic pentameter, or whatever. In that sense Jeremy's music and poems, like

Writing a poem is like making an artifact. It is making something physical out of words.

—Galway Kinnell

Creativity is inherent in playing, and perhaps not to be found elsewhere.

—D. W. Winnicott

the potions, were intensely personal creations that were free of external rules.

I think Jeremy is going to become a marine biologist or maybe an environmental scientist but this other side of him, this poet self that he has developed, will continue to express and be a part of his life in many important ways. I don't think Jeremy is going to be a world-famous poet, but it is clear to me that his creative impulse is a core part of who he is.

It is unlikely that anyone using this book will become a world-famous poet, but that is not our purpose here; the intent of this book is to foster our creative delight in making "potions," a delight we probably enjoyed as children but then lost track of over the years. Why is it important to recapture the joy of creativity? Why begin the journey of poem-making if your goal is not necessarily to be a recognized poet?

There are many reasons. To begin with, you may indeed become a good poet. You may find deeper and deeper layers in your writing that will free your voice to articulate astonishing things. This is definitely possible. You may even publish some poems. And you may find that, like most "famous" poets, you write only a few lines here and there, now and then, that ring with perfection. But to write just those few lines is well worth it.

Your attraction to poetry writing may be the need to speak in your distinct voice about your unique experience. You may feel that there is no other way to speak about what is usually considered "unspeakable." You may delight in writing a poem to a loved one. You may be in love with words; and there is no better place to learn to love words than by writing a poem. You may wish to become a voice for justice, for those unable to speak. You may feel compelled to write during difficult times in your life, and you may learn that your poems help you to heal. And finally, you may just want to experiment with your poetic potential—out of curiosity and the challenge of exploring something new.

All of these reasons may be true for you at different times and in different places in your life, and all are good reasons to begin. Reading this book will put you in touch with people

He said he should prefer not to know the sources of the Nile, and that there should be some unknown regions preserved as hunting-grounds for the poetic imagination.

—George Eliot

The imagination is the secret and marrow of civilization.

—Henry Ward Beecher

whose lives have been broken at times, but who were deepened, healed, and renewed through writing poetry and discovering their poet within. It will also introduce you to those who have felt the enlivening joy and playfulness that writing poetry can give.

I have heard men and women on plane trips, in lines at the post office and photocopy store, in the classroom, in public workshops, on the phone, on walks by San Francisco Bay, in correspondence, and in cafés tell me their stories and share their poems. My experience is that these stories and poems not only come from the heart, but *are* the heart of these people's life stories.

The women and men in this book come from all walks of life, all lines of work, and gravitated to poetry for different reasons. Yet, through their writing, each has found what can only be called their unique and true words, culled from all the words they have ever learned over their lifetime. Writing poetry has made it possible for them to free their imagination and to express the full and amazing range of human feelings, insights, and questions.

Hurt, passion, courage, despair, joy, sadness, delight, fear, humor, anger, love, irony, whimsy, wonder, compassion—any of these emotions might be at the core of your poem. Your truth, whatever it might be, can find its most natural expression in the poem you write.

When we begin making poems, we begin sensing our world in a new way. We're struck by the poetic voice that resides within us all. Octavio Paz put it this way:

> *Between what I see and what I say,*
> *between what I say and what I keep silent,*
> *between what I keep silent and what I dream,*
> *between what I dream and what I forget:*
> *poetry*

Poetry-writing is a pathway to a place within yourself of sensitivity, growth, and transformation. Your writing can encourage a renewed connectedness with nature, with your most essential self, with your daily life, with those you love, with your community, and perhaps with God. By such connection, I'm not suggesting that writing poetry suddenly makes everything wonderful or easy. But when your poems become the "container" of your truest feelings, you will begin to experience and integrate those feelings more consciously.

Making poetry part of your life can give you a kind of peripheral vision, a new way to see your life and the path you are taking.

Just the other day, I received a letter from a student in the graduate psychology course I teach at John F. Kennedy University near San Francisco that describes her adventure of opening up to poetry. Marla is getting her counseling degree in the expressive arts:

> *I left your class with an expanded awareness of the depth and power of each simple word. Suddenly, the lyrics in songs on the radio are imbued with a depth I had not noticed before. Suddenly, I am thinking in more colorful language. Suddenly, I am creating poems spontaneously in response to the situations in my life; in response to the environment around me. I am discovering how poetry heals and expands the possibilities for growth and change and appreciation in my life.*

There are a number of books available on poetic craft, and many of them are excellent. This book will help your writing in that way, but it will do much more. It will connect you to the deep places of the heart and to the joy of making "potions" that is natural to us all. It will invite you to a hands-on experience with poetry, the insights from which can be applied to your life as a whole. The poems in this book represent a wide range of writing ability—from Nobel Prize winners to first-time poets. I have included all of them because their authenticity will inspire you to add your unique voice to this fellowship of poets. As you'll soon discover, poetry is within each of us. It's there waiting for you to find what you never really lost.

A good poet's made as well as born.

—Ben Jonson

[The function of poetry is] to nourish the spirit of man by giving him the cosmos to suckle.

—Francis Ponge

. . . Poets are not gnats in the wind.
They are dragonflies from the sun.
Come, burn your bliss in midair.
You are more needed than you know.
Be arsonists of the phoenix nest
          and glow!
                    —*James Broughton*

Return to the Most Human

The Need for Poem-Making in Our Lives

Our deepest desire is to share our riches, and this desire is rooted in the dynamics of the cosmos. What began as an outward expansion of the universe in the fireball ripens into your desire to flood all things with goodness. Whenever you are filled with a desire to fling your gifts into the world, you have become this cosmic dynamic of celebration, feeling its urgency to pour forth just as the stars felt the same urgency to pour themselves out.

——Thomas Berry

The poet is, after all, very human, a person who deals with the truth as he/she sees it, who writes about those special moments in life which have given him/her excruciating pain or joy.

——Judith Minty

To realize originality one has to have the courage to be an amateur.
——Marianne Moore

Return to the Most Human

Across the wall of the world,
A River sings a beautiful song. It says,
Come, rest here by my side.

. . .

Lift up your eyes
Upon this day breaking for you.
Give birth again
To the dream.
—*Maya Angelou*
    from On the Pulse of Morning

These lines from Angelou's poem are a reminder: being open to the language of your heart is a pathway to seeing life anew. The process of writing invites us to draw near to this river of inspiration. Your poetic words can give expression to all that you are. They can reach down into your dark hours, whisper the direct or mysterious language of your truth, reveal your tenderness and joy, shape a new consciousness through your creative imagination.

Rather than eliminating life's contradictions, poetry helps us integrate sorrow and joy, horror and humor with compassionate awareness. Through its condensation of language, poetry guides us to an understanding of the underlying unity in opposites which permeates our existence. And the sounds of poetry reach us at a depth that cognitive thinking cannot. Through poetry we enter spiritual passageways to the essence of what we feel. Your poetic voice can help you find your way, through dark and light. May Sarton speaks of this paradoxical journey in her poem, "Santos: New Mexico":

> *. . . We must go down into the dungeons of the heart,*
> *To the dark places where modern mind imprisons*
> *All that is not defined and thought apart:*
> *We must let out the terrible creative visions.*

I listen so that I may decipher the mystery of myself and become more whole.

—*Richard Moss*

Return to the most human, nothing less
Will teach the angry spirit, the bewildered heart,
The torn mind to accept the whole of its duress,
And, pierced with anguish, at last act for love.

Writing poetry can return you to your "most human." It can provide a meadow in which to share your love and joy, your loneliness and longing. A home for your bewilderment. A healing place for your anger. The paper on which you inscribe your poetry is a safe haven. It will not strike back at you; rather, it will give your imagination and feelings the space they need to breathe and wander, laugh and wail. Poetry draws out *your* unique voice and reaches *your* deepest feelings.

Truth and morning become light with time.
—*Ethiopian Proverb*

Ben's Story: "May I Read This to You?"

I was flying home to California from Baltimore, Maryland, and my seatmate was a businessman computing figures on his laptop computer. That moment in the flight when we realized we were sitting together in a fairly fragile space moving 30,000 feet up in the air, we began to talk and get to know one another. Ben ran a company that made specialized circuit boards for personal computers. When the conversation turned to me, I told him I was a poet. I told him that I showed people how they could use their own words to speak their truth, deepen their self-understanding, and expand their creative imagination. I was aware of how different our personal stories were. I said at that point, "I've found that most people, although they don't talk about it, have in some way or another been affected at a deep level by poetry or have written poetry themselves at significant times in their lives."

Ben became very quiet. His jaw softened. He looked into my eyes in a way that said he had suddenly recognized a friend. It was a vulnerable look that men do not often reveal to one another. His eyes said he had found someone who could listen to a wilder part of himself. Ben suddenly wheeled his burly body out of the seat and rummaged in the overhead bin. He sat down with a worn envelope in his hand and pulled out a folded piece of pa-

When a man does not write his poetry, it escapes by other vents through him.
—*Ralph Waldo Emerson*

per. I noticed the paper was fragile, old. I could see it had been through a lot. Yet I also sensed an enormous strength in what he was holding. I sensed it was a source of strength for him. The paper opened in Ben's hands like a bird's wings.

Ben asked, "May I read this to you?" "Yes, I wish you would," I said. Ben read a poem he had written, a poem about ardent memories of his youth. It was remarkable how fresh his memories sounded. Halfway through, the poem took a hard turn into his present midlife crisis. He looked directly at that crisis with those words on the page. It was not a remarkable poem in terms of craft, but in his awkward and lumbering effort to peel away somber layers of male silence, Ben had done a remarkable job. The poem described the terrain of youthful, inspired love and then the difficult but honored path of thirty-five years of marriage and the raising of children. In the writing of his poem, Ben had jumped into the void of the unknown that men fear most. He explored that country *between his dreams and his life*. He flew over it. He walked down into its valleys. He hiked to its peaks. And in the process, he had gathered something valuable. His words bridged a gap in his life that only he could traverse.

Ben read the poem to me but I knew he was delivering an important message to himself. No one else could have put these words into the unique pattern they formed. No one else could have spoken these words as he spoke them. No one else could communicate so intimately to him as he himself had done.

It was a joy for Ben to find someone who spoke a language seldom spoken, the language of poetry. Although we were strangers who spent only a few hours together, Ben and I were able to get beyond small talk and speak to each other from a deeper place within ourselves.

When we arrived at the San Francisco airport and saw one another standing at the baggage claim, we knew there was a simple but extraordinary knowledge that we now shared. It wasn't just that we had met and had conversation. On our flight together, we had visited a place not on our itinerary. What happened to us? The Swedish poet Tomas Tranströmer reflected on such an exchange: "The lesson of official life goes rumbling on. We send inspired notes to one another."

Then there is the listening at the gates of the heart which has been closed for so long, and waiting for that mysterious inner voice to speak. When we hear it, we know it is the truth to which we must now surrender our lives.

—Beth Ferris

A man who has no imagination has no wings.

—Muhammad Ali

Ben and I stood there for a few moments, waiting to pick up our luggage and go on with our lives—aware that by sharing a poem, we had broken through some ancient wall that no longer stood between us.

Finding Poetry in Our Everyday Life

When power leads man toward arrogance, poetry reminds him of his limitations. When power narrows the areas of man's concern, poetry reminds him of the richness and diversity of his existence. When power corrupts, poetry cleanses, for art establishes the basic human truths which must serve as the touchstone of our judgement.

—John Fitzgerald Kennedy at the dedication of the Robert Frost Library, October 26, 1963, Amherst College

We are deepened and enriched as a society when we value poetry and make time for it in our lives. Happily, there is a great renaissance occurring at the moment, as more poetry appears in public places and is exchanged among people in the course of their daily lives. Young people are flocking to coffeehouse poetry readings, former President Jimmy Carter is enjoying success as the author of a best-selling book of poetry, and Poets in the Schools programs are flourishing across America. And in every community throughout the country there are many more examples of how poetry's presence is being felt:

Human salvation lies in the hands of the creatively maladjusted.

—Martin Luther King, Jr.

ᘐ Patrice works in the district office of a large hi-tech organization. She and her co-workers struggled with a stubborn copy machine that kept breaking down in various fits. The corporation made commitments to replace the copier, but it was the "tomorrow that never came." Finally, Patrice and her officemates, in a moment of inspiration and exasperation, composed a poem as a way to once again make their request to the corporate office. Lo and behold, very soon after the delivery of their poetic plea, the copier was replaced. What's more, Patrice and her co-workers received a friendly poem from corporate headquarters in response to theirs.

- The city of Atlanta has constructed a contemplative seating arena featuring twelve bronze plaques with poems etched into them in their Detention Center Plaza. These original poems by Atlanta residents speak to themes such as facing hardship, making changes, and renewing one's life.

- In Philadelphia, Power 99 FM, one of the nation's largest urban contemporary radio stations, used prose passages and poetry from a book of African-American writings entitled *I Hear a Symphony* as part of their Black History Month presentation.

- Debra works at a book distributorship and takes orders over the phone. In the message area of the order form, she sometimes writes a few lines of poetry for the enjoyment of the warehouse staff, who read Debra's poems as they fill orders. Debra once wrote "god said eat more popcorn, it smells good." That line eventually became one in a series of poetry postcards that Debra now sells!

- In Washington, D.C., Andrew Carroll has created a nationwide volunteer effort called The American Poetry and Literacy Project. The project gives away new books of poetry to prisons, hospitals, public libraries, homeless shelters, nursing homes, schools, and other public places. The idea was initiated in 1992 by Nobel winner and former American Poet Laureate Joseph Brodsky. Brodsky and Carroll got together and the project has been running successfully with direction and inspiration by Andy Carroll ever since. So far, the project has distributed over 50,000 books of poetry across the country.

- Two U.S. Forest Service park rangers in northern California bring poetry writing into their work with park visitors. Ranger Roger Abe is third generation Japanese and a writer of haiku. He tells visitors at Alum Rock State Park, near San Jose, that blending haiku and nature walks will allow them to "explore the park and yourself at the same time, to reach a deeper you." The unlikely site of Ranger Mary Schumacher's

Poetry is written or read for real people: it should be a part of the gatherings where we make decisions about what to do about uncontrolled growth or local power plants, and who's going to be observer at the next county supervisor's meeting. Poets shine a little ray of myth on things; memory turning to legend.

—Gary Snyder

"poetry writing walks" is the infamous Alcatraz Island in San Francisco Bay. Ranger Schumacher says, "We could do this in Muir Woods, with all the drippy trees and the ferns, and it would have been a snap. You just walk into Muir Woods, and it's poetic. I want to find something challenging."

W Charles Rossiter, Ph.D., of Albany, New York, has created community-access television programming called *Poetry Motel*. Funded by the New York State Council on the Arts, programs are distributed to community stations in upstate New York, Long Island, and Massachusetts. Originated by Charlie in 1989, over a hundred programs of *Poetry Motel* have featured the works of local poets, regional poets, and poets of national renown.

W In Minneapolis, a poem by John Ashbery is inscribed on the girders on both sides of a pedestrian walkway that stretches across a busy highway, so that bridge walkers are able to read the poem coming and going.

One of the most significant and widespread ways that poetry is entering into public use is the increasing recognition of its healing power. Poetry to enhance healing is being written by people in diverse settings. Chapter Eight is dedicated to the specific topic of poetry therapy and healing, but at this point it's essential to acknowledge how valuable poetry can be in transforming our lives. The following story illustrates how learning to approach the world around us with a poet's sensibility can be a life-changing experience—even for those least likely to ever change. If poetic words have the capacity to make a difference in a circumstance such as the one that follows, imagine how it might make an even greater difference in your own life, contributing to the grace, wisdom, and enjoyment of living your life well.

A man's work is nothing but the slow trek to rediscover, through the detours of art, those two or three great and simple images in whose presence his heart first opened.

—*Albert Camus*

A Place for Miracles

. . . The instant
trivial as it is
is all we have
unless—unless
things the imagination feeds upon,
the scent of the rose,
startle us anew.
—William Carlos Williams

These lines from the William Carlos Williams poem, "Shadows," remind me of an astonishing story I heard from a colleague working in the field of poetry therapy. Val is the activities director in a convalescent hospital and frequently works with Alzheimer patients. It seems unlikely that something like poetry could make a difference for people with this reality-shattering condition, but the experience of one of Val's clients, a woman I'll call Pamela, proves otherwise. Pamela had not spoken a word to anyone for many years. Val tells what happened one day:

Pamela attends my poetry group at the convalescent hospital. Her tall, thin frame is usually slumped to one side of her huge, reclining wheelchair, and her left arm constantly sweeps over her head. She rarely opens her eyes and has not spoken in years. Her beauty speaks to you through her soft, white skin that has few wrinkles and bears the high cheekbones of regal elegance. She often wears a bright pink sweat suit that makes her fragile frame come alive.

During the group, which is meant to stimulate the five senses, I brought in a fresh rose and described it to her—the rich, red color of the petals, how they looked like velvet—and guided her hand to touch them. I likened the color to claret wine, expressing the sensation of its taste on the tongue. I held the flower close to her nose and encouraged her to smell the wonderful fragrance. I contrasted for her the difference between the softness of the petals and the roughness of

*B*eauty challenges the force of gravity. . . . To savour the beautiful means to glimpse complete goodness, an unconditional yes to life.

—Piero Ferrucci

the stem and its thorns. How the color of the leaves played their role in framing its beauty.

As I moved away toward another woman in the group, Pamela sat bolt upright in her wheelchair and said, "Yes, it is beautiful." These words echoed from one soul to another. She had found her voice through the sensation of descriptive feeling and the language of poetry.

At the end of each session, we sit in a circle and I read poetry, chosing at random from a selection of poems. As I read "An Autumn Morning" by Adeline White, the usual calm descended on the group. As I finished the last line, Pamela asked, "What is that poem called?" Her hearing of the poetry brought back her voice and literally opened her eyes to the world she had forgotten.

In hearing both Pamela's and Ben's story we might consider our real potential for awakening our poetic voice. For too long we have waited and allowed ourselves to live life without the scent of roses, without using our voices to respond to life's beauty—or to speak of our pain.

Three Things to Practice

A meditative practice of three dynamically interrelated activities will help awaken the poetic voice within you:

⩔ Breathing
⩔ Stillness
⩔ Listening

Poetry is a kind of meditation that slows me down and brings me back to myself.

—Allen Ginsberg

Breathing

A conscious awareness of breath in the creative process will give your writing power to go directly to the heart. You will find greater access to the power of poetry by practicing some form of meditation.

Attention to the breath brings us into the moment, and in the moment we have contact with feelings and sensations. In this way we become attuned to all the particulars of life. Such particulars—a cat's paw, the sound of the wind, the people assembled around your kitchen table—are what makes a poem sharply focused.

Breath infuses words with life. Words are made of more than syllables, more even than sound; you cannot speak a word without breath. Breath makes words alive; your words are made of your breath.

When you write, send your breath into your words. Do this by speaking your writing out loud. You will naturally be putting your breath into the words you write. Touch each line of a poem, or anything you write, with the signature of your breath.

Feel the unique life-breath of whatever you are writing about. For instance, if you write about a cat, sensitively tune in to the breathing of that cat. Through greater awareness of breath, you will develop a more intimate relationship with all that inhabits your daily life. Use your breath to feel and sense your way in the making of your poems.

> . . . *I sensed the surrounding expanse of forest-covered hills as if they were my own skin, feeling upon them the presence and movement of bobcat, deer, possum, turkey, beaver, and other creatures within the mile or two region that this tree had somehow brought within me. Like an artery delivering oxygen to constituent cells, I felt the river below breathing energy upward into the moonlit air.*
> —*Ken Carey, from* Flat Rock Journal

EXERCISES

Conscious Breathing

Read the passage by Ken Carey about his experience feeling the river "breathing" near his home in the Ozark Mountains. Just as he does, try to feel the breathing of someone, someplace, or something, and tune in to that breathing. What is the rhythm and quality of that breathing? How does it connect with your own feelings? How does it affect the atmosphere around you?

I will ask you to write down your impressions, but before you do so, take some time to become aware of your breathing. Let your awareness settle into your natural process of breathing. Don't attempt to "do" anything but *notice* the in-breath and out-breath. Allow your breath to flow naturally. Awareness of your incoming and outgoing breath provides a way to feel or cradle something in your mind and heart so that your newly conceived reveries can gestate, change, and flourish in a creative act.

_____

_____

_____

_____

Stillness

Stillness is where you meet with the essence of things. A natural result of noticing the flow of your breath is developing more inward and outward stillness. In stillness we can begin to let go of external voices, stereotypes, and clichés that crowd out original, personal, and internal feeling voices. Those discordant outer voices fade away in stillness. Stillness is a place of rooting oneself in a much larger field of being.

So often, we find ourselves imprisoned by the self we present to the world. We may know that we like to wear colorful T-shirts and old shorts, take walks on an empty beach in the morning, and ruminate haiku in our heads—as well as play the agile thinking corporate sophisticate in the meeting room. But in our pursuit of a career, that beachcomber-for-poems part of ourselves may recede from view. We forget to make time for the poet within.

There is a constant swarm of activity in our daily lives. When we vibrate to the same activity-buzz as everyone and everything around us, we lose touch with the remarkable inner place that can be an instant retreat, a place we can go to meet ourselves and God once again.

Loraine, who works in the fast-paced business of radio broadcasting, tells me she has memorized "The Lake Isle of Innisfree" by William Butler Yeats. She has spoken that poem aloud to herself so many times that the tranquil "Isle of Innisfree" has literally become an interior place for her, a place she knows like she knows her own home. She uses this poem to keep herself centered. She keeps a copy of it on her desk. She says it helps her to

When we understand how precious each moment is, we can treat each breath, each moment, as a newborn baby. Awareness can become that tender.

—Michelle McDonald

recall a sense of stillness. It becomes a source of inspiration and sustenance to her.

Stillness comes when one quiets the mind. Meditative breathing can help you to develop stillness. Without the practice of stillness, it is difficult to listen or hear. With the practice of stillness, listening becomes a joy.

While it may not be possible to retreat to the mountains or walk along the beach as often as you might like, it is certainly possible to take breaks that will help you recover a sense of inner peace and stillness. Making some kind of contact with nature is immensely renewing. You might begin by simply paying attention to your own nature—as expressed in your breathing.

> *Nothing but stillness can remain when hearts are full of their own sweetness, bodies of their loveliness.*
>
> —*W. B. Yeats*

Developing Stillness

Ⱳ Take a moment to *feel* your breathing. As you inhale, feel the sensations of your breath as it enters the nostrils. Perhaps it is cool. Allow your breath to fill your belly. As you exhale, breathe out the chatter in the mind. As you continue this mindful breathing, allow yourself to settle into a sense of stillness. Feel that just behind the ripple of your thoughts there is a deep stillness, like a still lake.

As you settle into this stillness, watch your sensitivity to feeling. Practice listening to the stillness. Sounds may come up but let them go. Feel the stillness from which those sounds arose. Do not strain to accomplish or think of anything, only attend to your next breath and sensitively feel. As you exhale, enter into the stillness. Allow your mind to quiet. Listen to and feel the voice of silence and stillness.

> *I swear, there is in me no wizardry of words.*
> *I speak to you with silence like a cloud or a tree.*
> —*Czeslaw Milosz*

Ⱳ The next time you find yourself near a tree or a rosebush, even if it grows on a city street, stand by it and *feel*. Slow down your pace, just be. Observe a bouquet of flowers at your home or in the office. Stop for a moment, feel the stillness that permeates the petals. Find a secluded place to sit by a lake or in a field. Pay attention to your breathing. Take your time. You might even do this while driving in the countryside. See and feel all of what is before you and within you. Let your breath flow and merge with the stillness. Be present with the form, colors, activity, and life-force of living things. Enter into the stillness one moment at a time. Feel the presence of everything that is alive within the stillness.

Listening

Listening is the path to intimacy. The practice of intimate listening reveals the interrelationship between all aspects of perception: thought, feeling, sensation, intuition, and spirit. Listening is a way to go beyond the rational, chattering, divisive mind and feel the language of connectedness among all things. Practicing this kind of deep listening helps your choice of words to be fresh and original:

> LISTEN
>
> *She is a woman*
>   *a woman with stars in her ears,*
> *Made just for listening*
>   *to unseen voices and unknown songs*
>
> *Listen . . .*
>
> *Listen to the willowtree sing*
>   *of sky reach and dark earth food*
> *An unwritten painting*
>   *of iridescent feathers and tickling worms*
>
> *Listen . . .*
>
> *Listen to the leggy foal play*
>   *cloudshadow chasing to hot milk*
> *It's an unsung drawing*
>   *of jumpgallopkick and mothersafe*
>
> *Listen . . .*
>
> *Listen to her very bones ache*
>   *at a scattered lifestretch*
> *Concealed wishes,*
>
>   *tasks incomplete, dreams still to do.*
>   —*Carole Dwinell*

The event of creation did not take place so many kalpas or aeons ago, astronomically or biologically speaking. Creation is taking place every moment of our lives.

—*D. T. Suzuki*

Nobody sees a flower— really—it is so small—we haven't time—and to see takes time like to have a friend takes time.

—*Georgia O'Keeffe*

Because everything is interrelated, in this listening and renewal of our own self, life itself is renewed. Hermann Hesse wrote this beautiful passage about the process of intimate listening and renewal in his classic book, *Journey to the East:*

> *As I approached the house of which I now knew every crack and fissure in its grey-green plaster, I heard the tune whistled of a little song or dance, a popular tune, coming from the upper window. I did not know anything yet, but I listened. The tune stirred my memory and some dormant recollections came to the fore. The music was banal but the whistling was wonderfully sweet, with soft and pleasing notes, unusually pure, as happy and as natural as the songs of birds. I stood and listened, enchanted, and at the same time strangely moved without, however, having any kind of accompanying thoughts. Or if I did, it was perhaps that it must be a very happy and amiable man who could whistle like that. For several minutes I stood there rooted to the spot and listened. An old man with a sick, sunken face went by. He saw me standing and listened too, just for a moment, then smiled at me with understanding as he went on. His beautiful, far-seeing old man's look seemed to say: "You stay there, one does not hear whistling like that every day." The old man's glance cheered me. I was sorry when he went past. At the same moment, however, I immediately realized that this whistling was the fulfillment of all my wishes, that the whistler must be Leo.*

I remember attending a spiritual conference many years ago at which the philosopher, writer, and founder of the Findhorn Community, David Spangler, was one of the major speakers. Those who had spoken prior to him had been very inspiring and the atmosphere was rich with a sense of brotherhood and spirit. Spangler stood quietly at the lectern in front of a thousand people, looking out at us for many moments before speaking. Then he simply said: "At a time like this, I want to be very, very quiet." Everyone in the auditorium sensed the profound, lovely intimacy of listening together.

There are many times in our day when we might simply listen to "the willowtree sing" or to our "very bones ache." When we might stand before life and say, "At a time like this, I want to be very, very quiet."

It is in those moments of listening we can begin to catch word phrases, feelings, and images—the suggestions of a poem's initial impulse. The first word of something already whole, something that will speak to you if you listen.

If one aspires to understanding and clarity in communication, one must first learn to listen with healing awareness, free from internal or external distractions. In this way opposites can be brought into balance and one may hear more directly the subtle messages of the Self, whether audible or inaudible.

—Frances Vaughn

Poetry is sometimes like going along in a big rig with no one else on the roads, no smoke, no stops by the wayside, going on with no cargo, the radio quiet, only the sound of your own voice trying to get in touch.

—Frank Stanford

EXERCISES FOR DEEP LISTENING

1. Take ten minutes, wherever you are, and practice listening. You can do it waiting for the bus, at work, at your kitchen table—anywhere. Feel that your listening is like a net you have cast out around you. Sounds are like tiny fish able to flow through your net of listening. Pay attention. Enjoy the process. Allow all these sounds to swim and flow through your net, and simply make note of them: Speaking sounds. Movement sounds. Doors opening and closing. Cars accelerating. Laundry sounds. Kitchen sounds. Office sounds. Nature sounds. Dogs barking. Planes overhead. Go beyond identifying the particular origins of these sounds and just listen to the ebb and flow of various sounds as if you were listening to a symphony. Listen attentively to the moment-by-moment frequencies and structures of the particular sounds you hear. Let them come and go.

    Now focus on one or two sounds as if they were a big enough fish to be caught in your net of listening. Listen intently to these sounds. Feel them. Let's say you hear a jet flying in the sky or dishes being washed in the sink. Where do you *feel* these sounds in your body? Can you feel the sounds of a jet engine rumbling low in your solar plexus or of kitchen plates clattering somewhere between your ears? Listen for how sounds can correspond to places in your body. Write down your impressions and feelings, exploring connections between sounds and where you feel them in your body.

2. Sit in a restaurant and listen to the people talking around you. Listen for the range of emotional tone in their voices. Do you hear boredom, curiosity, passion, light-heartedness, anger, hurt, distraction, happiness? Now listen to the various emotions expressed through their choice of words. Do the emotional tones of people's voices match the particular words

they choose? Listen also for expressive modes of speech: slang, idioms, accents, tones of voice.

3. Listen for how particular words feel to you—not just their meaning, but primarily their sound and how they move. For instance, words like "grace" and "harsh." What does the sound of the word "grace" feel like when you hear it? Is it fixed in space—like the word "rock"—or does it flow and spread out in a more subtle way? What image illustrates the *sound* of the word "grace"? What about the word "harsh"? Is it a word that sounds rough? Cutting? Hard? Do the consonants at the end of "harsh" press it down into a tight space in your mouth? What kind of image does the sound of the word "harsh" bring up?

    If you were to make hand movements to demonstrate visually the sounds made by the words "grace" and "harsh," what would those movements look like? If a word could come alive and dance, what would its dance be? Experiment with listening to and getting to know the sounds of words—not just what they mean, but how they feel and move *based on their sound*.

Receptivity and Permission

Receptivity

I offer you two general suggestions for beginning the writing process and for keeping the flow of creativity as active as possible. The first suggestion is: Receptivity.

The greatest writers of all time had to deal with exactly the same thing as you when it came to putting a word down on an empty page. Each time they sat down, they also had to trust that the words would come to them—once they became receptive:

I never know when I sit down just what I am going to write. I make no plan. It just comes and I don't know where it comes from.
—D. H. Lawrence

You can consciously prepare yourself to practice trust and receptivity. Sink into your center with meditative breathing. Practice stillness and listening. Let yourself open in this way to each moment. Let your awareness gradually become keen and still. As you become still, concentrate on what is happening right now, what is coming up in the moment. Listen to what the Quakers call "the still small voice." Pay attention to what Zen Master Suzuki Roshi calls your "big mind"; observe and listen to what is happening. Open to your feeling; allow yourself to free-associate.

> That everything is included within your mind is the essence of mind. To experience this is to have religious feeling.
>
> —Shunryu Suzuki Roshi

Here is how one poet describes the methods she uses to enter into her writing. Her simple words are comparable to the practice of meditation that will allow you to tap into your "big mind":

> Concentration; observation; losing myself.
>
> —Sandra McPherson

How can you set this process of receptivity into motion? As you begin writing, you might want to use what is called an "entrance meditation." Entrance meditations act as affirmations or prayers to support the flow of your words. An entrance meditation is used to center yourself. It will help to focus your intention and allows you to concentrate on your writing process. Concentration and observation can be compared to threading a needle. Putting the thread through the eye of a needle is like losing yourself completely in whatever it is you wish to write about.

> Talking to paper is talking to the divine. It is talking to an ear that will understand even the most difficult things. Paper is infinitely patient.
>
> —Burghild Nina Holzer

An entrance meditation can be a simple and silent kind of prayer. Not a formal prayer, but a gesture to connect with your Muse. You will discover a way of doing this that is personal and especially right for you.

Over twenty years ago when I asked Ram Dass, my medita-

The absolute requirement for creativity is blindfolding the Judge. The first part of the creative process needs to be free of inhibitions. Later on, when ideas are fully formed, there is plenty of time to scrutinize them.

—Joan Borysenko

It is my heart that makes songs, not I.

—Sara Teasdale

tion teacher at that time, how to write poetry from a deeper place within myself, he said, "Take five deep breaths into your heart chakra and ask the ethers for poetry." His advice may sound a bit Eastern and esoteric for some, but I think his essential advice had to do with practicing receptivity.

HOW TO PRACTICE RECEPTIVITY

You can use the following as further guidelines for practicing receptivity:

⩗ Watch to see if an image flickers through your mind, because that is a good way to start a poem. If an image comes, ideas and feelings will be attached to that image. This "catching" of flying images takes practice. So practice!

⩗ Try to keep an image flow going. When we begin to write, the original impulse often gets lost and so do we. After you've got the initial feeling and image, sit very quietly and ask yourself: What do I really mean to say? What would I say if no one in the whole world but me were going to see this? What did I want to write about anyway?

⩗ Don't worry about big ideas or where you are going. If you knew where you were going, you wouldn't need to write a poem to find your way.

⩗ Keep your pen (or word processor) moving, even if what you write sounds silly. Be open to whatever flows from your thoughts, feelings, imagination.

⩗ Don't erase, don't worry about spelling or grammar.

⩗ And finally, don't feel you will always know at the time you write something how it is meant to turn out. An unused fragment from five months ago may suddenly call for your attention and be just the right piece to weave into a current piece of writing. Receptivity includes remaining open to your unused writing. For that reason, don't throw anything away. Keep your writing in a folder. Nothing is wasted.

The actual materials are important. A book at the nightstand is important—a light you can get at—or a flashlight as Kerouac had a brakeman's lantern.

—Allen Ginsberg

Permission

The next general suggestion for writing practice is to give yourself: Permission.

The key to writing isn't thinking or analyzing or planning. It's permission. Give yourself *permission*. I offer it to you with all my passion for this work and all the tenderness I have to encourage the emergence of your creative spirit.

But giving ourselves permission is not always an easy thing to practice. The process of writing, while helped by a meditative attitude of openness, does not always feel as open as we might wish. What we usually notice is that the biggest block to a receptive stance in writing is the insistent editorial drone that cuts off our initial impulses. The picayune nature of that editorial voice can be maddening and cause us to feel "What's the use?" or "Why even begin?" These are our "censor voices" that intimidate us with their puffed-up certainty.

One way to deal with your censor voices is to get clear about what their messages are—and talk back to them in a way that supports and bolsters your creative flow. Answering them clearly will help cancel out their power to enforce blocks on your creativity. Answering them directly will give you the permission you deserve to follow the flow of your imaginative ideas.

Talking Back to the Censor Voices

I once had a superb teacher who said that people who say they want to write but don't, don't write either because:

1. They don't want to write, or
2. They don't trust themselves to write.

Within those two reasons for not writing are a range of voices that make "reasonable excuses" for you. Perhaps the voice says you should only write if something significant or distressing happens in your life. Maybe it tells you you'll never produce anything publishable.

The fact that you've chosen to read this book means that, even if you don't quite trust yourself, you at least have the desire to write and perhaps you just need some assistance getting those inner critics off your back. When we distrust our creative impulses, it usually involves voices of shame and perfectionism.

Shame may sound something like this:

Ⱳ Why bother with anything as "intangible" as poetry? It's silly. Where is the money?

I willingly trust myself to chance. I let my thoughts wander, I digress, not only sitting at my work, but all day long, all night even. It often happens that a sentence suddenly runs through my head before I go to bed, or when I am unable to sleep, and I get up again and write it down.

—Simone de Beauvoir

The poet is the one who breaks through our habits.

—St. John Perse

- How can you spend time creating poems when there are so many more important things to do?
- Using poetic language just makes people uncomfortable. Expressing your insights and feelings makes them even more uncomfortable, and what's worse, it's self-indulgent!
- When will you grow up? Spouting off wild and weird musings was okay at twenty-one—but you need to start living in the *real* world!

Perfectionism tells you the following:

- You are never going to be good enough to be a "real" poet. Give it up.
- Look at that cliché! Look at that weak verb! Look at how that one phrase in your poem ruins *everything*. So what if you write many good lines and images! This poem is a *total* mess!
- I really want to do the very best I can. I am sincere, I really am. But I can't start writing, not just like that! I have to get ready first. There are some things I have to make sure I know really well before I begin. I need to read more books about craft. Listen to what experts have to say—then maybe I can start. But first, I'll make sure (once again) that this desk drawer is organized. . . .

There is a way to respond to these voices that prevent us from tapping our creativity. After we've let them clearly state their reasons for standing in our way, we can talk back to them. Let's listen to some more of these "censor" voices as well as some empowering "permission" responses:

Censor Voices	Permission Voices
What I have to say is not worth anything.	No one else can say what you have to say. Your thoughts and feelings are nowhere else to be found.
I have no imagination.	Your imagination is a birthright. You cannot lose it but you can forget you have it.
I can't write.	Was that a message you got in school? You do not have to please anyone else with your writing.
I got bad grades in English.	This is not an academic process. There are no grades.
I was so superb in English literature and criticism, I would feel embarrassed to attempt writing poetry myself. I know how great other writers are.	*To realize originality one has to have the courage to be an amateur.* *——Marianne Moore*
It's hard for me to get started.	There is no rush. Let the exercises in this book get you started.
I don't know if I want to share my writing.	You don't have to share. Write first for your own eyes. You may choose to share and find it liberating. Give your writing first to God, She's up all night anyway.
I am afraid of criticism.	First have the courage to accept your own writing. Then, you may choose to share it with people who will both strengthen and nurture your process of writing.
I don't understand poetry.	There is no one answer to what poetry is. It's like riding a bicycle—your emotional muscles will help you find your way.

I don't want to commit ugly feelings to paper.	Then why do you let these feelings stay rent-free in your head? Let them out, write them out and let them go.
Self-expression is not important to everyday life.	That may be true. But do you really want to live an "everyday" life?! Self-expression is what makes every day new.
I used to dream like a poet but I gave it up when I was young. Dreaming is not essential to my life now.	*Hold fast to dreams for if dreams die life is a broken winged bird that cannot fly.* *—Langston Hughes*
Writing about my feelings seems self-indulgent.	There is nothing self-indulgent about expressing feelings. You're worried about spending 89¢ for a notebook?
My writing never comes out good enough.	God didn't say "That's good!" until *after* he created everything. Don't let your perfectionism and judgmental mind interfere with the creative process.
My spelling is bad.	Your spelling does not matter in the writing process. This isn't school.

If there are "permission" responses listed here that speak to your issues about writing, write them down on a 3 × 5 card and keep them with you or put them wherever it is that you write. Memorize your permission responses. Say them out loud as an affirmation. The most powerful catalyst to begin the adventure of poetry writing is your desire to get on with it. It is that simple!

"O Life of the Questions . . ."

Resistance is not always something to discard in your writing. If the oyster cast every grain of sand out of its shell, it would be poor of pearls. *Writing* about that resistance may sometimes be a better solution to resistance than trying to cancel it out with an affirmation. Exploring your resistance may actually reveal that deep part of yourself that feels most passionate about poetry. It could be a place to dive for pearls. Your resistance may be close to the origin of your poet's voice.

What do I mean? The very place inside where you feel resistance toward poetry may be where your poet's voice was first awakened and still resides. Many people feel distant from poetry because in their first experience of expressing their poetic voice and truth, they felt neither listened to nor recognized. This may not be true for everyone, but it is for many of us.

What we were "taught" in school may have left us feeling cold. Teachers may not have realized that poetry has *first* to do with *your feelings*. They may not have treated poems or writing as if it has to do with *your real life experiences*. There may have been no attempt made to read poetry that related to what you might be feeling about life.

Perhaps you already had the sensitivity, imagination, and energy of a poet, but no one responded to you on that level.

I had an English teacher in high school who locked the door to the classroom after the bell rang. In many ways, he was an excellent teacher who demanded excellence of us, but his class was *very* serious business. I remember the way he leaned forward over his desk in an imposing way. He grasped a heavy Norton anthology in his hands as he sat there. We recited aloud long poems like "Snow-Bound" by John Greenleaf Whittier. To me, at the time, it was an old, long poem from another time. Worse, I was made to recite it even though I was petrified to speak in front of my classmates. I stuttered badly at that time and so I was embarrassed. Perhaps you were forced to memorize the words of poems but never encouraged to breathe in their inspiration. Inspiration was never talked about in my high school English class.

It was only later I realized that Mr. Crossman not only locked us *into* that room—he also locked us out of a meaningful relationship to poetry. This wasn't just poetry for prisoners—he also made us prisoners of poetry! No wonder people grow up feeling poetry is dull and irrelevant.

I also had marvelous teachers who were tremendously supportive of my poetry writing and who served as mentors during high school, teachers to whom I still feel a deep sense of grati-

Education is not the filling of a bucket but the lighting of a fire.

—*W. B. Yeats*

The sublimest song to be heard on earth is the lisping of the human soul on the lips of children.

—*Victor Hugo*

tude. Seeking those teachers out, letting them know how important poetry was to me, is what made the difference.

But many of us were not given the chance to discover the kind of fierceness, joy, and passion that poetry offers. In the movie *Dead Poets Society,* Professor John Keating, played by actor Robin Williams, speaks of this passion:

> . . . *You will learn to savor words and language. No matter what anybody tells you, words and ideas can teach the world. We don't read and write poetry because it is cute. We read and write poetry because we are members of the human race. And the human race is filled with passion. Medicine, law, business, engineering—these are noble pursuits and necessary to sustain life. But poetry, beauty, romance, love—these are what we stay alive for. A quote from Whitman: "O, me. O life of the questions. Of these recurring. Of the endless trains of the faithless. Of cities filled with the foolish. What good amid these O me? O life." Answer? That you are here and life exists. Identity. That the powerful play goes on and you may contribute a verse. What will your verse be?*

The pressure of daily living often makes it difficult to pay attention to the deep beauty poetry celebrates or to answer the question; *what will your verse be?* Working hard and dealing with life's challenges often claims our lives to the extent that our poetic voice remains submerged. It is often during times of distress, when our heart has been wounded, that we find that voice once again.

A Part That Usually Remains Hidden

What we don't learn in school is that poetry and poem-making is related to the soul. The Sufi teacher, musician, and poet, Hazrat Inayat Khan, said:

> *In poetry the rhythm of the poet's soul is expressed. There are moments in the life of every human being when the soul feels itself rhythmic. At such moments children, who are beyond the conven-*

*tionalities of life, begin to dance, to speak in words that rhyme, or
to repeat phrases that resemble each other and harmonize together.
It is a moment of the soul's awakening. . . .*

*Among all the valuable things of this world the word is the
most precious. For in the word one can find a light that gems and
jewels do not possess; a word may contain such life that it can heal
the wounds of the heart.*

We sense that poetry is related in some essential way to spir-
ituality. It is because of our inborn sensitivity to this that we are
attracted to the creative use of language. Our soul responds with
energy to our desire to grow—and creates poetry. Poetry says
things in ways that no other kind of communication can. When
we write poetry, it is possible to not only "heal the wounds of the
heart," but liberate our imagination. Reading and writing poetry
is a secret bridge to a part of ourselves that is sacred. Someone
once wrote to me about how my poetry had made a difference
in her life:

*I know that your sensitivity and beautiful poetry help me to con-
nect with the very same in myself, a part that usually remains hid-
den, silent, and well protected. Your courage to open and share such
a personal and vulnerable part of the soul is a gift and inspira-
tion.*

Giving voice to those aspects of ourselves which usually re-
main hidden—the sensitive, beautiful, vulnerable, and coura-
geous as well as the dark, the shadow, the rage, the anguish—this
is what our attraction to poetry is all about. Our connection to
poetry is deep and very personal. We are not likely to reveal this
depth readily to others, if at all. Whether we're a successful,
powerful person or someone struggling with self-doubt and lack
of direction, this hidden part of ourselves is essential to our be-
ing. It takes great courage to reveal this side to others—or even
to ourselves.

There is another word to remember in addition to permission
and receptivity. That word is: Aliveness. Onie Kriegler, a work-

*Fortune sides with he who
dares.*

—*Virgil*

*That is at bottom the only
courage demanded of us: to
have courage for the most
strange, the most singular and
the most inexplicable that we
may encounter.*

—*Rainer Maria Rilke*

shop student, wrote a poem about the courage to feel what she called "this living."

> There are a few ways at least to ride this ride.
>   This living,
> mouth wide open. Knuckle's white, hair defying gravity
> for a time. A few ways at least,
> feet aloft, sensations surging through bodies
> like they are blood. Fingering old bruises
> to feel safe. A few ways at least to ride this ride.
>
> Hard cold metal, soft grips for hands, is there a
> soft grip for my heart?
> Captive for a time in a spinning chaos, holding on for
> dear life,
>   Dear Life, are you worth holding on to?
> Once I let you go for a time, this releasing
>   created the courage to keep on riding.

Poetry is a real feeling flowing within each of us: "sensations surging through bodies / like they are blood." We need the poetic in our lives to be fully nourished. This need is as real as the need of cells in our body for food and the ocean's need for rivers.

EXERCISE: POETRY AND THE LANGUAGE OF THE SOUL

Say this poem by Langston Hughes aloud to yourself and feel the words flow within you, like your blood. Notice the way the spaces in the poem on the page make its emphasis clear. Take time to memorize part of this poem. Let your voice flow like a river as you say it:

THE NEGRO SPEAKS OF RIVERS

I've known rivers:
I've known rivers ancient as the world and older than the
flow of human blood in human veins.

My soul has grown deep like the rivers.

I bathed in the Euphrates when dawns were young.
I built my hut near the Congo and it lulled me to sleep.
I looked upon the Nile and raised the pyramids above it.
I heard the singing of the Mississippi when Abe Lincoln
went down to New Orleans, and I've seen its muddy
     bosom turn all golden in the sunset.

I've known rivers:
Ancient, dusky rivers.

My soul has grown deep like the rivers.

                                    —*Langston Hughes*

"In the Belly of the Beast, the Heart Sits Just Above"

You are invited to explore this ancient river of yourself and your world, drawing from the creative and healing energies of other poets and poetry. Your own writing will be a path to finding and developing qualities we all have within us: sensitivity, strength, passion, clarity, and courage.

I mentioned earlier the radio news director in a major East Coast city who memorized the Yeats poem. Loraine heard me speak about the healing nature of poetry and wrote to me about why she feels poetry is vitally important in her life. I think her unglamorous comments are significant because she lives inside the media beast which has such a pervasive impact on our lives:

> *Each morning I read a litany of the world's pain. Tens of thousands of Rwandan refugees dying . . . six-year-old girl shot and killed after celebrating her birthday. The news provides an entirely negative filter on reality. The worst thing is, this suffering is never touched by the heart. The phrase I can think of is: "life out of balance."*

Literature is news that stays news.

                                    —*Ezra Pound*

Poetry opens up my peripheral vision. As a broadcaster I know I'm really narrowcasting—presenting a scene of reality reduced to three minutes including sports and weather. Poetry takes me to the undiscovered places in my heart and mind. It's a place to travel after I've slogged through yet another story on O. J. Simpson. It's a place to release pent-up feelings.

This woman's frank comments about "narrowcasting" the news of our world and her desire to find meaning in her personal world through poetry remind me that we all might listen for "the heart" in the midst of painful change. Mary Kelly, a therapist and maker of ceremonial masks and dolls, writes of the importance of this deep presence of heart:

In the belly of the beast
   the heart sits just above.
      Beating
      Reminding
I am here. I am here.

Through the storms,
   the knots, the
      gnashing teeth
I am here. I am here.

Disappointment, hurt, frustration howl.
I am here. I am here.
   I stretch. I hold it all.
I embrace your pain. I
      enfold
your fury.
      I am here.
         I am here.

The voice of the poet that says, *"I am here."* Why should this matter to us? Perhaps, after all, it is about simplicity, as poet Gary Snyder reminds us:

In this era of light shows, huge movie screens and quadraphonic sound systems, it is striking that an audience will still come to hear a plain, ordinary unaugmented human being using nothing but voice and language. That tells us that people do appreciate the compression, the elegance, and the myriad imageries that come out of this art of distilling language and giving it measure which is called poetry.

T w o

Leaving the Roots on Your Writing

Revealing Yourself in Your Poems

A good word is like a good tree whose root is firmly fixed and whose top is in the sky.

—The Koran

You can smell a poem before you can see it.

—Denise Levertov

A little too abstract, a little too wise,
It is time for us to kiss the earth again,
It is time to let the leaves rain from the skies,
Let the rich life run to the roots again . . .
—Robinson Jeffers

Just to Make It Clear

THESE DAYS

whatever you have to say, leave
the roots on, let them
dangle

> And the dirt
>> Just to make clear
>> where they come from
>>> —Charles Olson

This chapter will explore the many ways of getting into your feelings so that your poems will be vibrant and alive. Olson's poem welcomes our truth. It invites us to tell about those aspects of ourselves we tend to conceal. It asks us to get to the root of our story, even if it's about the darkness or the shadows, the unpleasant underpinnings, the dirt. You can write about everything fecund and juicy. You can write what is wild for you. You can show where your roots go.

Olson is also saying to use words that are alive. Poetry need not be soft, sentimental, or sweet. Olson's image of dangling roots and clinging dirt reminds us that our words are more than just ink on the page, more than just a thought about something.

The sound of the word, like the root of a plant, is essential. A word *is* sound. Listen to the sounds of words you choose—say them out loud. Do they help you to feel the roots of what you are expressing? Even if you didn't speak English, would you be able to sense part of the meaning of your poem from its sounds?

EXERCISE: ESTABLISHING SOUND ROOTS IN YOUR WRITING

Take words like green pepper. Say "green pepper." Say it until it becomes just a sound: green pepper, GREEN PEPPER, *green pepper* . . . let your tongue and lips roll over both words. Imagine that you are holding a green pepper, or get a green pepper and hold it. As you feel it, breathe in. Feel its weight. Its curvaceous shape. The spaciousness inside. The smoothness of its skin. The vivid green. Can you see hues of purple and red? Feel its sensual, even erotic, symmetry? Smell and taste the refreshing tang. Sense the green pepper so that the words you choose to describe it help you to feel its green pepperness.

Words That Flare Out of Experience

When I lead workshops and people share their spontaneous poems, one of the first qualities people recognize in the atmosphere of the place we are gathered is that there is a deepened level of genuine intimacy. People begin to leave "roots" and "dirt" on their words. This intimacy is first a self-honesty, which then extends into the group experience.

The words of the workshop members become imbued with feeling, and an alignment with authenticity grows. What members share is more than the words on the page. Their words flare out of the fire of their experience. What follows are the poems and stories of Rosemary, Jeremy, Mary-Lee, Connie, and John, and their experiences of writing from their roots.

ROSEMARY

Rosemary Sharon MacKenzie writes during a major transition in her life about going down into a dark place to wait, to feel her roots:

> THE SOLSTICE
>
> pressing in dark, heavy, black
> as ink; enveloping, closing in,
> descending down; to squeeze out
> the last of the light.
>
> what to do but wait.
> wait until the dark
> has its way.
>
> wait until it can get no darker
> no blacker, and no
> more oppressive.

It is with words as with sunbeams. The more they are condensed, the deeper they burn.

—Robert Southey

Poetry is a human art, and we're really talking about our lives, and poetry which is most readable is that which is most intimate and touching.

—Diane Wakoski

then it will turn.
then the whole earth will turn.
a seed of light will shimmer
between the cracks in the rock
and grow.

it will grow, and gain in strength,
put down roots until a leaf
of light bursts free
to hold the frightened world.

Deep silence was felt in the pauses between the lines and stanzas of Rosemary's poem as she read it. The silences had the same value as the lines of her poem, and like each breath, drew us more deeply into contact with the experience of her life. We felt the noble capacity of the human being to trust an unknown, inner process. We felt behind the poem the alluring mystery of darkness and light, death and life, roots and leaves.

Knowing how to listen to and be fully present in life, with your senses, heart, and mind, is the key to writing with this kind of intimacy. Deeply listening to what is within and around us changes us. And listening and intimacy are related—like the body and breath. Intimacy in your writing means you're communicating on the deepest level with whoever hears or reads your poem—even if the only one to hear it is you.

How to encourage more roots in your writing? How to know intimately who you are? *How to hold the frightened world?* Writing about painful circumstances that we see around us is one way. When we deal in our writing with the disquieting truths about the world in which we live—truths others may wish to avoid—such an experience is a way of keeping ourselves spiritually alive.

JEREMY

Jeremy Eddy, the young poet whose story I told in the Introduction, wrote a powerful poem about a dying man he got to know on a city street. Notice how deeply Jeremy *sees* another human being, how he sees this man just as he is, without

---

The woman's place of power within each of us is neither white nor surface; it is dark, it is ancient, it is deep.

—Audre Lorde

Almost all of our sadnesses are moments of paralysis of feeling when we can no longer hear our surprised feelings living.

—Rainer Maria Rilke

shying away from what is unpleasant. Seeing this man's life as it is both honors that man and somehow brings the poet closer to himself:

WALTER?

I know the AIDS man is dead
His face was dirty black; his eyes red
I know he's dead; I can feel it

He used to stand on the corners of streets
Leaning into the world; he used to
Hold his hand outstretched; sad-like and infinite

He'd stop me and we'd talk sometimes
I think his name was Walter
Just to hear him talk was like listening

To an ancient motion picture; a movie view
Of the life I never knew, like a hundred
Gospel singers, lined up in rows

Singing him to heaven.
His spirit roams the gutters of his own
Empty streets. His jive soul strollin'

Through the heat of the night. I remember
Times he'd smell like death but he'd hang
on and talk to me; spin those golden

Stories like threads in a man's tapestry;
His only possession in this cold world.
And I'm buying him food; talking

Politics and still I watch him die
I watch him die, the death of a man
With nothing but pride and a tattered

Coffee cup he holds in the street; he holds
Out to the world and says, "Please,
Will you help me?"

The lines "He used to stand on the corners of streets / Leaning into the world; he used to / Hold his hand outstretched; sadlike and infinite," would not enter our hearts in such a deep and powerful way if they didn't touch on some common ground. The words "leaning" and "infinite" come from truly seeing this man, the kind of seeing we miss when we pass and disguise our annoyance or hurriedly drop a coin in his cup.

Another place to find our roots is when we begin to love ourselves. Stephen Levine says that the person we most want to hear say "I love you" is *ourself.* Learning to accept ourselves "with no part left out" is gradual work. Times of disappointment, rejection, and despair offer us the painful opportunities to do this difficult work. Dropped into the abyss, we must give ourselves time to find our wings and sing.

MARY-LEE

Mary-Lee McNeal tells her story of being torn apart by grief and then healing herself through the renewing spirit of poetry. She tells of roots that were born of a human cry, of profound primal sound. This cry is the essence of her reclaiming. In fact, the Latin word *reclamare* means "to cry out." Mary-Lee says:

> When I was flattened with grief a few years ago, I turned to poetry the way the faithful turn to religion, and in the reading and later the writing of poetry, I found a way to survive.
>
> It happened one day when I stood staring out a window, watching the rain. I was so overcome with the loss of someone I'd loved that I wondered how I would take the next breath. I turned to the bookshelf where my Norton anthology sat. (It isn't that I hadn't read and enjoyed poetry, or even written it before this time, but poetry was one of life's pleasures—something very different from what it became that day.) I opened the book to a poem I'd studied in a class some months before, and something happened.

The only thing that can save the world is the reclaiming of the awareness of the world. That is what poetry does.

—Allen Ginsberg

It is possible that the scream comes from the forsaken body, the scream that manifests in a symptom is the cry of the soul that can find no other way to be heard. If we have lived behind a mask all of our lives, sooner or later—if we are lucky—that mask will be smashed.

—Marion Woodman

The poem was Robert Graves's "Lost Love." Its hyperbolic language became an arrow that pierced a membrane I'd worn around my life until that moment. Waters came rushing out, tears I'd stored for a lifetime. Graves was describing a person so "quickened by grief" that he saw through flint walls, he heard grass drinking, he heard ants groan. I was no longer alone. And I was no longer flattened by my grief, I was quickened.

It was from this quickening, from her tears, that Mary-Lee's poem emerged:

THE POET'S VOICE IS KNOCKING

She cannot breathe   she is
surrounded by swelling shoulders
monstrous crowd of faceless humans
They elbow past and press upon her
pushing   kneading   knocking
They reek of need   enormity of their
collective need is what takes air from her
she is drowning   like water they push
past   around   over her
she cannot meet their pressing
she feels herself go down

    The dream is familiar, the difference being
    this time she doesn't suffocate in silence
    this time she screams
    wild strong leaping screams that frighten her
    and then   screams that keep coming   with
    just enough space between them to
    suck breath and scream again

But somewhere below her deepening dream
the poet's voice is knocking.

    She never hears its echo
    but her screams begin to change

slowly
first they   begin to   elongate   to
stretch   not yet to song
but to a keening cry   sweet and long

In its streaming length she begins to hear a new
music   which first sounds like
flutes but then becomes   human
she is stunned to hear it comes from her
she opens her mouth wider
her eyes close   her neck arches
sacred sounds fill the space between her
and the crowd   she senses them become
faced   they stop   wait   listen with her
to a song she begins to imagine even while it
rises from her open throat   an exquisite wailing
so high   it   cracks   her own heart

Mary-Lee's words are spare. They are born of anguish and sound—sound that comes from her deepest roots, her most honest voice. By expressing her most desperate feelings, she draws sustenance from the cleansing and empowering act of poem-making. Mary-Lee had the courage to leave the roots on her poem. Go over her poem and highlight words or phrases that have power for you. It may just be one word in a line that gives the entire passage a visceral energy.

Sometimes, perhaps more frequently than not, the transformation that poetry offers will come by surprise. We may not even be thinking of a poem—and suddenly we discover one is coming to us almost faster than we can write.

CONNIE

Connie Smith Siegel found writing poetry to be a source of renewal after a personal disillusionment. Her poem comes to her quietly—unexpectedly, simply, suddenly—as she looks at lilies outside her window:

For years I have endeavored to calm an impetuous tide— laboring to make my feelings take an orderly course—it was striving against the stream.

—Mary Wollstonecraft

NAKED LADIES

They call them naked ladies
Pink lilies that appear like magic
At summer's end when all the green has gone
They rise alone from stalks in hardened ground
Against the golden grass long dry from summer heat
A chorus of rosy voices
Singing of spring in a dying season

Like phantom daydreams growing
From dusty ground of half-lived lives
A hopeful glimpse of light
In gardens long since past
They pass, as daydreams must, when seasons move

But for this moment in the soft September light
Their brave foolishness creates a magic spell
Where dreams still live and love still grows

Connie's reflections on her poem:

"Naked Ladies" was a major source of healing for me. I had been feeling very desolate after a phone call had made it clear that a relationship built from hopes would not materialize. I felt a tremendous sense of loss, and worse, deep embarrassment verging on shame, that I had been so misled by my fantasies and dreams. With a certain bitterness I began writing in my journal about the death of this dream when I noticed the pink lilies in my back yard standing out against the dry grass. I started a poem about these flowers, and was amazed at how much further this metaphor could carry my feelings, and then, unexpectedly, transform them. Identifying with the lilies, I could admire their brave foolishness, which was poignant, but not a flaw. Feeling much different, I walked for a long time in the hills, sometimes with tears, but knowing I was part of a larger, more abundant reality.

The extraordinary capacity of Connie's poem to hold paradox in a way that heals rather than fractures is clear in the last stanza.

Nothing is linear in the poem. Rather there is a mixing of textures and colors: "golden grass long dry" and "rosy voices." There is little that is extra in the poem. She keeps our senses in contact with hardened ground, summer heat, and pink lilies. Such sensual detail permits us to enter that dimension of life which is held in the heart of the moment yet always renews itself:

Where dreams still live and love still grows.

Although walking in the hills expanded her feelings, it was the poem that changed them, making a place for her heart to walk, to cry out on the page, and be revitalized. Like her cleansing tears, her poem distilled and then cleansed her experience of painful loss.

There is a great price we pay for denying our connection to nature, our ability to perceive the extraordinary in the ordinary, our sensitivity to others. It's the price of being shut off from the things and people we really love. This painful sense of loss can be particularly acute and numbing for men.

John

John Enright paid this price for forty-six years or more. Intellect and reasoning were the prizes he sought. His logic teacher at Yale, the famous F. S. C. Northrup, gave John a grade of 98, telling him it was the highest grade he had given anyone in twenty years of teaching logic. John pursued the remaining 2 percent for many years. He's now glad he never found it.

When John began to write poetry at the age of sixty-four, it wasn't logic that seemed to matter anymore. He heard wilder voices. He began to face his mortality and to consider what he had missed in his measured, logical existence.

Goodbye

How can I say goodbye . . .
To the places I never have been?
To the magical lands I read of when young,

To forget all we believe and know may be impossible. But we can, at least for a miraculous moment, put all explanations aside and look with innocent eyes.

—*Piero Ferrucci*

Any original and wholehearted response to life carries the capacity to shift the energy of consciousness, and the result is transformation of one degree or another.

—*Richard Moss*

The people, the scenes, the beasts that I dreamed of
I was new, and young world was beckoning.

How can I say goodbye . . .
To the places I went, but wasn't?
So caught up in fear and trying to impress;
Busy living out images dreamed by others,
That nothing quite real—truly mine—was occurring.

How can I say goodbye . . .
To the people I never did meet?
Those I admired, sensed the chances of kinship.
Kept away by false images, fears and unworthiness.
So I never could take the great step.

How can I say goodbye . . .
To those I did meet but didn't let in?
So full of conviction that they wouldn't see me,
So fearful of what they might say, think, or do
That I kept all exchange on the surface. . . .

How can I say goodbye . . .
To those parts of me that never were used?
The drummer, the hero, magician, the chief.
Yes, beggar and trickster, the juggler and thief
Kept locked in my attic by fear or by grief.

This poem of "goodbyes" is one many men might have written. The last line of each stanza is a progressive summary of the phases in many men's lives: The turning points that were missed. The consequences of taking the road *most* traveled. The regret. The experience of being everyone else but yourself. As the poem progresses, it becomes increasingly full of grief and finality. But the *exploration* of the word "goodbye" is not a despairing or a final act at all. The first line is a question, a kind of "what if?" As in *The Christmas Carol,* where Scrooge is given another chance, this poem is a conscious reordering of priorities.

It was not a physical homesickness from which the poet suffered, it was something far more fundamental—the nostalgia of the soul.

—Rabindranath Tagore

"Goodbye" was a great step forward, the beginning of more writing for John. Now on the latter part of his path, he is increasingly able to welcome the unknown, that formerly unwelcome intruder in the sterile home of "logical" existence. John's life has transformed, and poetry was the catalyst. He tells his story this way:

> In 1992, a friend introduced me to Carl Sandburg's "Wilderness." I was entranced, and longed to touch that until-now foreign domain of poetry.

There is a wolf in me . . . fangs pointed for tearing gashes . . . and a red tongue for raw meat . . . and the hot lapping of blood—I keep this wolf because the wilderness gave it to me and wilderness will not let it go.

There is a fox in me . . . a silver-gray fox I sniff and guess . . . I pick things out of the wind and air . . . I nose in the dark night and take sleepers and eat them and hide the feathers . . . I circle and loop and double-cross.

                              . . .

There is a fish in me . . . I know I came from salt-blue water-gates . . . I scurried with shoals of herring . . . I blew waterspouts with porpoises . . . before land was . . . before the water went down . . . before Noah . . . before the first chapter of Genesis.
                              —from "Wilderness" by Carl Sandburg

> The wilderness is not where I had been in my life. That there might be some "self" beyond the narrow verbal realm I lived in was a concept totally foreign to the world I grew up in.
>
> Increasingly, I have felt something from these poems penetrate me. Not as "insight," because often it cannot be put into words or concepts. It is almost as though these are "personal myths" that deliver their messages in a right-brain, holistic way rather than in left-brain, analytic modes. Frequently, I felt touched to tears writing or even reading my poems; I could not tell you why or how, just that some possibilities opened up or some barriers dropped.

In Kyoto with their begging bowls
I remember Buddhist Monks.
I sensed even then they were more free
Than I was with my loaded trunks.
                              —*John Enright*

Watching for the Light Through the Cracks in Our Lives

Rosemary, Jeremy, Mary-Lee, Connie, and John all began the poetic process by feeling down to their roots. For every one of them, this feeling appeared almost by surprise, as if some light had suddenly shone through from somewhere else. Etched in the beams of that light of feeling was a poem. For Rosemary, it was trusting her ability to go into the dark and wait for a "leaf of light" to burst free. For Jeremy, opening up to the suffering of another person and seeing things as they are gave him inspiration. For Mary-Lee, watching the rain and reading the grief poem "Lost Love" by Robert Graves helped her grieve and reclaim her voice. For Connie, allowing lilies blooming in the dry grass to reach her heart. And for John, it was responding to the wild cry of the wolf heard in the Sandburg poem. Through each of these moments of feeling and perception, something transpired that changed each of these individuals. Writing their poem was a way of making that change manifest.

It takes courage to grow up and turn out to be who you really are.

                              —*e. e. cummings*

   The songwriter and poet Leonard Cohen wrote a lovely song about the grace of the "cracks" in our lives: "There is a crack in everything and that is how the light gets in." Where are your cracks? Where does the light of feeling and poetic perception get in?

Catching Light Through the Cracks

Write freely in answering the following questions. Remember, leave the roots on.

What scares you? _____

_____

What angers you? _____

_____

What saddens you? _____

_____

What delights you? _____

_____

What intrigues you? _____

_____

What do you appreciate about the person you are? _____

_____

Create a dramatic dialogue between two or three of these questions. Follow the trail of a particularly strong response to one of the questions and develop it further. Use details to illustrate. If you could give a metaphoric identity to your sadness or intrigue, what would it be? What kind of voice would it have?

Listening to Music

Poetic consciousness lives in all our tissues, like a baby, who barely distinguishes between his joy and the breast that has given it. To live poetically is to experience as meaningful all that the organism is and does.

—*M. C. Richard*

I almost always listen to classical music when I write. While I was working on Sueños *in New Hampshire, I listened to Mahler. The first movement of his Ninth Symphony. Over and over again. Loud. On a cheap stereo purchased with trading stamps. To get just an iota of the greatness of such music into poetry has always been my ambition.*

—*James Reiss*

Music can help to evoke your feelings at the roots. The poet Laura Chester wrote a profoundly touching poem about a friend's daughter who died of leukemia. She describes how music helped her to stay close to her original feelings while writing:

I put on the piece of Ravel's music we had listened to earlier and which had been such a perfect complement to my melancholy, a combination of weepiness and frustration. As the music played, I wrote in longhand, letting the music ground the feelings I had to negotiate, something I had to uncover in myself by assuming my friend's loss as a mother. I don't usually write to music but this piece sang so perfectly what I needed to express in words, that it helped to guide the flow without interfering.

Laura Chester also found that Ravel's music made it easier to re-connect with the initial intent of the poem during the process of rewriting. The music became her ally as she wrote:

In the early stages of rewriting "Pavane," I continued to play the music that helped stir it. It allowed me to sink back into the same place more easily, and when I rewrite I have to retrieve that original urge otherwise it becomes mere correction and something vital is lost.

Poetry atrophies when it gets too far from music.

—Ezra Pound

Listen to a variety of musical pieces and styles as you explore and write about the range of your feelings. Let your response to the music guide your images and words. As you listen, open yourself to the music. Sink into the sounds and flow with them. Does the music evoke sadness . . . delight . . . exuberance . . . peace? Are there combinations of different feelings? Is it energetic . . . languid? Can you give the sound of the music an image? Is the sound large like an oak tree or refined and delicate as a bird's wing? Is it bright like clear dew sliding along a green leaf or somber as sea waves on a slate-gray morning? Does the music move sturdily like a bear in the forest or is it more evanescent and quick, flashing like a fast river? If you could be an instrument in this particular piece of music, what instrument would you be? How would being that instrument affect how you interacted with the world—your language, your movement, your sexuality, your sense of humor?

Here are some musical pieces that I have found to be evocative and moving. You will of course have your own favorites. The music on this list is intended to elicit your creative language. You can use these pieces either to inspire a poem, or as appropriate background to support what you choose to write about:

Bach: Suite no. 2 for flute and strings
Concerto in F, for oboe, strings, and continuo
Ariosa

Beethoven:	Sonata for violincello and piano no. 5 in D major, opus 102, 1
	Moonlight Sonata
	Ninth Symphony
Coltrane:	A Love Supreme
Debussy:	Claire de Lune
	Prélude à l'Après-Midi d'un Faune
Fauré:	Requiem
	Sicilienne
Rainer:	Songs of the Indian Flute
Ravel:	Pavane pour une Infante défunte
Sachdev:	Bansuri East Indian flute music
Vivaldi:	Concerto in C for piccolo blockflöte
Vaughan Williams:	Lark Ascending

Leonard Cohen, Sinead O'Connor, Enya, Beatles, Judy Collins, B.B. King, Bob Dylan, Grateful Dead, and many others.

Do not commit your poems to pages alone. Sing them, I pray you.

—*Virgil*

Memorizing Poems: Gaining More Grace in Your Life

Memorizing poems is an excellent way to bring quickly to mind those values and gems of wisdom that guide, delight, and center you. Poems called up from memory can instantly transport you to any place you choose to go or evoke any feeling you want to call up. Perhaps it is a place of tranquility that you want to visit. Yeats's "Lake Isle of Innisfree" is perfect:

THE LAKE ISLE OF INNISFREE

I will arise and go now, and go to Innisfree,
And a small cabin build there, of clay and wattles made:
Nine bean-rows will I have there, a hive for the honey-bee,
And live alone in the bee-loud glade.

And I shall have some peace there, for peace comes dropping slow,
Dropping from the veils of the morning to where the cricket sings;
There midnight's all a glimmer, and noon a purple glow,
And evening full of the linnet's wings.

I will arise and go now, for always night and day
I hear lake water lapping with low sounds by the shore;

Language shapes consciousness, and the use of language to shape consciousness is an important branch of magic.

—*Starhawk*

While I stand on the roadway, or on the pavements grey,
I hear it in the deep heart's core.

Memorizing a poem is a matter of practice and choice. This is no longer the forced memorizations from high school! Choose poems that you enjoy. A businessman I know has memorized numerous poems by the Sufi mystic poet Jelaluddin Rumi because he enjoys them and because they remind him of a place of centeredness and wisdom within himself; a centeredness that is incredibly helpful in handling a very successful business. Many of Rumi's poems are short and perfect for easy recall.

Come to the orchard in Spring.
There is light and wine, and sweethearts in the pomegranate
    flowers.
If you do not come, these do not matter.
If you do come, these do not matter.

If you want to memorize longer poems, there are a number of handles that can help you to do so. Various aspects of the poem—images and sounds, the rhythms, and sometimes the rhyme—can be keys to support your remembering. When reciting an image such as, "I hear lake water lapping with low sounds by the shore," make that a concrete image in your mind and link it with the words. Sound allows you to take something in beneath a cognitive level and learn it almost by osmosis. In the Yeats poem there are the melodic *l*'s and *o*'s which can help to make memorization easier. Feel the "music" of those sounds as you recite and memorize the poem—it will help, in the same way music and rhyme help us remember jingles and commercials.

Another helpful method is to write down longer poems on 3 × 5 index cards. You can break the poem down by stanzas or groups of lines. Go over each stanza many times. As you begin to learn one section almost completely, go to the next and work on that one until you feel you've almost got it. Then say them together a number of times and move on to the next stanza or group of lines, and so on. Don't just memorize by rote. Tune into the flow of the poem so that you can use your

In a poem the word should be as pleasing to the ear as the meaning is to the mind.

——*Marianne Moore*

The poet speaks to all men of that other life of theirs that they have smothered and forgotten.

——*Edith Sitwell*

I have never started a poem yet whose end I knew. Writing a poem is discovery.

     —Robert Frost

Courage faces fear and thereby masters it.

    —Martin Luther King, Jr.

feeling of it to keep you on track. Cards are helpful because you can put the cards in your pocket or purse and easily get them out at convenient times. After a while, just put the cards away and each time you speak your poem, speak it with renewed feeling.

There are many ways to make the memorization of a poem enjoyable. I was able to learn many poems by Yeats by checking out a cassette recording of his poetry from the library and listening to it a number of times. By listening to a skilled reader, I was able to absorb the whole poem rather than learn it in pieces by going over the words on the page. There are many recordings of poetry read by the poets themselves as well as by skilled readers and actors.

We all have our own tricks for things like memorizing. You should use what works for you. The important thing is that the poems you memorize will make your life richer and more graceful. But I'll suggest one more idea for how to memorize. Let me know if you try this one!

When she was seventeen, my friend Adrian Griffin memorized a long poem called "Silent in America," by the poet Philip Levine, in a unique way. The poem is thirty-eight stanzas long, of about four to eight lines each. Adrian went well beyond using 3 × 5 cards. She wrote the poem in black felt pen on the walls of her bedroom! She literally *lived* inside that poem for a while. Some seventeen years later, she can still recite it from memory.

We humans are at our best when we enjoy poetry. Sometimes all you need is to reflect in your mind one poem that says, "I can make it through."

    —Maya Angelou

Choose a few favorite poems you'd like to memorize. Try the poems by Yeats and Rumi in this section just for practice. Poems that are connected somehow with circumstances in your life might be particularly compelling and easy to memorize. Listen to tapes, use the 3 × 5 cards, or simply read the poem out of the book until you "get it." Say the poem to yourself just for the sheer enjoyment. Speak your poems to an interested friend or family member!

Meditation

In Chapter One, I wrote that developing a meditative stance, by focusing on *breathing, stillness,* and *listening,* is helpful for becoming more aware of your inner voice and the world around you. This sensitivity and awareness will in turn flow into your writing. You needn't think of writing only about "peaceful" things! To the contrary, meditation practice can encourage you to draw from deep within yourself, to see all that you are, and that includes giving yourself permission to make room in your writing for your full emotional range.

Spiritual growth is achieved with passion, difficulty, and intensity as much as it is achieved by peace, silence, and love.
— *Carolyn Forché*

You might want to consider extending this meditative approach further. It could be useful, if you are attracted to do so, to consider meditating with others. I've participated in various ongoing meditation groups for over twenty years and it has been an essential part of my life and writing. For the past seven years, I've meditated with a small group of five to eight people. Our format is simple: we gather at an agreed-upon time (Sunday evening) and the host has always lit a candle before we sit together. That's it. In addition to meditating together we have included a time after meditation for speaking to one another "from the silence." The speaking we do is not any kind of "channeling" hocus pocus but a very simple sharing. Rather than opinions, what we speak is language from the open heart. Our words come up from the silence and are shared with respect for everyone present. The experience of meditation and speaking together is very special and, as you can imagine, can be an oasis in the midst of the routine busyness of living. Consider developing such a gathering yourself.

The poem is an expression of your whole being at the moment of vision.
— *Richard Eberhart*

Energy is eternal delight.
— *William Blake*

It is the soul's duty to be loyal to its own desires. It must abandon itself to its master passion.
— *Rebecca West*

Drinking from Your Root System: What Are Your First Thoughts?

Take time to write your responses to the following words. Meditate on each word for a little while. *What are your first thoughts?*

silence	attraction	the unknown
shame	fear	courage
trust	passion	inner voice

What does "trust" say to you? What does "shame" say? Use your words to paint a picture of trust and shame—or any of the other words listed above.

If your *inner voice* or *courage* were represented as an animal or as something else in nature what would they be?

This exercise can help you to explore the roots of these words. Write quickly. *Be tangible, specific, and use detail*—as much as possible. Don't hesitate to use words and phrases that are unusual. Allow yourself to express what matters most to you. The following is an example to give you some idea of how to proceed. Notice the specific imagery.

> *Silence lives in a place that looks like my hands cupped together. When she is awake there, silence teaches bees to gather nectar. When she is asleep, silence dreams she holds thunder or a mountain.*
>
> *Silence is a gazelle hidden from harm in the tall dry grass.*

SILENCE

Silence lives in a place that looks like (describe everything you can about silence—where it lives, who it knows, what it wears, what work it does, how it plays. Use detail.):

_____

_____

_____

Using metaphor and simile,* describe what silence is like:

Silence is _____

Silence is like _____

If I could tell silence two things I would say:

1. _____

2. _____

*Metaphor is when you *equate* two things, such as "Silence is a cloud." Simile is when you *compare* two things using "like" or "as."

Silence helps me to tap into my creativity because:

1. _____
2. _____
3. _____

Experiences in my life where I have felt deep silence:

1. _____
2. _____
3. _____

ATTRACTION

Attraction lives in (describe everything you can about attraction—where it lives, who it knows, what it wears, what work it does, how it plays. Use detail.):

_____

_____

_____

_____

Name three people you admire and are attracted to:

1. _____
2. _____
3. _____

I would like to travel to_____

_____

_____

I want to experience _____

_____

_____

I want to learn more about _____

_____

I am attracted to the following places in nature: _____

_____

THE UNKNOWN

The unknown lives in (describe everything you can about the unknown—where it lives, who it knows, what it wears, what work it does, how it plays. Use detail.):

_____

_____

_____

_____

Use metaphor and simile to describe the unknown:

The unknown is _____

The unknown is like _____

The unknown is scary to me because of the following:

1. _____

2. _____

3. _____

The unknown is exciting to me because of the following:

1. _____

2. _____

3. _____

If I were to make a journey into the unknown I would take with me:

1. _____

2. _____

3. _____

SHAME

Shame lives in a place that looks like (describe everything you can about shame—where it lives, who it knows, what it wears, what work it does, how it plays. Use detail.):

_____

_____

_____

_____

Using metaphor and simile, describe shame:

Shame is_____

Shame is like _____

If I could tell shame two things I would say:

1. _____

2. _____

Three things that I know are healthy for me but which shame prevents me from doing are:

1. _____

2. _____

3. _____

FEAR

Fear lives in a place that looks like (describe everything you can about fear—where it lives, who it knows, what it wears, what work it does, how it plays. Use detail.):

_____

_____

_____

_____

Using metaphor and simile, describe fear:

Fear is _____

Fear is like _____

If I could tell fear two things I would say:

1. _____

2. _____

Three things fear prevents you from doing that would be a growth experience:

1. _____

2. _____

3. _____

COURAGE

Courage lives in a place that looks like (describe everything you can about courage—where it lives, who it knows, what it wears, what work it does, how it plays. Use detail.):

_____

_____

_____

_____

Using metaphor and simile, describe courage:

Courage is _____

Courage is like _____

If I could tell courage two things I would say:

1. _____

2. _____

Name three situations in your life that require courage from you:

1. _____

2. _____

3. _____

TRUST

Trust lives in a place that looks like (describe everything you can about trust—where it lives, who it knows, what it wears, what work it does, how it plays. Use detail.):

_____

_____

_____

_____

Using metaphor and simile describe trust:

Trust is _____

Trust is like _____

If I could tell trust two things I would say:

1. _____

2. _____

Name three situations in your life that ask for trust:

1. _____

2. _____

3. _____

PASSION

The place passion lives in looks like (describe everything you can about passion—where it lives, who it knows, what it wears, what work it does, how it plays. Use detail.):

_____

_____

_____

Using metaphor and simile, describe passion:

Passion is _____

Passion is like _____

If I could tell passion two things I would say:

1. _____

2. _____

Passion is important to me because:

1. _____

2. _____

Three ways that passion helps me are:

1. _____

2. _____

3. _____

Name three situations in your life that may need your passion:

1. _____

2. _____

3. _____

INNER VOICE

The place my inner voice lives looks like (describe everything you can about your inner voice—where it lives, who it knows, what it wears, what work it does, how it plays. Use detail.):

_____

_____

_____

_____

Name three things in nature or in your daily life that awaken and inspire your inner voice:

1. _____

2. _____

3. _____

Using metaphor and simile, describe your inner voice:

My inner voice is _____

My inner voice is like _____

I can hear my inner voice best when I am _____

_____

My inner voice tells me to write about these things in my life:

1. _____

2. _____

3. _____

Once you have gone through this exercise and are in touch with some of your feelings, put those feelings into images and poetic form—and begin to learn more about yourself. In responding to this exercise you will find fascinating material for your poems. Remember—leave the roots on your writing, "Just to make clear / where they came from." Express your unique truth and creativity in your poem-making.

Three

Gold in the Attic

Reconnecting with Your Natural Creativity

I pulled a book by Robinson Jeffers off the shelf one day. It was powerfully moving. Tears ran down my face. That's when I became a poet.

—William Everson

It is above all by the imagination that we achieve perception and compassion and hope.

—Ursula K. Le Guin

> *. . . my*
> *jaws ache for release, for*
> *words that will say*
>
> *anything. I force myself*
> *to remember*
> *who I am, what I am, and*
> *why I am here. . .*
> —Philip Levine

When someone deeply listens to you
it is like holding out a dented cup
you've had since childhood
and watching it fill up with
cold, fresh water.
When it balances on top of the brim,
you are understood.
When it overflows and touches your skin,
you are loved.

When someone deeply listens to you,
the room where you stay
starts a new life
and the place where you wrote
your first poem
begins to glow in your mind's eye.
It is as if gold has been discovered!

When someone deeply listens to you,
your bare feet are on the earth
and a beloved land that seemed distant
is now at home within you.

—John Fox

First Experiences That Opened the Door

I was being interviewed on a talk radio program one morning at rush hour. A woman called in and told how she had written poetry up in her room during her high school years—sometimes staying up all night. She said, "I never showed them to anybody, I just put the poems in a box. I think that box is still in the attic. You've inspired me to go back and dig it out again." She said she had been moved by my poem "When Someone Deeply Listens to

You," which I had read earlier in the program. I reminded her of
the second stanza:

> the room where you stay
> starts a new life
> and the place where you wrote
> your first poem
> begins to glow in your mind's eye.
> It is as if gold has been discovered!

Then I said to her, "It sounds like you may have gold up in the at-
tic." She said, "It just brings tears to my eyes."

> . . . Don't say, don't say there is no water.
> That fountain is there among its scalloped
> green and gray stones,
>
> it is still there and always there
> with its quiet song and strange power
> to spring in us,
> up and out through the rock.
> —Denise Levertov, from "The Fountain"

What were your early experiences of the imagination and the
music of life? What did you love that you were naturally attracted
to? What called to you? I remember being attracted to explo-
ration from as early as I can remember. Crawling through bushes
to get to the other side of our house was an amazing journey.
There were forests in the back of our house on the other side of
the creek—I wanted to go there. Exploring the unknown at-
tracted me.

What kinds of things awakened in you a spontaneous burst of
enthusiasm? These interests and attractions are essential routes
back to your inner poet. In those times of being filled with cre-
ative joy, when the earth and the universe spoke to you in ways
you found thrilling—what were you doing? What engaged you,
drew you into experience, to the extent that you threw yourself
into it with all of your energy and a sense of adventure?

*Whence come I? I come from
my childhood. I come from
childhood as from a
homeland.*

—Antoine de Saint-Exupéry

And as I was green and carefree, famous among the barns
About the happy yard and singing as the farm was home,
In the sun that is young once only,
Time let me play and be
Golden in the mercy of his means . . .
                                              —Dylan Thomas

When did you first hear an imaginative use of language? Perhaps nursery rhymes. Did your parents read storybooks to you or make up bedtime stories? What are your first memories of imaginative words, music, and singing?

At five or six, I loved to watch *The Shari Lewis Show* on TV. Through her banter with Lamb Chop, I began to enjoy making up language for different characters in order to tell a story. My friend David Sholle and I, when we weren't exploring caves and creek places, created puppet shows for ourselves and family. My mother made a puppet theater for me, complete with colored stage lights. I had a puppet, a sailor named GoGo, who could do whatever a hero needed to do.

At seven or eight, I remember seeing the Mitch Miller singers on TV, enjoying the syncopations and harmonies of their songs without knowing that was what they were called. My parents took us kids to church regularly and I sang in church choirs growing up. I resisted the regimentation of Sunday school, but the opportunity to sing was something I enjoyed. The choir director was an emotional man who did his best to shake music to life. He would stamp his foot as his hands sprang chords loose from the old piano in the church basement.

I had parts in musicals by Rogers and Hammerstein, lyrics linked to the action of life, music joined with telling a story. I loved acting in those plays. One could sing a song about walking through a storm with your head held high, or imagine the possibilities of a Wells Fargo wagon a'comin down the street—music was connected with life events, and that lyrical quality felt natural to me.

I remember being entranced by the music of cellist Pablo Casals when I was nine or ten. My parents gave me a record of the concert Casals gave at the Kennedy White House in 1963.

When you remember the play that lifted your heart as a child, you will know the heart of God. You will understand the motives behind this universal expression.

—Ken Carey

Thus childhood images, images which a child could make, images which a poet tells that a child has made, are, for us, manifestations of the permanent childhood.

—Gaston Bachelard

Something I noticed at some deep level, even then: Casals sighed, almost sobbed as he played. He was *in love* with the music. I studied cello from elementary through high school. My cello playing was only fair and eventually I stopped, but the experience left me with a permanent feeling for that instrument's depth and resonance. The cello was another connection I made with the heart of life.

My dad sometimes read to us children nineteenth-century poets like William Wordsworth and Edwin Arlington Robinson. In the mid 1960s, at eleven, I was taken to hear the famous Russian poet Yevgeny Yevtushenko read his poetry. I wasn't aware of politics at the time, only that here was a messenger from a far country. Yevtushenko stood on the stage alone—with only his voice—and he spoke with feeling.

It might have been any kind of artistry that tuned you in to the rhythm and grace of poetry. Did you dance, study ballet, ski, or skate when you were young? Did one of those activities thrill you in some way? Sports is full of poetic artistry. What fascinated you about baseball? Stealing a base is a kind of poetry in motion!

THE BASE STEALER

Poised between going on and back, pulled
Both ways taut like a tightrope-walker,
Fingertips pointing the opposites,
Now bouncing tiptoe like a dropped ball
Or a kid skipping rope, come on, come on,
Running a scattering of steps sidewise,
How he teeters, skitters, tingles, teases,
Taunts them, hovers like an ecstatic bird,
He's only flirting, crowd him, crowd him,
Delicate, delicate, delicate, delicate—now!
                              —*Robert Francis*

Or in football, was it when the quarterback and receiver were in such poetic sync that they could both foresee the precise spot where the football would magically appear in the receiver's hands? Did you run track, swim, or dance? Did movement and the rhythms of your body in motion fill you with energy and joy? One of the first clear memories I have is chasing a red ball that rolled down a little grassy hill. That moment is still full of brightness to me. The red of the ball, the green of the grass, the blue of sky—and me running to catch something, to catch that red ball, the image of that first rich feeling of aliveness.

Think back to when you were very young and caught the first sense of yourself as poetry in motion. What feelings, images, and words come up?

Science is permeated with artistry too. Exploring the elements. Mixing things together and experiencing interaction and change. Seeing entirely new things emerge from old things or nothing at all. This deep nonverbal language of interaction and change may have fed you with wonder. The sense of clarity and balance that comes from keen observation. Seeing connections in nature like the rhymes of a poem. Animals and the natural world also embody the music of life and its mysterious language.

Can you remember the initial experiences that opened the poetic door for you—the moments when you were greeted by a magical world? They may have been glimpses of different cultures, music, and languages within your own family or in places you visited. Or perhaps certain individuals first sparked your interest in creativity, friends or relatives who embodied a special kind of inventive, original vitality.

My astrologer and artist friend Mary Jones was deeply influenced by her uncle Victor, who was both artist and gardener. Uncle Victor created an artistic wonderland in his home garden outside of Boston, a garden that became a special place in Mary's childhood. Mary says of that garden:

> *The garden he designed was alive with his uniqueness as a human be-
> ing. It was lined with cobblestones and based on formal gardens he
> had visited in Italy and France. The cobblestones served as paths to
> the various parts of the garden—to the tomatoes, to the green beans.
> As I child, I would walk along these enchanted paths and meander
> from the green beans into a grove of full, ripe, red tomatoes. He also
> covered the gardens with oriental carpets—they became mulch over
> time! You would see the ripe, red tomatoes against the patterns of*

reds, purples, and maroons of a Turkish carpet. Most adults didn't understand, but for me that garden was a magical land of color, pattern, form—and nurturing.

Some adults may have thought her uncle odd, but those experiences were a creative doorway for Mary. Her Uncle Victor gave Mary the courage to claim the artist inside herself.

I would not measure thee by thy deeds but by thy vastest dreams.

—Kahlil Gibran

EXERCISE: EARLY EXPERIENCES OF BEING TOUCHED BY THE MUSE

Recall the times in your childhood when you felt the poetry of life. Take the time, all the time you want, to tell your story in the form of a poem. Think of anything that may have included movement, sound, rhythm, image, the imagination, keen observation, wonder, drama, the love and playfulness of language—any expression of these that reached quickly to your heart:

_____

_____

_____

_____

_____

EXERCISE: REMEMBERING THOSE WHO FED YOUR CREATIVE SPARK

Did a parent, friend, or teacher acknowledge your creative spark when you were a child and encourage your fledgling inner voice? Perhaps you had a teacher who taught you and then encouraged you to grow past them, so that you could move forward into your own destiny. It is helpful to recognize and honor such relationships because gratitude strengthens the gift we have been given and reminds us that we now have an opportunity to give to others.

Write a poem about someone who encouraged your creativity either in childhood or in your adolescence. That person may not have been aware that they were making a significant difference in your life. She may have just demonstrated her faith in you or shared her own enthusiasm for living and love of adventure. Perhaps that person showed you something about life that has always been very important to you. Include in your poem specific details and characteristics that make that person come alive and immediate for you. What was it about him that inspired you? What did he see and appreciate in you? Recall whatever is significant about your life back then and the person you were. Invite that important person who inspired or encouraged you into your poem and let him or her speak to you.

A workshop student, Margaret Barton, wrote a prose poem* about her favorite English teacher. Notice how her honesty and use of sharp detail bring this man to life:

My poet was born of your passion and frustration. You were an aging recovering alcoholic who paced my early grade classrooms like a tiger. Your confines were twenty teenage girls who encircled you, taunted you with their youth and uncaring summer faces.

I lived your sighs, your clicking fingers, your black spit-shined shoes as you paced the classroom. Your sudden whirl towards me haunts me as does your breath, your precision around words and their input and delivery.

Magic were the days when you dramatically flung the door open and words rushed ahead of you, filling empty spaces then and since and now.

You are dead and I am here, living and creating what was birthed and nurtured by us twenty-six years ago.

Living on we share together.

Children Guessed (But Only a Few)

As I grew up, I was determined to hold on to a sense of mystery. I wanted to be open to new ideas, creative possibilities, to explore life on my own. I wanted to retain the freedom I'd had in childhood to find my own answers. It was extremely difficult. It's hard to maintain that kind of determination, especially within an educational system that is designed to eliminate your inner quest as soon as possible.

What I discovered in poetry and writing was, in fact, an open doorway for that quest. That doorway accompanied me wherever I went. It opened in both directions: into my self and onto the world outside myself. I knew that doorway would keep *something* alive in me that was more important than anything else.

*A prose poem uses poetic language but is arranged in paragraph form, like prose.

That "something" is the voice of my soul.

What I saw happening as I reached the age of fourteen or fifteen was the conformity that takes over at that stage in our lives. People begin to move down the same road; "growing out" into the world and adjusting to it, rather than a "growing up" to create a world rooted within themselves.

Something happens in this "growing out" and I think most sensitive people feel it. It is that awful feeling of forgetting a sensitivity that once came from within. It's not the same as losing our innocence. That's a different story and an important part of the drama of being alive. But we don't lose our sensitivity toward life—we forget we have it. Our culture seems to demand that we forget this richness to a large degree. It takes almost everything we have to hold on to and remember our innate creative voice of truth.

But sensitivity can ripen in us and become a lasting part of our lives. The gift we were initially given by God is something we can now develop and give consciously to others. When life's responsibilities and struggles leave us feeling unfulfilled, do we fill ourselves with addictions or do we fill ourselves with what has spiritual resonance and meaning? When poetry fills the spaces in our lives, it makes a place for a ripened sensitivity to thrive.

We are meant to carry this sensitive awareness for the wonders of life with us forever—it is our vibrant connection with life's mystery. You won't be able to logically define this ineffable gift that is our birthright, but you can feel its presence, for example, in the poetry of e. e. cummings:

> *More than a mode of perception, poetry is above all a way of life, of integral life. The poet existed among the cavemen; he will exist among men of the atomic age, for he is an inherent part of man.*
>
> *—St. John Perse*

> children guessed (but only a few
> and down they forgot as up they grew
> autumn winter spring summer) . . .
>   .   .   .   .
>
> stars rain sun moon
> (and only the snow can begin to explain
> how children are apt to forget to remember
> with up so floating many bells down)
>   —e. e. cummings,
>   from "anyone lived in a pretty how town"

I must have guessed as a child and teenager. I listened to poets because they spoke about a world that was rich with what really mattered: insight, passion, beauty, truth, mystery. They created poems which brought these vague concepts alive. Here were adults who still valued their imagination! They guided me toward a world of truth and originality. I found a way out of conformity—a pathway to creativity and being true to myself. Using my own writing, I still struggle to find my way, but it is with an enthusiasm for a journey that poetry keeps alive.

Dylan Thomas offered students this insight: "To be nobody-but-yourself—in a world which is doing its best night and day to make you everyone else—means to fight the hardest battle which any human being can fight; and never stop fighting."

Dragonflies from the Sun

In the Introduction, I quoted the lines from the poet James Broughton:

> . . . *Poets are not gnats in the wind.*
> *They are dragonflies from the sun.*

We all strive for those moments when we feel like we're "dragonflies from the sun." We'll do just about anything to feel that way! What is it like to truly be a dragonfly from the sun? I feel it is a moment such as Audre Lorde experienced during her struggle with cancer:

> *Sometimes I feel like I'm the spoils in a battle between good and evil right now, or that I'm both sides doing the fighting, and I'm not even sure of the outcome nor the terms. But sometimes it comes into my head, like right now, what would you really give? And it feels like, even just musing, I could make a terrible and tragic error in judgement if I don't always keep my head and my priorities clear. It's as if the devil is really trying to buy my soul and pretending that it doesn't matter if I say yes because everybody knows*

he's not for real anyway. But I don't know that. And I don't think
this is all a dream at all, and no, I would not give up love.
      —Audre Lorde, from The Cancer Journals

Making a choice and keeping her priorities clear, Audre Lorde is a dragonfly from the sun. She has declared her mission: to use her voice to speak the truth. To make the concept of courage come alive. To overcome cynicism and speak with boldness. To live and see things with love.

When have you felt like a dragonfly from the sun? When have you most felt like "nobody-but-yourself"? It doesn't have to be during a time of crisis. It might happen on an ordinary morning when you wake up and see a simple yet miraculous shaft of sunlight through the window, and feel yourself to be in complete harmony with life the way it is.

As adults, such experiences of completeness often come unexpectedly: Walking in the woods and looking into a deer's eyes. Spending time with someone you love. Working in your garden and noticing the voluptuousness of a tomato. Standing on a street corner and feeling the movement of vehicles and bodies, the sounds and pulse of the city. Making love. Playing an instrument. Helping someone. Taking a courageous stand on a controversial issue and speaking out. Watching a baby sleep. Dancing.

Feeling awakened and fully alive can also be born of sorrow or difficulty. Perhaps you have had the experience of working through something painful yet feeling utterly present and in touch with yourself—a time when you didn't hide or disown yourself. Pregnancy and birth. Illness. The death of a loved one. Dealing with inner crises.

If you cannot remember a time when you felt this, *imagine* such a moment. Begin with something simple, a moment when you felt whole. Imagine yourself as a dragonfly from the sun. It's not cheating to imagine! The poet John Keats wrote in a letter: "I am certain of nothing but the holiness of the heart's affections and the truth of the imagination—*what the imagination seizes as beauty must be truth—whether it existed before or not.*"

EXERCISE: YOUR CONNECTION WITH LIFE

Write a letter or poem to yourself in which you describe your connection with life. What do you imagine your most essential connections to be? How is life connected to you? What and whom do you touch as you go about your day? It does not have to feel spectacular. It can be very ordinary—but it should resonate in your heart. What makes a difference in your life? Show in your letter or poem how sensitivity helps you to strengthen these connections. Why is sensitivity important in your life? As accurately as you can, tell your story. Here is a sample letter. Kimberley Nelson reflects on how the process of her writing and speaking involves a *relationship* with something inside her and with everything around her:

Reporting on the conflict between knowing and living, we speak. Demanding that the intangible is real, we speak. Dancing to the wild hive of bees, we speak. My poet is not personal, it is as if there were a we inside of me. The voice is my own but the consciousness behind it, urging it, IS greater than my own simple self. Likewise, I am responsible for what I say, but do not feel that the writing is me, it is something I wrote down. I am responsible for listening, for noticing the amalgamate images of experience. Metaphors are necessary to us because we truly apprehend things in relation to each other, not on their own. A tree is a tree by itself, and more when it is faced with a man, or a storm, or a Christmas tree farm, a desert, a child, or snow. I could not create these relationships alone.

love, Kimberley

All poets are creative, that is, able to make sustained raids on their private history.

—John Woods

Like the above exercises, all the exercises in this book are intended to help you find what you haven't lost. And once we've found our poet within—or at least heard whispers—what do we do next? I wonder if that woman I talked with on the radio went back to find those poems she stored up in her attic. I wonder if she followed through on her desire to reclaim the passion and feeling she poured into her writing so many years earlier. She could begin again in a new and different way. Once we have gone back to find the gold in our attic, once we have reconnected with those original places of joy, the next step is to make poetry a fulfilling and integral part of our lives.

Poetic Voices: The Doctor, the Weaver, the Broadcaster, and the Teacher

The following stories of four very different people remind us that as adults we do not have to give up our sensitivity—or our sense of responsibility. Our day-to-day life affords us endless opportunities for living creatively and drawing upon subject matter for poetry-making. Poetry is not an activity separate from life, with all its mistakes and successes. For these four people, poetry is in no way separate from their family life, work life, community or spiritual life.

> We have a lot of inhibitions that are thought to be shameful and private and unspeakable. But to reach another person, poetry has to be as open as possible. Then we discover that everyone's experience resembles everyone else's.
>
> —Galway Kinnell

What these four people have to say will guide you on your own path to a meaningful poem-making experience. The key is accurately listening to what is inside you and courageously writing what you hear.

MARY-LEE

Mary-Lee McNeal is married and the mother of two children. She teaches poetry through the Poets in the Schools Program at St. Elizabeth Seton School in Palo Alto, California, bringing poetry writing to poor children. Mary-Lee is a poet and fiction writer and is convinced that the study of poetry is essential to the art of writing fiction. We met Mary-Lee earlier in Chapter Two.

> *In poetry, you must love the words, the ideas, and the imagination, and the rhythms with all your capacity to love anything at all.*
>
> —Wallace Stevens

> I began writing poems in my head before I was old enough to put pencil to paper. I made up little rhymes which I repeated to myself—I loved the rhythms, the sounds of words. I thought of them as songs,

but I knew their music was different from the songs I heard on the radio and played on the piano. I never thought of giving my poems to anyone else. I was afraid someone would laugh at me.

Sometime during my adolescence I shared poems with a few girl-friends, and I remember those days as some of the happiest of my life. But as soon as I began to study poetry, I began to hide my own poems in notebooks and in drawers, unwilling to have them read or criticized, unable to admit I aspired to such lofty heights. It seemed the only people who had the right to call themselves poets were males of vastly superior intelligence who'd been dead for a long time. Or a few women who were destined to lives of reclusive loneliness. For someone like me, a girl bursting with the rawest kind of emotion, to call myself a poet seemed like some sort of sacrilege.

Nearly twenty years passed! I continued to write poems, but it was only my fiction that I would risk showing to others. One day I confessed to a woman who was telling me about her poetry class that I was "afraid of poetry." Her response was, "Oh, not me. I understand poetry." Something about the glibness of this casual remark changed everything. I suddenly understood the arrogance of our two polarized views. This woman's arrogance was to assume she could understand all the mystery of poetry; mine was to be afraid to understand any of its mystery. A short time later I took a handful of my poems to a poet I respected.

"A good start in poetry," she wrote, and that's all I needed. She hadn't said, "Stick to fiction; your poetry stinks." I looked at that word "start" and I started.

I wrote poem after poem, and I sent them to magazines. A few were accepted, most were not. But I kept writing and I read my poems aloud to friends. I began to put the reading and writing of poetry at the center of my life. A few years later I met a woman who voiced the same kind of fear I'd once known.

"I never say I'm a poet," she said, "because it's more humiliating to fail at poetry than any other form of art. Bad poetry is such a . . . desecration." I looked at this woman's sad, pinched face, I listened to her tight voice, and I was taken back to the girl I'd been, the one who wouldn't dare call herself a poet because she wasn't Pound, Yeats, or Eliot.

I resolved at that moment to do my part to help others avoid that

Developing a language of one's own, with distinct colors and nuances, with maps and charts and images that voice the self, takes a long time. It is a writer's lifelong work.

—Burghild Nina Holzer

fear at all costs. Since then I have taught poetry writing to all sorts of people, from six to sixty years old, from those who have never read poetry to those who are far better read than I, from those who strain for days to get a line right to those who seem to spill perfect lines with little effort.

None of us is any less aware of the sacredness of the best of poetry for having made our own humble attempts to write it.

INSIDE

I looked up. I still look up
to see him there behind her
at the stove.
Hunched in my corner,
pressing childbones to the heater
I looked up from my book
to see him there behind her
at the stove.

He, with his soft hat in his hand.
She, stirring, tilting her head
slightly to receive his kiss,
submitting somehow without moving
to his other hand
which slips silently to her thigh.
Pots bubble. A lid is lifted (by him?)
Steam rises. A spoon clinks.
Smells of coffee and onions frying

reach me.
The refrigerator hums at my back.

I wondered then, decades ago:
Why this slow rise of joy in my throat?
Because his hand on her proves they have
something strong and hot enough
to keep the scream of wind outside?
Because this book could transport me
to places high and strange and wild,

and yet I might nest, still, tonight
inside
this quiet evening kitchen?

Jack

Jack Coulehan is a physician, epidemiologist, and teacher of medical ethics at the State University of New York at Stony Brook. Dr. Coulehan's writings range from epidemiological studies of illness among Native Americans to essays on doctor-patient communication and symbolic healing. He is the author of *First Photographs of Heaven,* a book of poems largely about his work as a physician. Dr. Coulehan contributes articles to medical journals about the need for more poetry in the medical profession.

You can't depend on your judgment when your imagination is out of focus.
—Mark Twain

The writing of poetry is a discipline for many things.
—Muriel Rukeyser

Some think that poetry and medical practice make strange—perhaps even illicit—bedfellows. For example, Susan Sontag argues in Illness as Metaphor *that we should attempt to eliminate all metaphor from our thinking about illness. "Just the facts, ma'am." No frills. No cultural baggage. No connections with everyday experience. In an ideal world, we would reduce all illness and suffering to their biological components, avoiding any attribution of meaning. Cancer, for example, is simply and precisely a malignant transformation of certain tissue; it has no other meaning: it is not "the enemy within."*

Yet the search for human significance in illness motivates both patients and physicians. Illness cannot be reduced to a series of readings on machines, nor a biochemical process. Illness is part of a life story, a snag in the plot, an unpleasant theme, a mysterious villain. Like poets, physicians probe the complexities of human suffering, searching for the right image to express what they find, the right word to help make it better. Marc Straus, an oncologist and poet, wrote that physicians and poets are similar in that they both meditate "between a seen and unseen world, interpreting a hidden and mysterious world from clues found in the external world, and expressing that understanding." The domain of medicine, like that of literature, has both physical and spiritual dimensions.

Medical practice requires us to make "leaps of meaning" every day. The physician, in the midst of talking to a patient or thinking about a case, suddenly sees the problem in a different way. The diagnosis becomes clear. Or, after fruitless mucking around in the ambiguity of illness, the physician suddenly discovers the word that heals. We tend to call these leaps of meaning "intuition" or "clinical judgment" or "the art of medicine." These leaps are certainly subject to dissection and study. And the skills that allow us to make them can doubtless be taught. But the immediate "Eureka!" of seeing something in a new way is very much like experiencing a poem.

COMPLICATIONS

The last time Nate came in
he smelled like Grace did when
she worked door-to-door
for Avon. He had the one
pierced earring in, his beard
was trimmed, he had the cane
with a devil's head, the one
Grace had used to clobber him
the night she stroked. The last time
Nate came in the housing cops
had been there—took his two
big dogs. And then he was
alone. No matter what he did
the kids would bust his locks
and trash the place.

Nate found a woman half his age
or she found him. He wound up
in Baltimore, drunk, without
his bank account and by himself.
When he made it home
both guns were gone. Then Nate
was put in jail for D&D
a time or two. At the end
they phoned me from the morgue—
in his pockets the boys
found an old appointment card

Who, with a living heart, can live in this world as it is and not suffer and not experience pain? Who, with a tendency to feel, to sympathize, to love, does not go through pain? Who, with any sincerity in his nature, could experience daily the insincerity, falsehood, and crudity of human nature and yet avoid suffering?

—Hazrat Inayat Khan

and Nate's
"Certificate of Satisfactory Service"—
nothing else. They asked
if I would sign him out
and save the boys a trip?
I said, Sure! Let's give the man
a heart attack. *Then I thought*
of Grace's stroke, only I
didn't say a word about Grace,
just, Boys, the cause of death
was complications.

SAUNDRA

Saundra Lieberman is an accomplished spinner, weaver, artist, former art teacher, and is now embarking on a second career as a psychotherapist. She wove her first piece at eight years old on a four-harness loom her parents gave her. Saundra has a deep connection with the language of poetry through her love and knowledge of spinning and weaving. Her poem about winter sweaters is the remembrance of an annual ritual she performed for each of her children as they grew up.

Ahhhh . . . spinning. Spinning a yarn or spinning yarn. Two like phrases about two unlike processes, or are they? Spinning seems such an appropriate metaphor for how I feel about poetry. Spinning as a verb describes the feeling in my mind as thoughts race from topic to topic blending, teasing, relating and recalling ideas, impressions, and experiences.

Teasing wool, separating the fibers ever so gently to allow the undesired debris to fall to the floor, provides an image for the process of editing wherein words and phrases are dropped in an effort to weave clean concise expressions of thought. The synchronicity and similarity in creating poetry and spinning wool are uncanny.

The integrity of wool is established by the number of kinks per inch, the length and brittleness of fiber. Thirteen or more kinks suggest a strong fiber, three inches or better a good length, and the more lanolin the more workable and less brittle a fleece is. Poetry too must have integrity. Its strength is spun from fibers of content, intent, pur-

pose and persuasion, the number of lines, the choice of words, the image, the ahhhh . . .

Carding wool, brushing fibers, pulling them across piercing pointed needles, bent in wooden-handled paddles which smooth, comb, and transform massive tangles of fluff into straightened strands. Rolling the wool into logs to be stored in a basket next to the wheel. Smoothing rough spots, combing for words, working the idea and rolling into verse. The poem's intention is launched.

Spinning is when the rhythm commences. At the wheel the spinner sits on a stool, tapping her foot on the peddle . . . pressing a beat in four/four time. Softly relaxed, her hands gently caress the wool as she begins her performance; an age-old ritual. Fingers ever so finely pinch, draw, and release; pinch, draw, and release fibers as they twist into long thin cord which is fed to a hungry orifice that saves the yarn on a spindle. Words joined in thought and phrase, line and verse, spin a feeling, an experience, an image woven in content and saved in ink on a page:

Envision an image of spinning
if you will
long continuous thought connected sounds
which lead and follow up and down
round and round
Searching, working, styling ways
rhyming, timing thought in phrase
line to line silken words spill
as the poet's word sounds
the spindles whirl.

WINTER SWEATERS

Last spring's fleece
is being prepared
teased, carded and rolled into logs
awaiting to be spun.
Fingers in rhythm, dance
pinch draw release, pinch draw release
as the fibers spring
into woolen tentacles

wrapped tightly round the spindle
that saves them untangled.
Sweet smells of lanolin linger
and soften my hands
so as to honor
the wool as it passes through.
Fresh berries simmer on the stove
in kettles of white enamel.
After tepid baths of gentle dunking,
the wool is lowered into cooled pails
of blue, red and purple.
Thirsty and greedily
the wool is warmed with color
and hung to dry
in the tree outside my window.
Birds fly by to take a peck.
Nests in spring will remind me
of this season's spinning
and the children's winter sweaters
spun from last spring's
sheep coats.

TED

Ted Henry is a TV news anchor for a major midwest television station. He has been a journalist for thirty years. Ted helped to found an extraordinarily successful program for getting homeless families back into homes and steady work. Ted has been a regular participant in a poetry writing circle (see Chapter Seven) for over five years.

For me, writing the poem was the process by which I learned something about myself I had not previously known, at least not consciously.

—Richard Shelton

As a middle-aged male from mid-America, I was raised in the fifties when boys were instructed to conceal their feelings. It was then that I was taught the horrible notion that boys and men might not possess any feelings at all. Drawn out to its logical conclusion, I also figured that whatever intuitive urge I might have was baseless. Therefore, I dismissed such visceral impulses, until I discovered poetry.

I have discovered what might be the most wondrous tool of all, the intuitive voice. It was something I never knew I possessed, until po-

etry entered my life. The discovery of poetry and the intuitive voice has touched my newscasting work on deep levels.

I feel more genuine sadness or joy or chaos or even confusion depending on the nature of the news stories I am working with. I can feel myself reacting at a deeper level to the stories I am reading, and it's my belief that this extra depth of feeling is conveyed somehow through the camera's lens to the viewer. I am not suggesting that this gradual transformation in my news reporting represents a sense of self-righteousness, false empathy, or pushed compassion. I am only expressing a personal view that with the discovery of the poetic voice in my life I suddenly began to see the sum of life differently.

Each time I write a poem, I look forward to how I might be intuitively drawn to change or add to the poem, once I look at it again. The experience never fails me. I don't hear others talking much about this phenomenon and I sometimes wonder if I might have been the only child taught to suppress my feelings.

My hunch is that most poets merely take this feeling for granted. For me, it has become one of life's purest gifts. I'll spend an hour or two on a particular poem. I like what I see before me. And then I lay it down knowing that what's going to happen next is like kneaded dough baking in an oven: Its form is going to change.

When I return to the poem, whether it's while driving to work, in between household chores, or upon arising the next day, I am drawn like a knife to a magnet to reach out and strike this line, or delete that whole stanza or to add a new ending.

Poetry gives me the chance to see with greater clarity all that's on my mind, all that's important to me. And as it helps me to better identify where I am at any particular moment, it thereby helps me to be more attentive to my greatest needs.

Presence entails fully knowing that babies, women, and the old are starving and being maimed by militarism justified by high ideals; that forests and seas are dying; that there are fewer butterflies in our gardens, and more homeless on our streets.

—Don Hanlon Johnson

LATE NIGHT CYCLING

*The rushing night
is parted by his presence*

*warm waves lift him
in a glide*

all around
black curtains drape
the silent landscape

fir trees and tall grass
rest with eyes closed
and fail to notice
his whispered rush

the world quiets
to a crawl
wearing just a cloak
of summer sweet humidity

and for the moment
as dark becomes his friend
only he is alive

Poetry is the perfectly possible means of overcoming chaos.

—*I. A. Richards*

TELLING YOUR OWN STORY: "RECLAIMING YOUR INNER POET" QUESTIONNAIRE

This exercise encourages you to tell the story of your inner poet. The real beauty of this exercise is that it can be told differently each time you write. There is no "right answer," and in fact, your story may change from morning to night. Who you are as a poet could be expressed one way in the winter and another way in summer. What matters is that you are recognizing and discovering this creative, ever-renewing, multifaceted self. This exercise was created by my friend Perie Longo, a poetry therapist practicing in Santa Barbara, California.

General Guidelines

W You can link the questions together in a complete story or answer them individually. Answer those questions you feel most drawn to. Answer questions that are challenging or that seem like the most fun.

W Use your imagination but be specific in your naming: Include details of things, places, sense experiences, names, memories that tell the story of what your Inner Poet looks like, imagines, or must speak.

Before you begin, breathe and listen carefully. Let your voice and words flow.

What your inner poet looks like:

_____

_____

_____

What your inner poet feels like:

_____

_____

_____

Where your inner poet was born:

_____

_____

_____

What your inner poet sees:

_____

_____

_____

Where your inner poet is recognized:

_____

_____

_____

What your inner poet knows:

_____

_____

_____

_____

What your inner poet imagines:

_____

_____

_____

_____

Where your inner poet lives:

_____

_____

_____

_____

What your inner poet must speak:

_____

_____

_____

_____

Why your inner poet exists:

_____

_____

_____

_____

Here are some responses to this questionnaire:

My poet looks like the kind of Saturday morning that comes every once in a while—when you least expect it. He feels the sunlight trilling through each tree leaf, the emotion of ragged sea cliffs and palms that pulse and hold the birth of animals, raise sails and work towards the night of stars, mist, and silence. He lives for what matters most to me: wet leaves, fresh bread, and faces that have come through. These faces know me and say yes. And their yes becomes the choice to imagine my life as an ocean & wave that moves both inside & outside what I am, so where my poet lives, he arrives

with sweet sand clinging to his eyelids and what he must speak is
his breath, the salt, the water, the words: I am.

—*John Fox*

In spite of my best efforts to make him more presentable, my inner
poet is a word-binging drunkard, a cart-wheeling tap dancer
drumming magic, even out of stones. As for shape, form, or age—
asking him is as sensible as catching a cloud in a cricket cage. He's
resplendent in his manhood, as oiled as an athlete, hairless and
seamless as a boy, knotted and gnarled as an aging sailor.

No form contains him. He turns the sky purple by drawing a
single word across its surface and as a morning exercise he imag-
ines the birth and death of the universe, the ocean changing to sil-
ver, every heart on earth beating in unison, and the sun, her mask
off, opening glowing eyes. He is in awe of details: the curl of a rose
petal, a squirrel in mid-leap, a child's face watching butterflies. At-
tuned to the fine line between the expected and the worth notic-
ing, he is vastly amused that we lie to one another, so poorly and
so often.

In sixth grade a teacher managed to stop me from drawing,
erased my originality with her soft gum square. I learned to write
boring prose, dreary essays (about which I cared not a fig), and re-
search that no one read or needed.

My muse is born for liberation.

In my body he dances me till we fly. When I write well, he spurs
me on. Hot with his excitement, I write wildly. We become lovers.
His joy is huge when I exceed my boundaries. But when I'm more
worried about the price of the peso than the color of the sunrise,
he is gone.

He keeps me from standing in others' shadows. By speaking
truth larger than life, he envisions people better than they are. He
is an angel unwilling to let the world slide away, an inveterate op-
timist determined to stop it falling back into the sun.

—*Jim Fadiman*

My inner poet lives close to the skin and must be coaxed out with
delicacy. Only in the most trusting, serene circumstances, when
bathed in the warmth of the love of friends, she emerges. A shy pea-

The great instrument of
moral good is the imagination.
. . . Poetry strengthens that
faculty which is the organ of
the moral nature of man in
the same manner as exercise
strengthens a limb.

—*Percy Byssche Shelley*

cock, spreading her plumage. Losing inhibitions like shedding clothes with a lover, unbuttoning everything. Trance dreams and bones dance. Chrysalis unbinds and spins uncontrollably. Dizzy and laughter-drunk imagination pervades, blurring the distinction between fantasy and reality. Softening the boundaries between herself and everything, others and the world, you and me.

—Marla Lipschultz

f o u r

Language as Play

Experimenting with the Delights of Language

Children with the freshness of their senses come directly to the intimacy of this world. This is the first great gift they have.

          —Rabindranath Tagore

If you've ever listened to a very small child—if you are a mother, for instance—you know that they say some pretty strange and amazing things. That is because they are trying to tell us what the world looks like, seen for the first time, from a point of view that has never existed before! Great poets are people who have held on to that ability to see things new and say what they see. But we all had it once . . . original vision. A new way of seeing the world that was all your own.

            —Barbara Sher

Children move back and forth between the known and unknown minds with a minimum of fear.

            —Robert Bly

STALLIONS

*The galloping stallion runs
through the darkness into
the rainbow. The mist curls
around his feet like a cat
tracking a fly. It hears
singing like the music of
the hummingbird wings.
Like the sorrowful sound of
clover swaying in the wind.*
——Liz Brown, age 10

My imagination

is like a

tornado destroying

KA-BOOM.

problems and

hear a little

problem you

when I solve a

——Justin Petit, age 11

Raindrops shimmer down a dirty glass
And measle the windowpane.
Raindrops fall, breaking themselves into tiny china,
and run away like blood.
—*Ken Dickinson, age 10*

Look!
The clouds
are like
mashed potatoes!
—*Aaron Begg, age 2¹/₂*

The Inner Poet Is Our Youngest Part

The poet within us loves much of what the child loves: questioning, taking risks, imagining, exploring new possibilities, hugging life, playing! The poet within us also knows much of what the child knows: loneliness, hurt, the largeness of everything, fear of darkness, a longing to be heard. Yet beyond these, there is something else that the poet within us has in common with the child: a creative spark.

All these poems by children demonstrate a fresh sensibility and ingenuity which make things new. Their words show us that poetry makes comparison between vastly different things (potatoes and clouds!) as a way to help us understand life's mysteries—and in the process, it refreshes us with surprising turns of thought. Through poetry, we integrate once again the playfulness and curiosity of childhood into our adult lives.

Katrina writes about why her poet self is important in her busy life:

The inner poet is the youngest part of me. Forever young, I hope. My job keeps me on a short leash, so the inner poet often goes unheeded; brushed aside with hurried promises of "later." The inner poet knows

An excess of childhood is the germ of a poem.

—*Gaston Bachelard*

discovery and her purpose is to keep me from becoming a computer-
ized workaholic. She notices textures and small things. It is this part
of me that puts the decorations on our Christmas tree and plays tug-
of-war with our dog, Toki. It is the part of me that laughs at bad puns
and old elephant jokes.

Ted reflects on playfulness in his writing:

Some of the playful approaches I use in my poetry writing were
learned from other people, but surprisingly, many of them came to me
as sudden insights. And just the process of having and recognizing
these insights makes me think of the playfulness of creation.

His poem invites us to take notice of each miraculous mo-
ment:

TWILIGHT'S PEACE

When cream heavens
Lose their warmth
And turn cool pale

And the fat moon
Swollen in the bottom sky
Begins to ascend

It's nearly gone

The briefness
of cosmic
tranquility
                    —Ted Henry

Ted uses a handful of word combinations that are unusual in
sound and sense: cream heavens, cool pale, fat moon, bottom
sky. The long "oo" sounds of "lose," "cool," and "moon" are sooth-
ing. Are "cream," "bottom," and "fat" only fresh adjectives, or
could they also be used as nouns? In the case of cream and bot-

tom, even verbs? These kinds of transferences are not merely clever—they indicate real shifts in perception and offer new ways to discover the underlying relationship between things.

In the early stages of language, there was no rigid division between nouns and adjectives. The word "man" originally meant "intelligent." The word for "cow" could mean "that which provides nourishment." This adjectival character of nouns reflected the metaphoric and symbolic perceptions that were held by those who used ancient languages, such as Sanskrit. We've lost this spacious, symbolic use of language, and have replaced it with more static definitions. Poetry uses words in fresh ways to awaken within us these larger metaphoric connections.

Writing poetry will come naturally if you allow yourself to become as direct and free as a young child, if you can access a child's sense of curiosity and joy, a child's contact with feelings unfettered by analysis, as well as a child's ability to create metaphor by uninhibitedly making connections between everything seen and experienced. We can easily see all this in the children's poems that began this chapter!

You will create interesting word combinations by: reversing typical sequences of words; using unusual sounds to make dynamic images; putting together unexpected, even strange, word combinations; employing unusual adjectives and strong action verbs; turning nouns into adjectives, verbs into nouns, and nouns into verbs. Here are some exercises to experiment with. Remember—on the blank page, risk-taking is welcomed!

It is a very grave mistake to think that the enjoyment of seeing and searching can be promoted by means of coercion and a sense of duty.

—Albert Einstein

EXERCISES

Tag, You're It

1. Highlight the words or phrases in the children's poetry at the beginning of this chapter that impress you as new and exciting.
2. Highlight the words or phrases that remind you of your own childhood.
3. Write your own poem using your word and phrase choices or words that come to you as you consider the children's phrases and words.

Setting the Strawberry Alarm Clock:
Unusual Adjectives

Choose adjectives that sound unexpected and/or strange. Consider some of these famous examples from the 1960s: iron butterfly, strawberry alarm clock, surrealistic pillow. Here are others: feathered cadence, awkward star, spontaneous barn, sunburnt eyes, Christmas dust, chocolate childhood, wet jamboree. Make your own dynamic word combinations and then write a poem incorporating them.

Use unusual adjectives to:

ᴍ Wake your readers up so they'll perceive a particular "everyday" event in an entirely fresh way (as Ted does in his poem "Twilight's Peace")

ᴍ View a controversial social issue in a new way

ᴍ Write a daring, sensuous love poem

ᴍ Describe a spiritual experience without using the word "God"

ᴍ Make the reader laugh about an awkward situation

K-K-K-Katie, Beautiful K-Katie:
Repeating Sounds

Choose two particular sounds and use them repeatedly in a poem (e.g., a hard "a" or the long "oo"). You can use the words in the list below or make up your own. Use these repeating sounds in a poem that:

ᴍ Shows a correspondence to things you would normally think of as being separate

ᴍ Uses two sounds to represent two different emotions that speak to one another, without ever naming the emotions

$\bar{e}$	$\overline{oo}$	$\ddot{a}$	$\bar{o}$	$\bar{a}$
deem	flute	harvest	smoke	date
gleam	newt	car	flow	clay
seal	pool	harsh	loam	praying
between	jewel	operate	swollen	maiden
beets	dugong	gardenia	vote	scrape
sea	goo	barb	nomadic	race
cheap	moon	lobster	koan	wail

Shopping for Words

1. Go "shopping" through any magazine, book, or newspaper—or the dictionary—for words that interest or attract you. Write them down. Try not to "think" about them too much, just jot them down quickly, based upon your gut response.
2. Now put the words into three groups: nouns, adjectives, verbs.
3. Write a poem using the nouns as verbs, the verbs as adjectives, and the adjectives as nouns. For example:

Nouns	Adjectives	Verbs
belly	luminous	jump
cork	snappy	wrangle

With her jump face in place the luminous is
trying to belly to the wrangle mood
yearning to cork the snappy
before the snappy can belly luminous first.

A Bridge between the Sensibilities of Adult and Child

The prose poem below illustrates the crucial moment when a child, in a moment of awareness and aliveness, begins to consciously leave childhood, to become more aware of himself. Noah, a bright young poet of eleven, lives in San Francisco. He writes:

As I was walking home the other day I met my friends and we went and played baseball. As I was standing there on the field and the wind was blowing my soft T-shirt, I realized that this was my child-hood my only child-hood.

—*Noah Kircher-Allen, 5th grader*

I use sounds as it pleases my own ear. And my ear likes lots of sound. Sound and repetition. I like "music" in poems.

—*Charles Wright*

Noah moves through his known world—after-school time, friends, and baseball—and then, in a moment of keen awareness, stands within his unknown world. What is his unknown world? It is the magic sensation as the wind suddenly evokes for Noah his insight about childhood.

His fresh, sensory experience of the wind has an adult level of clarity, but it is connected to something more mysterious and lovely than most adults allow themselves to feel and reflect upon. How can we remember this?

> *We find that everywhere just beneath the surface of our conventional "objective" world lies waiting a forgotten world of overwhelming authenticity which is not alien but is ours.*
> —*Charles V. W. Brooks*

When Noah read his poem to people gathered at the National Poets in the Schools conference, there was an audible sigh as the adults in the room heard his last line. That sigh was a sign of longing for their own childlike sensibility, for the awe with which children relate to the world.

Too often, when we leave childhood, our awareness of the magic around us diminishes and we neglect the "forgotten world" Charles V. W. Brooks refers to. Discovering a way to reconnect with life's wonders and using language to reflect them is a joyful process.

All theory, dear friend, is grey, but the golden tree of actual life springs ever green.
—*Goethe*

SENSORY AWARENESS EXERCISE: FRESH FALLEN RAIN

This is an exercise to slow down and feel:

Take a walk after a fresh rain as the sun is just coming out. Wear whatever clothes you need to be comfortable, but allow for some open contact between the atmosphere, the earth, and your body. Go barefoot if you can. Let your face be in contact with the air. Walk slowly. Receive each moment openly and firmly as you take each step. What does the wet earth or pavement feel like underfoot? Feel the solidity of the earth under your feet as you take each step. Feel your senses open up as you walk, and allow them to be receptive. Stop from time to time and sense all that is around you. Go slowly. Feel the atmosphere. Does fresh fallen rain have a sound? A smell? Can you taste it? Don't try to label it, just feel it. Pick up some wet leaves from the ground and hold them in your hand or lightly skim your hand over the wet leaves of a tree. Close your eyes for a moment and feel fresh fallen rain sprinkle on your face. Let the rain-kissed atmosphere bring you a poem.

Write down your impressions in a notebook as you walk, or when you get home.

I Am a Piece of Paper, I Have Gushy, Gushy Comfort

Children are new to the world and express their unique sensory perceptions in a spontaneous way. A child's freedom from grammatical and literary standards is the very thing that makes language so enjoyable for them. We can learn a lot from their verbal playfulness:

> I am a piece of paper
> I have gushy gushy comfort
> I crackle
> A mean bully named hole puncher
> and I got in a fight
> He punched 3 holes in me
> Pssst . . . some poet just wrote on me.
> —Paul Green, 11 years

Paul probably didn't "know" his paper had "gushy gushy comfort" even one moment before he wrote that line. Once the word "gushy" was out on the page, though, he knew that he liked the sound and that it felt best to say "gushy" twice. *He felt it.* The next line of the poem snaps back immediately from that delicious-sounding gushy phrase to say, "I crackle." Paul did not consciously think, "Now I have to use a hard sounding, balancing word like 'crackle' because . . ." No. He intuitively explored the sounds and textures of words and "crackle" popped out. The poem sought a natural balancing point. *He let it.*

Take care of the sounds and the sense will take care of itself.

—Lewis Carroll

The unreasoned and immediate assurance is the deep thing in us, the reasoned argument is but surface exhibition. Instinct leads, intelligence does but follow.

—William James

Barking the Dog: Onomatopoeia

Have fun with words that sound like or close to what they mean, words like: whooosh, drip-drop drip-drop, zzzzzzzz, and bonk.

1. Write a poem in which half the words are onomatopoetic.
2. Make up your own "sounds just like it means" words and integrate them into a short poem.
3. Have one onomatopoetic word tell a detailed story of how it came into being. For example, how did the word "clunk" enter the language?

Shakespeare and I: Hyperbole

As an undergraduate I took a course in Shakespeare. In the early part of the semester, I asked the professor whether or not he thought Sir Francis Bacon might have written the plays of William Shakespeare. It's a popular esoteric notion—one I was interested in at the time. My freshman status was no protection for committing this inexcusable blunder: after ranting on for over ten minutes or more, my professor bluntly told the whole class that anyone asking such a question could be, at the very least, certifiably insane. I was a poor, duped fool to even consider such a thing!

Now, looking back, I find the event humorous. Even at the time, I can't say I was totally crushed by my professor's diatribe. There was something about it that I enjoyed. For all I know, he may have been hoping someone would ask such a question and permit him to perform thus. I think Professor Franklin was engaging in hyperbole at my expense. For whatever reason, he used my blunder to make his point by responding in an exaggerated way. I don't think anyone else in class attempted to stray far from the subject at hand after that!

Experiment with exaggerating by overstatement. Make your poem dramatic, funny, expressive. See how far you can extend your exaggeration to stretch the mind, to get the emotional impact of your essential message across, to make us laugh and see life's absurdities.

Think of an object, a circumstance, or a person in your life that could be well described by employing hyperbole. Make that object, circumstance, or person larger than life without losing track of its essential attributes. (Hyperbole can be serious as well as humorous. It can be used to describe sorrow and how the events of our lives are sometimes beyond understanding.) Create a poem from this description.

Describe in hyperbolic terms:

∿ Why your hometown sports team is so good (or bad)
∿ Your first date with your husband or wife, or with a lover

ᴡ Your exercise regimen

ᴡ The correctness of your political views

If you love things to be well-organized, write a hyperbolic poem proclaiming the benefits of disorganization. If you have a loose relationship to order, write a hyperbolic poem praising the attributes of a well-ordered life.

A Certain Openness to a Mysterious Process

Playfulness in using language occurs on many levels. There is the aspect of playfulness found in being original and inventive. But there is also a level of playfulness that goes to the core of being a writer—playfulness is a way to allow your writing to flow without judgment.

The poet William Stafford has some important comments to make on the place of "skill" in creative writing—that is, what people think of as knowing "how" to do something. For Stafford, it is not skill that gives us a place to start in our writing or that leads us forward, but receptivity and a certain openness to a mysterious process:

Finding ways to be sure that your ideas can flourish is necessary if the flow of ideas is to be maintained.

—James Fadiman

> . . . *They talk about "skills" in writing. Without denying that I do have experience, wide reading, automatic orthodoxies and maneuvers of various kinds, I still must insist that I am often baffled about what "skill" has to do with the precious little area of confusion when I do not know what I am going to say and then I find out what I am going to say. That precious interval I am unable to bridge by skill. What can I witness about it? It remains mysterious, just as all of us must feel puzzled about how we are so inventive as to be able to talk along through complexities with our friends, not needing to plan what we are going to say, but never stalled for long in our confident forward progress. Skill? If so, it is the skill we all have, something we must have learned before the age of three or four.*

What is needed in that "precious interval" of finding what it is you will say? It is a spirit of play, a willingness to follow your impulse, imagination, the wandering turn of your thought, the surprise that comes from opening up to what happens in your writing.

> *Only when I make room for the child's voice within me do I feel genuine and creative.*
>
> —*Alice Miller*

How did we play as children? We followed an impulse toward fun. We imagined that the toolbox our father had was not just a toolbox, it was *the* toolbox that serviced cars during the Indianapolis 500 and we were the head mechanics. Or we imagined that the open field and creek near our home was the playground for a legion of imaginary creatures, a place where we could become space aliens, good guys, cave dwellers, bad guys, wild horses, Amelia Earhart, and Mickey Mantle.

Poetic language offers us the opportunity to suspend a certain consensus of reality in order to invoke and experience a reality that is more deeply in tune with our feelings and our sense of who we are. In this way, we help imaginative poems to arise. All too often we are given the message to quit playing around and "get with the program." Sometimes, we wise up and transform "playing around" into creativity.

Carole Dwinell, a successful free-lance graphic designer, artist, and horsewoman, discovered the poet within in her mid-thirties. Carole says:

> *I worked as graphic designer for thirty years and chucked it because of deadlines. I just got tired of people putting things off until the last minute and then giving them to me and telling me to have it done tomorrow. So I stopped doing design on a regular basis. I work with horses now and only do graphic design when a project inspires me. Along with writing poetry, I am also returning after many years to painting and sculpture.*

Now in her fifties, Carole makes ample room for the child's sense of adventure and wonder, for her genuine and creative voice:

MOONSTRUCK

i am
older and wiser now,
it's true.

but i have a secret.
it's the moon.
believe me,
it doesn't just
hang in the sky
with footprints in moondust
and litter of rockets.

no.

it's a cookie.

crisp, cold silver sugar
to melt

in my mouth.

placed on the skyshelf
and hid until dark

untouched.

then each month
you can eat it.

one small bite at a time.

In Carole's poem there are images taken from the real world we all know about—footprints of astronauts and litter of rockets—but those physical facts are only used as a backlight to illuminate her imagination which reveals: the moon is a cookie! Carole says:

My poems usually start as a combination of feeling and idea that has sufficient intensity to transform itself into two or three phrases. This transformation precedes a conscious decision to write.

—*Cynthia McDonald*

When I wrote down the initial thoughts that became this poem, I was camping. I was eating a sugar cookie one night and it was very cold outside. The cookie was cold too, but there was also something sensuous about it. It has that round shape. You take a bite out of it and it changes like the moon. Those first key words were: "crisp, cold silver sugar."

This poem has been through a lot of work. To find something that is universally fresh about the moon—about anything—it's important to step out of the way. But the poem itself is a step out of "reality." Writing the poem helped me to get out of the way. Essentially, the poem is about savoring the sameness of pleasure without trying to search out a new and better pleasure.

Laying the words of your poem out on the page is another opportunity to combine playfulness with the desire to accurately embody the reality about which you are writing.

Carole's poetry especially communicates through her line lengths. Notice how her words "move" across the page in this poem about e. e. cummings, master poet of playfulness:

> *e. e. cummings*
>
> *wordloose.*
> > *poet.*
> > *giddy with power and poemlove.*
> > > *Shooting down*
> > > > *all*
> > > > *the*
> > > > *rules*
> > > > *into*
> > > > *cheesecake.*
> *wordplay*
> > *for no one,*
> > *for everyone, for unicorns*
> > > *and city councilmen.*
>
> > > *A*
> > > *hidden*

e.e. man.

gigglewords.

Carole describes her process of choosing line lengths:

> *One of the ways I get line lengths and layout in my poems to work is I print the poem out just as I have it—even if I hate it as it is—and then cut the individual lines up into strips and play with them on a table. When I can move the lines around physically and feel the poem in a more kinesthetic and visual way, it works for me. I may need to change particular words on the line to get it to work when using this particular technique, but a sense for the poem's structure often comes forward strongly.*
>
> *All the changes I made in this poem had to do with finding its right shape on the page. Poetry is sometimes like making a puzzle but quite often if you put the puzzle pieces in different places than they are expected to fit, it looks* better.
>
> *I want to have the freedom when I write to try all kinds of styles. For instance, I make up words all the time. I wrote "e. e. cummings" in response to someone who said, a bit pompously I felt at the time, that I needed more structure and less foolishness in my poetry. So this poem is written for that part of us and of me that is quirky, that is silly, that doesn't conform. It's about freedom and that "e. e. man" who's there, hidden somewhere within us. We just don't let him out to play very often. And though we don't think about it very much, all of us seem to like those odd turns of phrase when we hear them. I think we are refreshed by them. And that is what poetry is all about.*

As in almost all of my writing, I was not aiming toward any reader: my entry into the process was through inward satisfactions I felt as the language led me onward.

—William Stafford

"Look, Think, Jump, Land . . ."

Consider the following possibilities for making line breaks:

- ⩊ To show the intervals of your breath, especially as impacted by various emotions
- ⩊ To show intervals of concise thought and/or image
- ⩊ To convey the natural flow of your everyday speech

- ⩗ To create a particular rhythm
- ⩗ As "enjambment"—an unfolding spillover of words from the end of one line to the beginning of the next to give the poem the feeling of an organism
- ⩗ Whatever feels right to you . . .

In my workshops, people experiment with wordplay, layout, and line lengths by first writing about a playful, energetic childhood experience in "regular" poetic form, depending on the words alone to convey the feeling of their experience. I then ask them to rework the layout in the poem, seeing how they can viscerally feel their experience by the way the poem is set out on the page.

Jack is in his late thirties and married. He is a systems analyst in the management information systems department of a large computer retail business. Jack's experience with poetry was minimal up to the time he took my workshop. Yet in his very first experiments with this exercise, he showed how natural it is to make words come alive on the page. Here is his first poem about a playful childhood experience, as it was written before he experimented with line lengths and page layout:

Rock Hopping Creek

Boys scramble out of camp
There is a new world to explore
Trees, trails, hills,   A CREEK!
The creek with water flowing
What's upstream? What's around the bend?
"I bet you get wet before I do"
We're at it, we jump, it's on!
The rocks are unevenly spaced
Some are far apart

Look, think, jump, land
Look, think, jump, land
Watch out for the slippery rocks

Jump, land   Jump, land   Jump, land
I see only the rocks, feel the cool air
Jump - Jump
Jump - Jump, Jump - Jump

Now I flow like water, but I stay dry!

Now look how the second layout of the poem on the page can reveal more of Jack's experience of "rock hopping," not just because he spreads words out wider on the page, but because in making this change, he creates more feeling of spontaneity and movement. If you read it aloud as it appears on the page, you can experience what Jack's rock-hopping adventure was like. The poem creates the texture of his whole escapade. Indeed, Jack's wonderful last two lines tell the whole story:

A poet needs to keep his wildness alive inside him.

—Stanley Kunitz

ROCK HOPPING CREEK

Boys scramble out of camp
      There is a new world to explore

Trees, trails, hills,   A CREEK!
      The creek with water flowing
            What's upstream? What's around the bend?

            "I bet you get wet before I do"

We're at it, we jump, it's on!
The rocks are unevenly spaced some are far apart
      Look, think,   jump,   land
            Look, think,   jump,   land
Watch out for the slippery rocks
      Jump, land
            Jump, land
            Jump, land

> I see only the rocks, FEEL the cool air
> Jump - Jump
> Jump - Jump - Jump - Jump
> Now I flow like water, but
> I stay dry!
> —Jack Winkle

Not all poems will be as physical as Jack's is in expressing movement through line breaks. It is a matter of sensing in your body and tuning to your feeling and perception about *what is right for a particular poem*. In order to make your poetic lines ring true, allow your poem to take the physical shape it demands.

EXERCISE: ALL ALONG THE LINE

Try experimenting with the following poem by varying the line breaks. Play with the lines until the "shape" of the poem pleases you.

PAH TEMPE, UTAH

Pale sliver of a moon
Almost unnoticed in the clouds
Still flying high from morning thunderstorms

Your luminescence woke me up last night
Making magic on the canyon walls
And shimmering on the flowing water
Warmed by hidden springs that touch
The ancient fires still burning in the earth
—Connie Smith Siegel

_____

_____

_____

_____

_____

Line breaks, perhaps more than anything else, will teach you to listen to your inmost voice, to the way the lines of a poem resonate with you, giving you a sense of spiritual alignment with your poem. Connie reflects on her experience of working on her poem long after she had left Pah Tempe: "I was still rearranging words and lines all across Nevada and well into Arizona."

Experimenting with line breaks is a way to discover on a visceral and intuitive level the heartbeat of your poem. Try Carole's line cutting technique (described on page 97) or other experimental ways of determining line breaks with your own poems.

On the purpose of lines in poetry:
Lines keep the motion of the poem going, both in terms of rhythm, sound, and in terms of meaning, denotative meaning.
—W. S. Merwin

"It Is the Best Way to Write Poetry, Letting Things Come . . ."

I can tell you the poet whose work first caught my ear when I was about five years old—Winnie-the-Pooh was a major "poet" of my childhood. From him I learned that play and creativity are the same thing. By spontaneously sitting down on stones in the middle of the stream and speaking his poems, Pooh gave the message: wherever you are, listen to your musings.

We can put Pooh's poetic philosophy into a more adult context because at the heart of it, his message applies to poets of any age.

First, let's hear about the creative process of poetry-making in this passage from A. A. Milne's *House at Pooh Corner:*

> *Tigger finished his last circle and came up to Pooh and Piglet.*
> *"Hot!" he explained with a large and friendly smile. "Come on!" and he rushed off.*

Pooh and Piglet walked slowly after him. And as they walked Piglet said nothing, because he couldn't think of anything, and Pooh said nothing, because he was thinking of a poem. And when he had thought of it he began:

> What shall we do about poor little Tigger?
> If he never eats nothing he'll never get bigger.
> He doesn't like honey and haycorns and thistles
> Because of the taste and because of the bristles.
> And all the good things which an animal likes
> Have the wrong sort of swallow or too many spikes.

"He's quite big enough anyhow," said Piglet.
"He isn't really very big."
"Well, he seems so."
Pooh was thoughtful when he heard this, and then he murmured to himself:

> But whatever his weight in pounds, shillings, and ounces,
> He always seems bigger because of his bounces.

"And that's the whole poem," he said. "Do you like it, Piglet?"
"All except the shillings," said Piglet. "I don't think they ought to be there."
"They wanted to come in after the pounds," explained Pooh, "so I let them. It is the best way to write poetry, letting things come."
"Oh, I didn't know," said Piglet.

What makes Pooh's poem delightful? It is the same element that makes any poet's work feel alive: *Pooh is receptive to what occurs in his life.* Receptivity allows originality to flow in. His poem comes from directly observing and being engaged in his experience.

The lines "because of the bristles," "Have the wrong sort of swallow or too many spikes," and "He always seems bigger because of his bounces" are magical not because A. A. Milne "decided" that these words were playful, but because, like Paul Green using the words "gushy gushy," Milne liked the way the words sounded in his mouth—they felt right and they worked. The rhythmic rolling *b*'s, the *buh buh buh*'s, feel good together, even humorous, when you say them. We delight in the phrases *because of the playfulness of the sounds*. The sense they make is important but secondary. Meaning arises from the sounds themselves, just as yeast makes bread rise.

Now let's listen again to the late, great poet William Stafford about "letting things come" in poetry. He speaks about his writing practice:

> *Back in school, from the first when I began to try to write things, I felt this richness. One thing would lead to another; the world would give and give. Now, after twenty years or so of trying, I live by that certain richness, an idea hard to pin, difficult to say, and perhaps offensive to some. For there are strange implications in it.*
>
> *One implication is the importance of just plain receptivity. When I write, I like to have an interval before me when I am not likely to be interrupted. For me, this means usually the early morning, before others are awake. I get pen and paper, take a glance out of the window (often it is dark out there), and wait. It is like fishing. But I do not wait very long, for there is always a nibble—and this is where receptivity comes in. To get started I will accept anything that occurs to me. Something always occurs, of course, to any of us. We can't keep from thinking. Maybe I have to settle for an immediate impression: it's cold, or hot, or dark, or bright, or in between! Or—well, the possibilities are endless. If I put down something, that thing will help the next thing to come, and I'm off. If I let the process go on, things will occur to me that were not at all in my mind when I started. These things, odd or trivial as they may be, are somehow connected. And if I let them string out, surprising things will happen.*

My reader is anyone who reads poetry but especially the woman who is too busy folding the laundry to read poetry and who reads it anyhow.

—*Nancy Willard*

EXERCISE: A PROGRAM TO INSPIRE IMPULSE WRITING

Let's see what surprising things can happen in your writing. Put your pen on the paper and write a poem about one or more of the following topics—or choose your own. Allow your words to play out freely on the page. Listen for sounds and rhythms as they come up—try words out in your mouth. Follow your impulses. Follow sounds and rhythms, colors and textures. Follow the trail of your wandering thoughts as you approach your subject. Let things connect and move you forward. As Pooh says, write your poem by "letting things come." Write everything you can about:

- ⩔ Doing the laundry
- ⩔ Working in your yard
- ⩔ Turkey (the bird, not the country)
- ⩔ Looking for something you've lost
- ⩔ Your most embarrassing moment as a child
- ⩔ Trying clothes on in a store
- ⩔ Things in the back half of your refrigerator
- ⩔ Changing the oil in your car
- ⩔ Your ideal Saturday
- ⩔ Your first kiss
- ⩔ Flying to the moon
- ⩔ Communicating with someone who doesn't speak English

When given a similar assignment in his fifth-grade class, ten-year-old Ian Begg came up with the following poem:

You

your lovely neck
your beautiful eyes
your gorgeous skin
your scrumptious legs
you, my Thanksgiving turkey
m m m m m m m h!

*L*anguage is not a cultural artifact that we learn the way we learn to tell time or how the federal government works. Instead it is a distinct piece of the biological makeup of our brains.

—Steven Pinker

The Language We Give Birth To: Playing with Sounds

The sounds words make evoke feeling and tone and add rhythm and texture to poetry. From the gross to the most refined, sound touches our deepest sense of self. Sound is the entire field of vibration from which grow particular words. Poets learn to vocalize, write, and play in that field of sound and appreciate every aspect of how words create verbal music.

Language sprouts from the cries of our infant delights and upsets. We respond to the sounds of language before we understand the words. Dylan Thomas offers us a priceless personal story about the sound of words:

> You want to know why and how I just began to write poetry. . . .
>
> To answer . . . this question, I should say I wanted to write poetry in the beginning because I had fallen in love with words. The first poems I knew were nursery rhymes, and before I could read them for myself I had come to love just the words of them, the words alone. What the words stood for, symbolized, or meant was of very secondary importance. What mattered to me was the sound of them as I heard them for the first time on the lips of the remote and incomprehensible grown-ups who seemed for some reason to be living in my world. And these words were, to me, as the notes of bells, the sounds of musical instruments, the noises of the wind, sea, and rain, the rattle of milkcarts, the clopping of hooves on cobbles, the fingering of branches on a window pane, might be to someone, deaf from birth, who has miraculously found his hearing. I did not care what the words said, overmuch, not what happened to Jack and Jill and the Mother Goose rest of them; I cared for the shapes of sound that their names and the words describing their actions, made in my ears, I cared for the colors the words cast in my eyes. I realize that I may be, as I think back all that way, romanticizing my reactions to the simple and beautiful words of those pure poems; but that is all I can honestly remember, however much time might have falsified my memory.

That early fascination with the sounds of language also includes the making up of words. Can you remember making up words as a child? What were they?

When as adults we experiment with making sounds, we take a major step toward connecting with the poet within. It means enjoying words for the way they pop, ring, reverberate in our ears. It means delighting in the nonmeaning aspect of words—

as a child does when he chants "Hickory dickory dock . . ." or "Fi Fie Fo Fum . . ."

I love to get adults involved in making up words. They will begin cautiously, not wanting to be seen by others as spouting nonsense, but soon—it's hard to stop them! Workshop participants create long lists of made-up words along with "real" words they like. We write them all down on a big piece of newsprint. Here is one such list:

Klakatats	Nettles	Quark	Kersplash	Slithery
Obsidian	Smorfly	Ketchikan	Smarms	Wallop
Trilliams	Floats	Zebra	Frangle	Woodchuck
Fractile	Fuzzy	Curvaceous	Seattle	Frabuloud
Malachite	Gragnex	Tuckfod	Ozone	Poozchita

Developing a poem from this list, I wrote:

OH, FRABULOUD DAY!

Oh, frabuloud day!
The fuzzy dandelion is tukfod, is klakatats,
is beige flour, is quinquamarine,
is blown into the curvaceous air—
a memorable irridescent frangle
floats into the velvet buzzing ozone, awakening
the incandescent & sweet sound
of small summer:
Slainte! Slainte! Slainte!

EXERCISE: JUST FOR THE SOUND OF IT

〜 Compile a list of both made-up words and real words that you enjoy saying. Include words that you remember making up as a child. Create a poem using the words on your list.

_____

_____

_____

〰 Read the following excerpt from Marilyn Krysl's superb poem, "Saying Things." Say the words out loud. Cast them into the air. Say-vor them.

> . . . *Say bellows, say sledge,*
> *say threshold, cottonmouth, Russian leather,*
> *say ash, picot, fallow deer, saxophone, say kitchen sink.*
> *This is a birthday party for the mouth—it's better than ice cream . . .*

〰 Find the entire poem "Saying Things" (it's in *The Discovery of Poetry* by Frances Mayes). Using it as an inspiration, make a regular practice of appreciating the sounds of words by saying them out loud, just for the pure auditory pleasure of it! Give your ears and mouth a birthday party and celebrate the difference they make in your life.

At this moment, I hear a plane overhead shaking the atmosphere with a low rumble. I can feel it in my toes. A train a few blocks away thunders forward, its wheels creating a palpable rolling vibration in the air that I can feel deep in my belly. My fingers click and clack lightly on the computer keyboard. I hear my breath stream in and out of my body. Sound is all around and inside me.

All things being derived from and formed of vibrations have sound hidden within them, as fire is hidden in flint, and each atom of the universe confesses by its tone, "My sole origin is sound."
> *—Hazrat Inayat Khan*

Words contain this fire of sound. Like the moving plane or the train or my fingers or my breath—words emit a sound that can be felt in the physical and emotional body. Sound and feeling come before image and meaning.

Take time during your day to listen to the sounds around you in all their variety and nuance. Listen to the words you speak and hear.

Blooming Berries, Winged Iris

The gift and enjoyment of sound was with us before we learned to write or spell or even to make sense. It was with us before we learned to organize our response to the world using labels and categories. To play with words, as 16-year-old Jamie Pearlstein does, is to remind ourselves of the magic language offers:

SPIDERY GRANDMOTHER

branching fingers revive
a smooth and gnarled
walking stick.
bark-colored eyes
thoughtful.
blackberry leaves scurry
over seasonal toes,
bony ankles.
resting
among klammath baskets
in the welcoming glance
of a red twiggy chair
within the dampness
of a soft shed
of wood.
waning
in pleasant new green.
blooming berries, winged iris,
persimmon, Sterling Silver
warm tomatoes.
Lazy Boy's wise purr
orbiting the wilted body
planting seeds
in grizzly hair
a chilled handle

belonging to a lazy watering can
awaits her kind paw
but saving water for June
grass clothed stepping stones
hiding the sing
of chirping crickets
tactile arms of old
sewn to the trunk of an apple tree
reaching above hovering
high walls
trespassing iron balconies
climbing offshoots
sifting out
angry calls of the street.
Pinnaroo's small melody
may be only a dim hum
but enough
to dry
damp, folded wings
of a zebra swallowtail.

From "bony ankles" to "Pinnaroo's small melody," from "grizzly hair" to "grass clothed stepping stones," from a "wise purr" to the "folded wings / of a zebra swallowtail," her rich flow of natural connections, tangible images, textures, and sounds make us aware that life is something miraculous. It demonstrates that the dynamic creation of which we are a part is filled with play, energy, rapture, and music.

Children have their active sub-conscious mind which, like a tree, has the power to draw food from the surrounding atmosphere. For them the atmosphere is a great deal more important than rules and methods, equipment, textbooks and lessons.

—Rabindranath Tagore

Play on Words:
Entering the Field of Your Imagination

Sometimes all you need to get started on a poem is one word or phrase. The following pages provide you with lots of words and phrases—endless possibilities for poem-making. This game is one of the most effective ways I've ever used to get people quickly making poems. The definition of the word "poet" is "maker." In mere moments, you can have access to your intuitive voice and imagination and be making your own unique poems.

One way to experience a sense of playfulness is to treat words as if they were objects you might find in nature: a shell, a stone, a palm frond, flower petals, some sage. Just as you could creatively put those natural objects together to form an interesting and attractive arrangement, so you can choose attractive words to arrange natural poems.

Another method is to treat the words as if they were paint, clay, or wood. Words thus become artistic material to be molded or chiseled or blended. You already have your materials, all you need now is to follow your imagination and your sense of what interests you.

EXERCISE: PLAY WITH WORDS

1. Make a photocopy on good cardstock of the words on the following pages.
2. Cut out the words using a paper cutter or scissors.
3. Put the words in a container.

You are ready to start! This game can be "played" with anyone: spouse, friends, lover, family, co-workers, people in your support group or just by yourself!

The essence of the game is to grab a handful of words, have fun playing around with them, and make poems! There are absolutely no rules to this game. You are the rule-maker! Here are some suggestions on how to get started:

- Spread your words out and see what you've got.
- Notice combinations of words that are unusual, interesting, provocative, funny, strange.
- Begin to arrange the words as you please, using all the words or only those that appeal to you.
- Choose new words from the bowl if you want.
- If you are playing this with others, trade words if you want.
- Add words that aren't in the bowl as you need them for your poem.
- If you need prepositions, connectives, articles, just add them.
- Change tenses of verbs as you desire.
- Let your poem take shape by moving the words around in ways that please you.
- Write your poem on a piece of paper once you've arranged it.

Remember: This is a spontaneous poem and does not need to look anything like the way you think a "real poem" should look. You can do anything you want. Be daring! If you feel that some words sound too strange to be linked together, try it anyway. Trust your intuition and visceral sense to guide you. Go with what feels right. Enjoy!

> *I don't believe in tame poetry.*
> —*Frank Stanford*

SAILS	TANGERINE	MONKEYS	GRACE
DANCE	DOVES	FEELING	NATURAL
LILAC	STARS	CRIES	WOW!
BRIDGE	SMILE	HUSH	DAWN
DRINK	MAGIC	EMERALDS	SWIMS
FLY	IN	RHAPSODY	ANIMAL
OOZES	IS	RETURNS	DREAMS
SHUDDER	RELISHED	SINK	RALLY
RECEIVED	CROWDING	PLUNGE	DASHING
CONCEAL	RANTING	WRESTLE	APPLAUD
SEEK	EDGED	AMAZE	CORRECT
SHINES	DEATH	SADNESS	PENGUINS
PLUCKS	MUSIC	FISHES	EARTH

CREATURES	RAINCOAT	BREATH	OPEN
HAIL	RESCUE	LOATHE	CHOOSE
ADORED	SAUNTER	BEND	TWIST
DEFILE	DEFEND	DIG OUT	RUSH
REVEAL	THUNDERS	FROM ME	SILENCES
BETRAY	SPINS	GROWS	PEOPLE
OCEAN	SEA	LEAVENS	SALT
DARK	EROTIC	LUCKY	GLISTENS
JUSTICE	BROTHER	TIGHT	SCARED
BESTOW	CARESS	CLING	GRATIFY
FRAGILE	CHILDREN	CHILD	ALONE
PIGS	DONKEYS	SWAN	TIGER
SUNSET	TRAMPLE	FINCHES	FLAT
SURPRISE	BOILS	HUMMINGBIRDS	FIRE
SHARING	SAND	LITTLE ISLAND	INFINITE
DRIPS	BEAUTIFUL	SUN & MOON	SHIPS
DESERT	RAINFOREST	CITIES	IMAGINE
DESTRUCTIVE	SNOW	RAIN	VENUS
DIAMONDS	WEEPS	MARRIAGE	RINGS
BLESS	GYPSIES	ASLEEP	CARS
HEALING	HANDS	FEET	SMOOTH
RELEASE	HARD	BANANA	FOOD
CHEERFUL	RISES	HORSES	APPLE
PEACE	WAR	ADULTS	ELDERS
DAUGHTERS	GRANDMOTHER	GRANDFATHER	NO
COOK	NUDE	TRUST	BRAMBLE
CRAZY	SAVING	BLACK	BLUE
ASHAMED	BONES	FIRELIGHT	BOAT

HUSBAND	LOVE	HOLY	CLOVER
BUBBLES	SORROWS	IS ALL	DESIRE
EVER AFTER	BLOOD	SEA SWEPT	WOODEN
REGRETS	JUGGLERS	CIRCUS	FARM
RURAL	SOUR	BROKEN	ADDICTED
BODY	DISSOLVES	LEAP	INSIDE
EXPLOSION	NATURE	ROCKS	ARTISTS
MOTHERS	DEATHLESS	LIFE	HEROINE
HERO	OPEN HANDED	PROWLING	ANGER
UNFOLDS	PETALS	POLLEN	INFANTS
LILIES	VOYAGE	LOVERS	HISSES
EROTIC	LOVEMAKING	DREAMS	LIGHT
SPILLING	BREASTS	FORGIVENESS	MUSIC
DEFENSELESS	ORDINARY	SNAKE	GRASS
SISTER	LISTEN	WOMB	CAT
FALLS	PURRS	CASCADING	ROOTS
URGE	LEAF	BUDS	RIVER
EMBRACE	INVITATION	GOD	COOKING
SIMPLE	UNWINDS	BARE	FEARLESS
UNKNOWN	TINIEST	AUTUMN	WINTER
STRUGGLE	LICKING	SPINNING	WHEEL

The following are some samples of this exercise . . . *anything is possible!*

> *Remember*
> *the fertile*
> *trees from*
> *where you*

and I
whisper into
the secret
place and
smile. The
old mill
now half-
covered with
moss had
that joyful
eeriness to
it that made
us wonder.
Wonder
what the
bluebird
used to
sing.
—Eric Kallman

Heartache fire looks for joy—
attains only struggle.
Here fragile petals smile
on just the grace to live.
                    —*John Fox*

Slavery takes away his right to choose.
He cannot go and praise the rich grass
            of the pasture
            if he chooses.
He is just a hard farm worker with
            waves of salt cakes
            on his hat.
Things must change in this land.
The slave will not wait for the grass is
calling him.
                    —*Matt Moore*

Above that ocean
    of winter marriage
    destructive cries
    frightened unity——no blessings.
Frightened winter cries
    above destructive oceans
    bless that marriage unity
Marriage cries winter,
    destructive, frightened
    above that ocean
Above winter cries
    destructive ocean
    frightened unity

Bless that marriage
Winter cries above
    that destructive frightened marriage

    Bless ocean unity

Ocean unity that blesses marriage
    gone the winter of
    destructive frightened cries.
            ——Judy Davidson

five

The Brain Is Just the Weight of God

Metaphor and Other Tools of Poem-Making

The brain is wider than the sky,
 For, put them side by side,
The one the other will include
 With ease, and you beside.

The brain is deeper than the sea,
 For, hold them, blue to blue,
The one the other will absorb,
 As sponges, buckets do.

The brain is just the weight of God,
 For, lift them, pound for pound,
And they will differ, if they do,
 As syllable from sound.
      —Emily Dickinson

Metaphor

Darmok and Jalad at Tenagra

There is a famous episode of *Star Trek: The Next Generation* called "Darmok" where Captain Jean-Luc Picard is beamed down to a planet with a Tamarian named Dathon. Dathon is also a ship's captain and, like Jean-Luc, is a leader of accomplishment and intelligence. Their goal is to develop bridges of understanding. But there is a real problem. Communication between the two is virtually impossible. Picard's thinking and speech is straightforward and rational. Dathon, on the other hand, can only think and speak in poetic terms.

When Dathon sees their campfire about to go out, he says something akin to, "Our stars are fading away." Picard has no idea what Dathon is talking about and is unable to recognize the link between the embers of the campfire and the stars. When Picard also notices the fire dying out and insists plainly that they gather wood, Dathon does not have a clue what Picard means because he is unable to link his inner poetic experience with practical action.

The story of Picard and Dathon is an excellent illustration of the split between the rational, logical mind and the creative, poetic soul. Jean-Luc kept trying to ascertain certain facts that would allow him to proceed logically in solving their dilemma; this only led him to further exasperation. Dathon, on the other hand, became more lonely and withdrawn as time went on. Unable to convey to Jean-Luc the fullness of all that he experienced and felt, he became depressed.

Finally, Picard, with his capacity for openness to new things, began to *listen* with his intuition. He saw the value and depth of Dathon's poetic communication. There began to be recognition: Dathon, for his part, saw that there was a way to put his inner world into action. It was through this process of recognition and connection that each became able to decipher the other's language, and their communication breakdown was bridged. This linking of seemingly different entities is the special, liberating role of *metaphor*. The making of metaphor opens a window where the inner and outer aspects of our lives can join.

The metaphoric voice contains the threads that join mind and soul, self and other, self and the natural world, self and God. What once seemed separate is revealed to be made of one fabric.

Poetic devices such as metaphor, simile, sound, and image allow us to make what is perceived within the heart come to light in our writing. Metaphors are capable of giving one a wholly new perspective; but they are not especially mysterious. Like Picard learning to communicate with Dathon, you can learn to make them.

Why are mysteries unpublishable? First because they cannot be put into words, at least not the kind of words which earned you your Phi Beta Kappa keys. Mysteries display themselves in words only if they can remain concealed: this is poetry, isn't it?

—*Norman O. Brown*

EXERCISE: "I AM A POMEGRANATE"

There is probably nothing more central to poetry than vibrant metaphors. Used with clarity and skill, they can make a poem breathe forever.

To do the following exercise, just ask yourself, "What do I want to be?"—something that is not obviously yourself. Do you want to be the mane on a wild horse? The color purple? An eggbeater? A salmon? Your pet? A drum? Your back yard? Your computer? Think of something particular in nature, a place that is special to you, an animal or part of an animal, an object in your home or from your place of work, a car, a weather condition, a spiritual symbol—anything at all.

Now write what you want to say about this thing that you are. Your writing should make it possible to *see, hear, touch, taste,* what you are. Remember you *are* this thing. Take some moments to *feel yourself* as the thing you have chosen. Imagine doing all the things you would do. How would you express yourself? How would you relate to your world? If I experienced you, what would my experience be? Here are two examples:

> *I am a pomegranate*
> *red and bursting*
> *full of*
> *surprise*
> *seeds of growth and bitterness*
> *I am difficult to eat*

take a lot of patience
I am messy
and will stain you
but my juice
is
   so
     sweet
      —Christine Stiegelmeyer

I am purple
vibrant
and whole
beauty and strength
radiate through me
I have presence
I will not be ignored
I do not have to shout
I surround your dreams
tinge your fantasies
I creep in at night
hold you in my arms
soothe you
   disturb you
      empty you
         complete you
I am purple
vibrant and whole
  —Christine Stiegelmeyer

Notice how Christine extends the metaphor to show us the many aspects of being a pomegranate and the color purple. Notice how she gets particular. Notice also how she offers nuances of each aspect and brings out the contrasts. The juice of the pomegranate will stain—but it is also sweet. Christine's color purple will not be ignored, yet does not have to shout to get attention. What a marvelous way to show us what the color purple is! Try it now yourself:

I am _____   I am _____

_____   _____

_____ _____
_____ _____
_____ _____
_____ _____

The Landscape of Possibility–Using Multiple Metaphors

Poet David Wiley refers to the blank piece of paper on which he writes as a series of metaphors. His provocative metaphors call upon us to see an ordinary piece of paper in entirely new ways:

> TO A PIECE OF PAPER
>
> _Here is the landscape of all possibility,_
> _whiter than the obverse of ether._
> _Here is the window of a universe unborn,_
> _where the mind's fugitive seed_
> _seeks a hidden orifice of Creation._
> _Here is the battlefield,_
> _here is the scented bed;_
> _here is the palace,_
> _dazzling in its lack of plumage,_
> _where something unknown_
> _wants to live._

Highlight the metaphors in David's poem. What _is_ a piece of paper? A piece of paper is: a landscape, window, battlefield, scented bed, and palace. In what way is paper a landscape? A landscape allows for a whole expanse of different things to be seen in one view. That's exactly the role of metaphor. And he goes on to name some of them. He says the paper is a window. Why is a window a good metaphor here? A piece of paper is a "window" that lets the light of your writing in and allows your eye to look through it—it is a place for what is within and with-out to interact, just as a window allows the wind to blow through. (Interesting! The word "window" comes from the Old Norse word, *vindauga,* or literally "wind eye.")

What about a battlefield? The paper is a place for opposing forces to gather, where you can grapple with what is real and what is not, with what is just and unjust. It is a place where your pain can go, where you can set yourself free.

A scented bed? We hardly need to be told about that metaphor! We can *feel* it. It's not just any bed, it's a *scented* bed. The choice of metaphor hints at the subtle fragrances of lovemaking in all its many forms.

What or whom do you love? The piece of paper is a place to be in love with your dreams and imagination. What voices will come together and speak on your page with their passion, with their strongest and most intimate cries? The page is a place to be with your beloved—whatever or whomever you write about.

The piece of paper is a palace inviting a sense of nobility and greatness. Yet, like the nuance of saying the *scented* bed, this palace catches our attention because of its *lack of plumage.* Your noblest and best thoughts can live royally on this startling blank page without being ostentatious.

What else could a piece of paper be? Using David Wiley's poem as a model, take some time to imagine for yourself other metaphoric possibilities. For instance, I wrote:

> Here is the garden of silence, the virgin soil
> of blossomed syllables and ripened cries.
> Here is the dance floor of all dreams,
> where the quickened feet of joy and grief
> trace out circles from the heartbeat of Creation.
> Here is the veiled chamber
> Here is the open hand
> Here is the sea foam
> shimmering against the dark shore of time
> where something unknown wants to live.

Now try your own metaphor poem about paper and what it is for your writing:

TO A PIECE OF PAPER

*Here is the*_____
_____
*Here is the*_____
where the _____
_____*of Creation.*
Here is _____
here is the _____
here is the _____
_____

where something unknown wants to live.

Poetry Is Pure White—Organic Metaphors

In his poem, David Wiley used multiple metaphors. Another approach is to use only one metaphor and thoroughly develop it. May Swenson has termed this "organic metaphor." She says, "Organic metaphor is where the metaphor moves all the way through the work, and it builds with just one metaphor." The challenge of this is to let that one metaphor grow. Remain close to the initial impulse of the poem and allow your one metaphor to develop—just as anything in nature develops and changes while still remaining essentially itself. Reading the end lines of such a poem, we should be able to remember the seed metaphor we started with. What we learn from this approach to a poem is that by staying with one metaphor, much depth and nuance can yield itself to you.

Here is a poem by Pablo Neruda that carries through on one organic metaphor:

When we see natural style we are quite amazed and delighted, because we expected to see an author and find a man.

—Blaise Pascal

In Praise of Ironing

Poetry is pure white:
it emerges from the water covered with drops,
all wrinkled, in a heap.
It has to be spread out, the skin of this planet,
has to be ironed, the sea in its whiteness;
and the hands keep on moving,
smoothing the holy surfaces.
So are things accomplished.
Each day, hands re-create the world,
fire is married to steel,
and the canvas, the linens and the cottons return
from the skirmishing of the laundries;
and out of light is born a dove.
Out of the froth once more comes chastity.

Throughout the poem we are reminded of one thing: whiteness. In the course of the poem, we hear about the skin, the sea, light, a dove, froth, chastity . . . but all of these white images refer back to the central metaphor of pure whiteness. The making of poems is being compared to the ironing of white cloth, made free of wrinkles by "smoothing the holy surfaces."

Neruda uses the whiteness metaphor at the end of the poem with the enchanting lines: "and the canvas, the linens and the cottons return / from the skirmishing of the laundries" as a way of comparing poem-making to the daily work of clothes laundering, work that can renew us with its transformative purity. We get to this depth of meaning by beginning with a single metaphor: *Poetry is pure whiteness.*

EXERCISE: DEVELOPING A METAPHOR

Let's explore how we can employ extended metaphor. In order to find one metaphor that will lend itself to sustained imagery in a poem, we need to experiment with various ideas.

Think about how Pablo Neruda brought in different aspects of both nature and the activities of washing and ironing to carry his metaphor of whiteness. Highlight the places where he refers to whiteness. How were these choices made? Here are some other metaphorical lines from poems by well-known poets. Use these examples to give you some ideas:

> *One must have the mind of winter . . .*
> *—Wallace Stevens*

> *I am the blossom pressed in a book*
> *and found again after 200 years . . .*
> *—Jane Kenyon*

> *We lodged in a street together,*
> *You, a sparrow on the housetop lonely,*
> *I, a lone she-bird of his feather . . .*
> *—Robert Browning*

> *i am a little church (no great cathedral) . . .*
> *—e. e. cummings*

How would it feel to have the mind of winter? What kind of thoughts might one have? In what way would they be winterlike? What else could you say about the metaphor of the "blossom pressed in a book" and the passage of 200 years?

Your metaphor could be of a particular season, person, thing, natural place, building, or anything else in the world. Write down a few possibilities and then use clusters of words, journal writing, list making, or free association to develop your metaphor. What are the implications of the metaphor you've chosen? Study it as you might study anything in nature. Observe it closely. Hold it in your mind's eye and turn it this way and that. Listen to it. Feel it. Write down everything you can possibly think of that relates to your metaphoric phrase. Catch the images that come up. Allow for unexpected, intuitive links. Peel away the layers of cliché, common meanings, and stale connections to get to the core of the metaphor you're exploring. Trust yourself. Experiment. Shape your metaphoric thoughts and images into a poem.

Simile

Bright Star! would I were steadfast as thou art—
                    —John Keats

There came a wind like a bugle;
It quivered through the grass . . .
                    —Emily Dickinson

*M*ost of my technical decisions in writing a poem are made intuitively, the way a basketball player puts a higher arc on his shot when he senses an opponent will jump high enough that the usual arc would result in the shot's being blocked. Such decisions are neither conscious nor unconscious. I suspect they are both.

                    —William Matthews

In contrast to metaphor, a simile is a more indirect or subtle comparison using "like" or "as." Keats longs to be steadfast *as* the star he addresses. Less powerful in its impact, the use of simile is nevertheless an extremely flexible and creative tool for likening but not actually equating two different things. Both Keats and the bright star retain their distinct outlines, their individual qualities, but a comparative link is made between the two; a relationship is formed—a creative tension the poet uses to enhance the vividness and significance of the image and the poem as a whole. Ezra Pound wrote a love poem in which he first invokes a striking simile and then reports on the "action" that took place:

ALBA

As cool as the pale wet leaves
            of lily-of-the-valley,
She lay beside me in the dawn.

If Pound had written the poem as follows, his poem would feel flat, without the same sense of lingering, dawning beauty that initially startles us:

She lay beside me in the dawn,
As cool as the pale wet leaves
            of lily-of-the-valley.

Here are some additional examples of simile:

Like the smooth sun-warmed river-granite curves
You hold me in your arms
against the rising tide.
　　　　　　——Ginny Fleming

Self-enclosed like a tulip
he is very shy.
　　　　　——Anonymous

Grandmother, acting like a child,
climbed the apple-tree in winter.
——Megan McEleney, 11 years old

Your mouth is like the delta
of summer night desires.
　　　　　——Anonymous

EXERCISE: MAKING AN IMAGE OF SOMEONE YOU LOVE

Using Pound's poem "Alba" and the other poems above as models, begin with an image from nature and compare it to someone you love or feel appreciation for. You can write an erotic love poem for a spouse or lover, or a poem of love for a grandparent, parent, sibling, friend, or child. Try a series of poems about people you are close to, using simile to explain what it is you love about them.

_____

_____

_____

_____

_____

_____

Sound

EXERCISE: AN INVENTORY OF WONDERS

What words do you like to say? Make a running list of your favorite words and phrases. Say them as you write them down. Let new words, unusual words, even strange words, spring forth. Your inner poet loves words like "Vivaldi," "jam," "twirl," "grapple," "ache," "snapshot," and "caress."

Turn the sound of those words around in your mouth. *Take your time saying them.* What sounds do *you* enjoy making? I enjoy saying these:

Miracle. Creek. Resonate. Geranium. Pistachio. Field mouse. Saturate. Golden corn. Fabric. Song. Agate stone. Elbow. Thunderstorm. Sandpipers. Birch bark. Walrus. Shoulder blade. Intone. Everglades. Human tears. Kiss.

The Kentucky poet-farmer Wendell Berry writes about such "wonders." He says, "Poetry keeps an inventory of wonder / and uncommercial goods." Keep a running inventory of words you enjoy. Draw material from this list to use in your writing.

Inventory of Favorite Words

1. _____ 11. _____
2. _____ 12. _____
3. _____ 13. _____
4. _____ 14. _____
5. _____ 15. _____
6. _____ 16. _____
7. _____ 17. _____
8. _____ 18. _____
9. _____ 19. _____
10. _____ 20. _____

The Force of Magic in Your Voice

After you write your inventory of wonders, speak your words out loud. Savor the experience. Make your mouth wet with the words you say. Jut your jaw out for a moment to make more room for your words. Turn your tongue about as if to till it like a fertile field. Stretch out your throat and larynx. Open your mouth wide. Tense the muscles in your throat for a moment and then relax them. Breathe deep into your chest. Make nonsense sounds to mulch the ground of your voice: "Smarl, smush, grash, and grum. Frash, galooo, and harrumm" . . . be silly! Enjoy. Breathe—fill your chest full. Slow down and take your time to speak your words out loud. There is no rush. I remember my friend John Blake's saying, "Slow is fast."

You may feel funny or odd at first, but go ahead anyway. "Step barefoot into reality." Release your poetic cry into your body. Let it out into the open air. Feel the tone and quality of your voice as you name your inventory of wonder. Is the sound only up in your head? Does it sound nasal? What is going on in your throat? Do you feel connected with your chest, heart, and belly when you speak? Or does it feel like the word-bridge is impassable between your head and the rest of your body?

Be gentle—the throat is a place in many people that needs care and attention. It is a place where the expression of feelings becomes blocked. You can use your exploration of poetry to uncover the potentials of your voice. Your voice is a beautiful place to experiment with expressing your truth and creativity. The Trobriand Islanders of the South Pacific say about the voice: "The force of magic resides within man . . . and can escape only through his voice." Magic is within you. Play with words. Note what is happening in your body as you speak.

Listen to and feel the consonants you make—let them pop out of your mouth like pine cones bursting in a fire. Say this: *Pine Cone.* Pop the *P* and the *C* of pine cone through your tongue, mouth, and teeth. Say this: *Breeze.* Spill your vowels out like a breeze. Let the feathers of your breath fly on all those liberated *e*'s. Experiment! Play the instrument of your voice.

Savor vowels, appreciate consonants.

—*Allen Ginsberg*

I have found that the deepest levels of shamanic experience are associated with the liberation of the voice. I have found that the most powerful connections with soul are made with the voice, and this accounts for the intense resistance that many of us have to free vocal expression.

—*Shaun McNiff*

Image

PRAYERWHEEL FOR WILLIAM

you worked alongside men
   riding the fishwheel
      down
    the trickster tides
       of summer

your boy hands hurrying hurrying
   baskets tossing
     splashing
     salmon
onto the birchwood raft

   your cut-up windburnt hands
    that loved the violin
     smelling of fish
     and woodsmoke

tall and awkward Indian boy
   arms too long
     hair always falling
      into your blackberry eyes
  drifting with the river
   turning with the fishwheel
    my prayers of you
     are turning
     turning
      —Mary TallMountain

Mary TallMountain, born in 1914 along the Yukon River, weaves the image of her younger brother William, a "tall and awkward Indian boy" into images of the drifting river, salmon, violin, and fishwheel—and into her own turning prayers. "A

Prayerwheel for William" is a rare poem in that it is written about one sibling's love for another. Mary's choice of images and her eye for them are informed by the feelings of an older sister. The image of her prayers "turning" for her brother merges into the fishwheel he tends. One turning, circular image nests inside the other and both strengthen the poem. Mary's images are also enhanced by the way the poem drifts narrowly down the page; the line breaks and layout are like a river flowing. All of these aspects of her poem work together, and the fact that they do gives the images clarity, authenticity, and strength. We enter each image and experience the poem as if we were right beside the other fishermen, feeling and smelling the splashing movement of the fish and the water. Creative images have this kind of power. And it is within our power to craft them.

Images are the heart of poetry. And this is not tricks. Images come from the unconscious. Imagination and the unconscious are one and the same. You're not a poet without imagery.

—Anne Sexton

EXERCISE: IMAGE-MAKING

Name three things in your life that you care about, and describe them using words you've never used in describing these things before. Turn "seeing my garden" into "meeting my chrysanthemums in the cool dawn." Name things as particularly as you can. Sharpen your focus. Make images that enable others to sensually experience your thoughts and ideas.

1. _____

_____

2. _____

_____

3. _____

Read Mary TallMountain's poem again and notice how the description of her brother William flows out, building the whole image, as if unfolding out of the "fishwheel." Next, choose the image phrase that you are especially pleased with from the image-making exercise. Tap into a center place in *that* image and allow the impulses of that image, the hints it offers to you, to guide your writing as you shape a poem.

Connie: The Sounds of the River Came In

*I*mages are the midwives
between experience and
language.

——Matthew Fox

One of the lovely things about making images is that they help to close the imagined gap between the particular and universal, the tangible and intangible, the inner and outer. Poetic imagery has the capability of joining disparate elements to make spiritual, intellectual, or emotional connections. These aspects of ourselves, so often relegated to ill-fitting compartments, are capable, through poetry, of communicating to one another in ways that can be utterly frank, life-affirming, spontaneous, and revelatory. Through images and the distillation of language, we enter into deeper relationships with life.

Thus the "divided self" is made whole. Listen to Izumi Shikibu, a lady and poet of the Japanese court writing a thousand years ago:

*T*he image is a kind of
emotional shorthand.

——Erica Jong

> *Watching the moon*
> *at dawn*
> *solitary, mid-sky,*
> *I knew myself completely:*
> *no part left out.*

The singular image of the moon not only connects Shikibu to the entire universe, but makes her feel whole. Make room in your writing for more expansive images; allow your inner poet to notice relationships between the intricate web of elements that your own life comprises. Dare to veer off the well-trodden path of perceiving things too literally.

Connie did. Connie is an accomplished professional painter in her fifties. Her paintings communicate vibrancy and aliveness. She teaches painting at John F. Kennedy University, one of the most progressive universities in the country. She has also written a lot about painting and considers herself very verbal. Yet up to the time she began to write poetry, she says that she literally hated writing.

Connie had rigid expectations of how perfect her writing had to be. There was a hard edge to her approach to words that came out sounding fine, but the actual process of creation was no fun.

Connie says, "The words I used had to be like good soldiers. Or, worse, I felt as if I were in prison when I wrote."

Connie goes on, "When I was in grade school, I had written religious poems. But soon after that, I had a sense that I could no longer be a poet. I would have felt too pretentious. Then for various reasons, at this later time in my life, poems started to come again."

It was on a painting trip to New Mexico that Connie began to discover what a companion poetry writing could be.

> I was driving in the Chama River Valley in New Mexico, a day after thunderstorms had turned sections of the road into impassable mud beds. I barely slid through a very tough place on a cliff and knew I couldn't go back again. So I decided to spend the night in the valley and let the roads dry out. That night I felt isolated and fearful, and could have gone into the van, locked the door, and slept. Instead I sat outside, looking at the moon, and writing directly out of what I was seeing, picking up the threads of all my sensations, and letting the words follow. When the sounds of the river came in, the poem started having a life of its own, and began to connect with my life in a very poignant way.
>
> It got quite personal and moved beyond just description of the place into the voices of my heart. Feeling the river as metaphor allowed the personal feelings to evolve in surprising ways. I was quite drawn into the writing, as if a friend had come to visit with me. The whole process of writing transformed my relationship to that desert place. I felt welcomed and nourished by it.

Just as the moon served as a potent symbol for the tenth-century Japanese lady of the court, the "half moon rising" was the catalyst for Connie's engagement with language:

RIO CHAMA

Half moon rising out of purple twilight
Shining on the rocks and distant cliffs
Blue black swallows rosy glow and stars appear
I hear the sound of water on the banks of Rio Chama
On a clear August night.

Anyone who wants to experience beauty must first of all abandon all preconceived ideas and perceptual frameworks.

—Piero Ferrucci

Life's picture is constantly undergoing change. The spirit beholds a new world every moment.

—Rumi

I was enthralled with Rio Chama
Along the rutted road I saw the grey-green water
Edged by bright green willows
Part the orange cliffs above and stretching far beyond
Keeping their distance, yet present in their light.

Are you the river place I always search for
The one that nurtures me and strengthens both?
If only the road were shorter, smoother
Or less impassable with rain
A little more comfortable, predictable
Then I would take you to my heart
Be loyal all year round.

Yet now I sleep beside you river
Your sound comes in—the distance gone
The echo of your voice is in me river
A sound of searching, wanting to be home.
A place, a person; what in this whole earth
Can hold me, take my heart, wake my soul
Or do I keep on traveling like the river
Arriving home, but always moving on.

Connie further describes her experience of writing this poem:

The last stanza was a total surprise. I had started to talk to the river in poetry. Once the river metaphor jumped in . . . the rhythm and cadence seemed to pull me in like a magnet. Things—insights and feelings—rushed over and stuck to it. I chewed on those last two lines all day long! It was such a joy. The making of language took me to a whole new place. A place that was deeply integrated and alive.

Just months before, Connie had considered her relationship with words adversarial at best, and she had not written poetry since grade school! Give yourself the opportunity to be delighted by your own words. The sounds. The images. The surprises. The connections.

Read Connie's poem again. Imagine a place you could go to hear something as magical as the River Chama. Write a poem to show us a place that has special meaning for you. A place that would sweep you away—or pull you in like a magnet.

Here is another example of a poem about a beloved place by a workshop student. First, Ginny wrote in her journal everything she could think of about a place she loved called Winecoop:

The old wooden steps on the house, the area drenched with sun and fruit and flower, rich country quiet. A place to visit, to be, simply, on a summer's day. I remember loving it so, visiting with Mike and the other brothers, playing, exploring, butterflies and lovely woods, deep in a quiet Virginia, my heart state. And the bees, the honey warmth, my deep innocence. That playful spirit so way inside, that silly girl with the weird haircut, toothless smile, and gangly legs. The innocence of the place and the girl, long ago. Winecoop was the place where chinchillas were raised, briefly I recall. And I have always loved the name—Winecoop. It was somehow owned by the Trappists and used when families visited. A place for a child to be a child in full wildness and innocence.

Poetry is the language in which man explores his own amazement.

—Christopher Fry

Ginny gathered a wealth of images from her memories of Winecoop. Even though she didn't use these particular images in her poem, writing freely generated such poetic phrases as: "my heart state," "honey warmth," "a child in full wildness," and "deep in a quiet Virginia," which is of course her name as well as the state she was visiting. She can now use these lines for another poem. What the revision process brought was a distillation of the images of bees and honey. Here is the poem that Ginny drew from her journaling piece. The poem was written within about twenty minutes:

WINECOOP

Blackberry brambles blossom heavy
Sweet honey soaking through me, in sunlight unfiltered
A child unhampered, in her element
Within the circle.

Entering Images—A Poetic and Spiritual Practice

When the soul wishes to experience something she throws an image of the experience out before her and enters into her own image.

—*Meister Eckhart*

Poetry provides a focus for this image-throwing, this technique of expressing what's in your soul. Your own images may provide a guide for entering a new dimension of your life, that place you begin to communicate with, as Connie did sitting near the Rio Chama, or as Mary Tall-Mountain did when she conjured up the fishwheel tended by her brother William.

The following exercise will help you to "enter images" and experience them more fully. You can experiment with this by being someone or something other than yourself; you can imagine yourself as a bear, for instance. What is it like when you become a bear? Or a season, an element in nature, an object? You could be many things. How would you describe your new identity? Come up with an image that appeals to you and allow it to teach you more about yourself and life by describing it in poetic terms.

> *. . . I am circling around God, around the ancient tower,*
> *and I have been circling for a thousand years,*
> *and I still don't know if I am a falcon, or a storm,*
> *or a great song.*
>
> —*Rainer Maria Rilke*

Meditate, one at a time, on five images you would like to enter into and become.

I enter and become my image of _____.
(Sit with this for a while. Feel it. Write your experience.)

I enter and become my image of _____.
(Sit with this for a while. Feel it. Write your experience.)

I enter and become my image of _____.
(Sit with this for a while. Feel it. Write your experience.)

I enter and become my image of _____.
(Sit with this for a while. Feel it. Write your experience.)

I enter and become my image of _____.
(Sit with this for a while. Feel it. Write your experience.)

Take just one of your images and develop it more fully. Listen to it. Enter into it again and again. Focus on what it feels like. As you do this, feel it with all your senses. Observe it. Act it out in movement. Illustrate the story of that image. Let your words flow out into a poem. Walk toward your image in your heart's eye. Enter it and breathe. See what happens.

Rational answers do not contain our feelings—or our poems. But if you follow a thread of an image (like the gradual ripening of fruit follows the turn of the seasons), you may discover an enormous amount about who you are and what is in your world. Write down images as they come up during the day—give them a place of "containment" on the page.

Catching the Image: More Poetry-Making Exercises

1. Like the sound of the Rio Chama, each pulse of your own heart is an invitation to see and listen to your world in a fresh way. Your pathway through your world up to this very moment is suffused with the sound of your own heart. Since your earliest moments, your heart has done a crucial job for you. Listen to it. Feel it. Place your hand over your heart right now. As your fingers press slightly into your flesh on the left side of your breastbone, take a breath.

2. Continue to place your hand to your heart. Feel it. Feel it in your body. Take five deep breaths and ask the Muses for images. Allow images to come to mind. What images arise? Let them drift up. Speak them: drum, river, moon. Thunder, morning, night. Cave, meadow, dancers. Let them come and go. Speak them again: hungry child, tears, chasm. Sit with these heart images awhile. Begin to record them. Write them down. Once you write them down, speak them aloud.

3. Make a list of three experiences you remember from your childhood, youth, or more recently. What are the sensations of those things—use all your senses: smell, taste, touch, sight, and hearing. For this exercise, choose an experience you feel positive about. Distill that experience into one image. Remember yourself at that moment. Recall the flow of your feeling. Let analysis go for the moment and stick with your senses. Feel that place inside your body where you take a deep breath. Begin with an image that is very simple. See into it as precisely as you can.

4. Catch an image. Watch it in your mind's eye very closely. Describe these experiences quickly, letting words flow, with detail given to sense and richness of feeling. If your writing takes off into unexpected directions, flow with it.

The image that came to student Chip Raman was of being out in a rowboat with his father as a small child:

> The sweet scent of fresh cut grass
> lining the water's edge, mixing

with pungent air of lily pads, mud and muck
and thick wisps of Papa's cigar smoke.
Dusk is in full-bloom.
Reflections of a setting orange sun
on water broken by the slap of oars.
Strong arms pull the craft forward
in a steady glide.
Whirlpools twist and leave their trace behind us . . .
Water droplets hang precariously
on the edge of well worn wood.
Temperature is falling with the light.
Crickets chirp.
Birds call from the bank.
Dragonflies make easy prey for hungry fish
rising above the surface every here and there.
A chilly breeze crosses my stubby hair,
the moisture and the motion bring up goose flesh,
careening toward the landing dock,
drifting in an arc on even keel,
I spot the first star in the mountain sky.
Our rowboat clunks into the post,
wet rope wrapped around
holds our place,
gentle rocking holding still.
Papa leans forward to fetch his son,
firm hands grasp my underarms——
lift me high
into a rising cloud of burnt tobacco:
a cough, a shiver.
He places me down
socks and sneakers dampened,
leave silhouetted footprints on
wooden planks,
proof positive we're safe on shore,
leaving behind a crooked invisible line
where we rode the lake at twilight.

Journey into a Postcard

Begin to gather a collection of interesting postcards and photographs. Bookstores, the kind with cafés, sometimes carry particularly artistic and evocative ones. Choose those that are especially interesting to you. They can picture people or scenes from around the world and might be contemporary, or decades old. Look for unusual perspectives, photographs that show particular insight into human beings and the earth. You can also collect photographs from magazines and newspapers. Gather images that evoke feeling. As you gather these images, you can work with this exercise in many different ways.

ᚹ Feel the subject of the picture and listen to what it tells you about yourself. What does it say to you? If you could speak to the subject of this picture, what would you say? Use the imagery of the picture as a catalyst to connect with your own internal imagery and language. Allow the image to really touch you. Feel as if you were hearing from this image for the very first time. Make a list of feeling words or images that come up. Draw from this in making your poem.

ᚹ Imagine you *are* the subject of the picture. How do you feel? What do you want to say? What are your hurts? What are your joys? Where have you traveled on your journey? Whom have you touched in your life? What or who has touched you? Perhaps you are lending your voice to an animal. Use the words you imagine this person, animal, or place might use. Use a different language if you like. Use sounds, if that feels right. Describe the images, sounds, textures, smells, and terrain of this subject, and speak in its voice, with its heart and gut.

Here is a student experiment with this postcard journey, based on a stunning photograph by the famous photographer Edward F. Curtis, of the face of an elder man of the Kwakiutl people. The Kwakiutls are a Northwest Indian tribe who live on a north corner of Vancouver Island in British Columbia, and who are known especially for their extraordinary wooden masks. Their name *Kwakiutl* means, "beach at the north side of the river." In this poem, Kathy Carlson first speaks in her own voice about the man in the postcard, then speaks in his voice, and then goes back to her own voice to reflect on what the man has said:

I find some poems arriving in voices. Some part of the psyche splits off and becomes an autonomous personality with its own vocabulary, mannerisms, physical characteristics, and obsessions.

—Peter Klappert

Old like trees,
like deep pools in a clearing.

Year after year
of rain of hunger of laughter of death.
Marks left on your face, time tracks
eternal eyes, worn down
through passion and seasons.
Paper-thin frail leathery
patient quiet
ground into incandescence.
Keeper of memory
of times when we walked quieter here
times before speed before numbness before cities.

Part tree part animal part river part night sky.
Seer with quiet eyes animal eyes mountain eyes.
What passions burned in you in younger years?
What follies and pain brought you
to that endless tolerant smile?

Rain fell on me.
Tears came and went.
Times rose and times fell.
I remember: clear autumn hunting days.
Hot sun on backs bent to earth.
Corn in wooden bowls.
Dreams, wood smoke, a good woman dying.
Babies, morning light.

Worn down to the shine
light as a feather,
the quiet rolls off you
inviting me to drown in those eyes
to sit with you for hours
in silence on the cold ground
to still my impatient mind
my leaping heart
to sit and watch the quality of light on your hands
your tender solid dark hands

the damp smell of woods
the cold seeping up from the ground
your way of rooting into the earth
and becoming rock and tree.
I sigh at my own hurry, my youth
though I did not think myself young
until I sat with you,
you who goes on forever,
just sitting just smiling just watching.

Partner Exercise: Feeling-Place Poem

You can adapt the directions in this next exercise in such a way that you can do it with yourself, but it works best if you have a partner.

I developed this exercise with my friend and colleague in the California Poets in the Schools Program, Kimberley Nelson. It involves both the organic development of your poetry and sharing it with another so you can discover how it is heard. It will help you hone your ability to be particular and at the same time explore your creative imagination by letting go of some control. Your partner will help you in this exploration and clarification.

You are going to name a place in this exercise and then write about it. This could be a place that is very special to you, or an ordinary place. It could be a particular mountaintop, or your desk at work, your back yard, apartment balcony, a park bench, or a seat on the bus. You can experiment with the "special" and the "ordinary" and see what happens as you write.

If you choose a painful place, ask yourself first if you are comfortable proceeding before you begin. You should have appropriate support for going deeply into the exercise in this way.

You can do this exercise in a large group or with just one other person.

1. In the corner of their paper, both partners write a word that expresses a feeling or quality.
2. Now write the name of a place, connected with that feeling, in that same corner.
3. Free-write, describing that place as if it personified that feeling, *without ever using the feeling word you have chosen.* Write a poem telling about this place and the feeling you have chosen, but do not use the actual feeling word. Be particular and detailed.
4. After writing your poem, get together with your partner. Choose who will be "A" and "B" and who will go first.
5. A reads his or her poem to B—at least three times. The listener, or B, should listen deeply but not talk about the poem, label it, or analyze it. Stay with your "feeling response" to what you have just heard from A's reading.

6. B circles what he/she feels are the five or six key words in A's poem. Circle no more than six words.

7. Reverse the process: Now B reads his or her poem to A three times.

8. A silently reads B's poem and circles five to six key words.

9. Both partners use the key words chosen by their partner from their own poem to write a new poem. Take time to write this new poem, putting the words that your partner has selected into your new poem. Your new poem may follow the thread of your original poem or start off in some new direction. Trust your process. Take ten to fifteen minutes.

10. Repeat another cycle of choosing key words, exactly as before, between A and B. Write another poem using the key words your partner has chosen.

11. Read your final poems (this will be the third poem of the series) to one another. Listen closely.

12. Closure: Now talk together about what the writing and reading process was like for you in terms of trust, what it was like to move from the first poem to the third, what it was like to have someone else be a part of your writing process.

One of my workshop students, Phyllis Williams, tells about her experience with this exercise:

Writing my poem using the key words chosen by my partner put me in touch with an unexpected experience of grief over the death of my cousin. It made me go deeper in successive poems. My cousin died many years after our time together in 1939 at Lake Sutherland in Washington State, the subject of my first poem, but because it was an accidental and sudden death, I never fully grieved or had the opportunity to attend his funeral. This stored-up grief came out in the process of writing this poem series. This was surprising to me because it had started out as a fond remembrance. [The words Phyllis's partner chose for her are underlined.]

1939

Sunset as Lake Sutherland stretches taut
Its wet mirror, reflecting persimmon
And the paleness of peach-colored skies.

Black licorice sticks interrupt sleek surface:
Dock and pilings where we'll walk

When everything is black, except
Summer stars too close for possibility.

Then I and my best cousin, Clydie,
Who knows about such things, will marvel
At streaks of phosphorous flash
Here and there beneath the water,
Instantly, magically,
Like minute versions of sheet lightning.

In motionless air that wraps us in its quiet,
We'll listen to young trout jump for joy
As they slip in and out of paradise.
We'll strain to hear the whispered lap, lapping
Our lake does because it cannot purr.

My writing partner circled "phosphorous" and "black." These images in particular affected my sense of time as I began to recall the experience so deeply that it felt like only yesterday that Clydie and I had walked together on that pier. Going into the second poem, I began to peel away many more layers than had been revealed in the first—it reflected both my unexpressed grief looking back and the wonder I felt at the time of the experience. I was nine years old at the time and I had never seen phosphorous in the water at night. To have my cousin show me these flashes by dipping the oars in the water felt like a miracle to me.

In the second poem, I was in touch with deeper underpinnings of my experience at Lake Sutherland. Everything condensed down in this second poem. The outwardly idyllic, lovely qualities of Lake Sutherland slipped away and all I was left with was a sense of the dark, the persimmon silence, the phosphorescence and closeness to this important cousin. I internalized all of these in the second poem and distilled them inside—a place where time didn't seem to matter:

CLYDIE

It doesn't matter.
Time doesn't matter.

We're still there, you and I,
Waiting in the persimmon silence,
Closer than Peter and Wendy,
Waiting for the dark,
For flashes of phosphorous underwater,
The hushed lapping of the lake.

The distillation and revision process led me to a third poem. The flashes of phosphorous underwater, in the dark, became the metaphor for the wonder of the time I got to spend with Clydie and also the quickness of his lifetime. There is a new line in this third poem that refers to Clydie's coming death and my loss. "Would vanish faster than the stars swooping down to greet us," made it possible for me to say something about his loss without stepping out of the presence the poem had created: the fact that I had in all my sense of wonder at nine no idea that these precious moments were so fleeting. Now at sixty-four, partly through writing this poem, I realize how important it is to love and bless:

COUSIN CLYDIE

If I had known how short our time would be,
That I would lose you and the closeness we had
There, at the lake, at dark, long ago in persimmon silence,
There as I reveled in your big-brother nearness,
As we played on the dock, rowed out onto black water,
Sang "Three Little Fishies" while real fish jumped all around,
There as we marveled at the phosphorous
Quick-flashing under the surface;
As the lake rocked us,
Lap, lapping against our boat.

If somehow I had known how
The shelter of you, fairest and best you,
Would vanish faster than stars swooping down to greet us,
Somehow, somehow I would have said goodbye,
Sent angels for your journey,
Blessed you on your way.

Phyllis comments on her experience of doing the dyad exercise:

> I've done this two-person, three-part exercise many times. Each time the dynamic of being with someone else who listens and zeros in on the key words makes me feel heard in a different way than when I am reading a poem to a group. Sometimes I feel I am too close to my writing to pick out the kernel that I need to go for. That other person often has the distance to see it. This exercise works so well because it involves listening rather than analyzing. I am also providing the distance to help the other person choose their key elements and this mutuality is creative.

The images and ideas that dreams contact cannot possibly be explained solely in terms of memory. They express new thoughts that have never reached the threshold of consciousness.

—Carl Jung

Dream Time Images

What if you slept, and what if in your sleep you dreamed, and what if in your dream you went to heaven and there plucked a strange and beautiful flower, and what if when you awoke you had the flower in your hand. Ah, what then?

—Samuel Taylor Coleridge

Don't dreams, images, and metaphors come from the same place, the same ground? The place where we experience a certain kind of truth?

1. Plan for one night a week to devote your energy to your dreams. Write down your dreams the next morning or when you wake during the night. When you are ready to work on creating a poem, note three specific images from your dream material that seem especially potent. Write these three images down and, keeping in mind the "plot" of the dream, use your imagination in the waking state to link the images together into a poem. If you only remember a fragment of the dream and no continuous plot, that's all right. Often it is only fragments that are recalled. Essentially, the exercise is the same in either case. Take whatever images you remember and shape them with your waking imagination.
2. Take one of your dreams and observe the predominant feeling tone in the dream. Was the feeling tone neutral? Scared? Angry? Joyful? Excited? Keeping in mind the feeling tone that you have identified, reenter your dream and connect once again with its images. Now make a poem from those images, speaking from the perspective of that feeling.
3. Hypnogogic hallucinations occur just as you are falling asleep. These are the "snapshots," or little dream vignettes that appear as one falls asleep. These images may also appear as you wake up, but this is a less frequent occurrence for most people. Almost always in these brief

"dreamlets," the dreamer is a pure observer. Such images are excellent sources of creativity because they are often pure image, that is, there are no words, no plot—just a quick image. You can take one of these images, write it down literally, and then amplify it, building more detail (imaginative and/or factual) to make a poem. Here are a few examples of hypnogogic hallucinations: "I am pushing a full shopping cart in a supermarket. It goes faster and faster and flies out the front window." "A big golden disk with hieroglyphics all over it is rising out of an indigo blue sea."

What do metaphor, simile, sound, and image have to do with our real lives? When we write poetry, even as we struggle to write it well, we get in touch with our interrelationship to life. Through these poetic tools, we perceive unexpected connections. Poetry is a way to include in our lives the priceless gifts that headlines, deadlines, and bottom-lines cut out: sensing the heart of our world, of another, of ourselves; knowing that your voice of truth and creativity is unique and important.

When we discover the secret relationships of meanings and traverse them deeply we'll emerge in another sort of clearing that is Poetry.

—*Odysseus Elytis*

Keep in the Heart the Journal

Making Poems from Your Journal Entries

The journal is like the moon, emitting a magnetic tug that draws information from your subconscious and unconscious minds and brings it to the surface, where you can work at the conscious level.

—*Kathleen Adams, author,* Journal to the Self

And if I tell them that they wrote poems, they often say, no, that couldn't be because they don't like poetry. So I don't tell them for a while. I merely point out to them that they have just found one more way to write in a journal.

—*Burghild Nina Holzer, author,*
A Walk Between Heaven and Earth

That is my essential reason for writing, not for fame, not to be celebrated after death, but to heighten and create life all around me. . . . I also write because when I am writing I reach the high moment of fusion sought by the mystics, the poets, the lovers, a sense of communion with the universe.

—*Anaïs Nin, from her* Diary, 1939–1944

The Journal:
A Trusted and Versatile Traveling Companion

The essential intent in journal writing is self-understanding. Your journal is a perfect guide: It listens without judgment and reflects who you are back to you when you read it. It is a trusted and versatile traveling companion that will be a true friend along your life's path.

The simplicity of the journal is beyond compare. It consists simply of a blank book (or blank computer screen) and a pen or pencil (or keyboard). The only necessities for keeping a journal are: the blank page, something to write or type on, and yourself.

This chapter encourages you to explore the relationship between journal writing and the making of poems. It will suggest reasons for why the journal provides an incredibly rich place to discover poems. It will also offer some maps and examples for moving from journal to poetry writing.

Why use journal writing as a source from which to draw poetry? The journal allows us to express *everything* about ourselves on different levels and in a wide variety of ways. A poem condenses language and experience. Used together, these two forms of writing create a powerful tandem for discovering yourself through writing.

For those who write already in journals and occasionally also write poetry, this chapter offers an opportunity for you to *enhance* the poem-making process and the enjoyment that can be had from the special powers of poetry.

For journal writers who regularly draw the material for their poems from their journal books, the examples and exercises given here will extend that practice in fresh ways.

The brilliance of the journal is that it invites you—in a totally nonjudgmental way—to stop and talk to yourself. You can ask yourself anything you can think of or imagine. And how you respond may often surprise you.

EXERCISE: SENTENCE STEMS

Through the journal device of "sentence stems," you can find out a lot about yourself. Finish the following simple phrases. Be as particular and specific as you can in your responses. Don't hesitate to use unusual word combinations, to be very frank, to be as unexpected, off the wall, fun, and creative as you would like to be:

I enjoy _____

I hate _____

I like to talk about_____

I am sad because of _____

I am awed by _____

I am angered by _____

I am wary of_____

I am delighted when _____

My humor is awakened by _____

My spirit is made strong by _____

My life today was touched by_____

My dreams for the future are _____

My answer to the question "Who am I?" is _____

"Home" for me means_____

You can begin to develop poems from these sentence stems. Expand the exercise to include a half-dozen different answers to just one of the questions, using the opening part of the sentence as a repeating refrain in the poem.

Here are a few examples:

> *I am wary of*
> *frothy ads that promise me the earth and sky*
> *big barking dogs and fast-talking politicians*

I am awed by
young children who expertly flip and tumble in gymnastics
two lions fighting in the African sun

The Journal:
From the Tao Te Ching to a Whole Earth Catalog

The journal provides a place to ask yourself what you want to do with your life. Margaret and Jeff tell how journal and poetry writing give them an absolutely necessary sounding board for their souls:

> *I literally woke up one day, bought a notebook and haven't stopped writing since. I write or think about writing constantly. It is a background "hum" to my existence. I have made considerable life changes and see my written expression as paramount.*
>
> *—Margaret*

> *Having participated in the Vietnam war, I shut off most of my feelings some years back. After I wrote poetry about my experiences I began to heal the trauma of war. Poetry is the soul truth we all can benefit from.*
>
> *—Jeff*

The journal provides a simple point of direct contact between you and the adventure of your life. It helps to put your hand, your heart, and your brain in harmony with one another and to get your thoughts moving. It is a place to hear, to experiment with who you are. You can write your own version of the *Tao Te Ching* or the *Whole Earth Catalog*. In other words, the journal is for your most sublime intuitions as well as your everyday practical thoughts.

> *Writing naturally means that you allow yourself to use your journal as a blank canvas onto which the rich intricate portrait of your life can be painted as it organically emerges.*
>
> *—Kathleen Adams*

Creating a poem from your journal writing is like the process of pruning and cultivating a garden. If a poem is the ripe fruit of language, a journal is the soil where your garden of language evolves into that fruit.

In a journal, all your thoughts become mulch for growing a poem. You can work in your journal to pull out the weeds in your life. It is the place you can pray for rain. The journal is also a place to allow your poetic language to lie fallow for a time. There is no rush to become a poet, you are one, always; trust the process and just keep writing. Your journal will naturally become an excellent source for releasing the seeds of poems.

> *Keep in the heart the journal nature keeps.*
> —*Conrad Aiken*

In anything that grows, the element of surprise is part of the process. You never know quite what might happen through your journaling. One word or phrase may suddenly explode free from the page and catch the wind of the Muse. It will land like a seed and start to grow into a poem. You'll see this journal-to-poem process in action through examples in this chapter.

Everything you feel an inclination to write about is worthy of your journal. Through this inclusive process, you'll find the material for future poems. Inclusiveness is the perfect attitude for allowing a creative flow. The journal is a place to go to discover your poetry-making ability, a way to give yourself permission to write—no matter what comes out.

Journal writing is also a way to allow your language to develop. You can be experimental without feeling self-conscious. Turn your words and thoughts around this way and that. Get to know your unique writing style and voice.

In other words, you can bang around pretty good writing in your journal—throw your words and ideas around, knock into them, bounce them, flex them, test them out in various ways.

The openness of the journal gives you an opportunity to delve more deeply into things you wouldn't necessarily consider "poetry material." It's a place to go to find out *what really interests you*—both in terms of subject matter and language.

Finding ways to be sure that your ideas can flourish is necessary if the flow of ideas is to be maintained.

—*James Fadiman*

You may be surprised to find that a very mundane thought or response to something or even particular phrase fascinates and attracts you. An image that seemed inconsequential at first may suddenly come alive.

The process of journaling allows you to write about everything that occurs to you—you are free to write your most original thoughts as well as clichés. It is an unconditional place to be truthful, fantastic, off-the-wall, dreamy, romantic, practical, philosophical, boring, and confused. There will be times when you'll be insightful, dramatic, and incredibly creative—and days when you'll be dull and uninspired. *All of it is all right and all of it can be worthwhile.* Living side by side in your journal, this disparate chorus of voices inside you will begin to resonate more clearly. You'll hear their tones at times clashing, at times in harmony. You'll sense their moods. Spread out in your journal, and you'll begin to find room for all of your voices.

Listening for the Poet in Your Journal

I think I am searching in the journal for something that can't evolve until I write about it.

—Beth Ferris

As you write in your journal, you may begin to notice part of yourself that might find even greater expression through poetry-making. What should you listen for?

⋁ *Listen* to the places in your journal where your words seem to "sing." (You can explore this by reading your journal out loud.) By "singing" I mean that the words have a resonance, a rhythm, an attractive sound, a strangeness, a quirkiness, a flowing, lyric quality. There may only be hints of this music. You might be "singing" about your morning breakfast, a recent walk in the city at noon, or the ache in your back. But in each instance, it is the rhythm and sound in your words that catches your ear.

⋁ *Listen* to the places where your *feelings* are described in ways that are deeply meaningful to you, where the feelings you are expressing ask you to plumb them even more deeply in a focused and particular way.

- ☡ *Listen* for those places where your naming and description of objects, people, settings is especially acute, writing in which your senses are particularly honed and alive.

- ☡ *Listen* for captured core moments that have remained hidden or tucked away as if for safe-keeping. Core moments are your central life issues. These may be experiences that feel too private to develop further; but at some point, they will become available to you as material for a poem.

- ☡ *Listen* to everything in your journal as if it were someone you might meet who had an unexpected message for you. The most ordinary journal entry might offer a place to start a superb poem.

Listen to the past, future, and present right where you are. Listen with your whole body, not only with your ears, but with your hands, your face, and the back of your neck.

—Natalie Goldberg

The most unlikely incident can suggest to me the most unexpected ideas.

—Joan Miró

Here is an example of a mundane incident that elicited material for a poem. One of my students is a counselor in a group home for teenage girls. Anne wrote in her journal about a day she went to court with one of her girls; the court was determining where the girl would live—with her foster parents or in a group home. Note Anne's lively and descriptive words:

For work today, I went to the court at San Jose. Myriads of elliptical faces, kaleidoscopic shifts of features, as multi-raced streams of people flow past the door where a rigid policeman with knife-sharp words tells me to hand over my belongings for his caustic perusal. Would I really sneak in a bomb or a gun?

A long rectangular windowless room where we sit, with many people in rainbow colors, amidst lots of grey and black. We wait for the judge to decide this child's "fate." Who will she live with? I see one girl, clad in deep forest green velvet—her voice is shrill like a peacock's. She talks and talks. Another girl, enfolded in my heart because we're

> *close—the one I came with—says nothing. We wait, trying to ignore the harsh reality we are here for.*
>
> *The black-robed judge, perched like an avenging desert bird, talks with sand-dry words to decide her home, which will be our group home. My girl's hair is blue-green prism colors, her limpid eyes clash with her sharp tiger words—her razored words pour forth like jagged rain. But I know that frightened deer within, shunted to a small corner by past abuse.*

This is the "poem fragment" Anne drew out from her journal entry:

> *Razored words pour forth like jagged rain*
> *The blue-green rainbow hues*
> *A small water-fall down her back*
> *As she sits, defiant, careless.*
> *And the frightened deer behind her eyes*
> *Afraid to show its limpid open heart*
> *Hides . . .*
>
> *—Anne*

Oftentimes we start out looking for big ideas to use in writing poems when it is in fact the seemingly insignificant detail that can provide the most interesting place to start. The blue-green of the teenage girl's hairstyle became a small waterfall down her back.

The journal is a place to allow oneself the freedom to give voice to the whole of one's life—including those areas we often ignore. Kathleen Adams, a master journal teacher, writes in her book *Journal to the Self*:

> *Even the most maudlin, the most inane, the most abstract journal entries can contain seeds for future insight; the tapestry of your life will be woven with the weaker entries punctuating the stronger. Unfinished lists, a letter that started out all wrong, a paragraph that ends mid phrase can relay significant information about your personal process.*

Think of a poem "seed" as something *particular* resting in the body of your journal, waiting for just the right time to burst and take root. Indeed, your journal "seeds" may range in subject from surreal to domestic to spiritual to socially conscious—some may represent core issues in your life, some may just describe how your body is feeling at that very moment. In each of these instances, it is possible to gather the language you need for poem-making. Let's take a look at another example.

In midlife, Phyllis Williams began a career as a therapist. Now in her sixties, she is a woman of energetic spirit and imagination. A prolific writer, she regularly gathers poetic material from her journal entries. But it isn't just the "poetic" Phyllis writes about. Her journal is a place where she notices everything. In the following example we can see how her everyday observations influence aspects of the poem-to-be:

> *My body is so sore. Especially my back, right in the middle between the shoulders. When I came home last night at 9:00, I felt so stiff and restless. I took a brisk walk around the block in the dark. Low in the sky, hovering over the western hills, there was a Gypsy moon augmented by a single star shining brighter than all the others. Somehow, a sliver of a moon that still shows the suggestion of an outline of its dark side, reminds me of a Gypsy fortune teller.*

Taking the above journal entry as a starting point, Phyllis wrote a poem that uses many of the same images and issues about the mysterious process of aging and finding a path to do this gracefully. But unlike the journal language, everything in the poem is condensed and charged. Phyllis dove into the prosaic waters of her journal and came up with a pearl:

> *A single star, like a beauty mark,*
> *Augments a Gypsy moon, as it leans over hills*
> *That sleep entwined like Matisse nudes.*
> *Her white crescent circles round to highlight*
> *A dark side, ripe and full,*
> *As she waits to tell my fortune.*

Personal writing affirms the relationship, for it includes these implied warnings: this is what I think at this moment, this is what I remember now, continuing to grow and change.

—*Mary Catherine Bateson*

Perhaps her crystal ball will know
Who orchestrates my moods,
My high tide and my low,
Now that I've no seeds to grow.

Get a highlighter and note the images, words, and feelings that link the journal pieces by Phyllis and Laurie to their poems. Track themes that appear in the journal and then in the poem:

Journal Comments   Connections in the Poem

_____

_____

_____

"To Know in Detail, Minutely, What I Was Talking About..."

Poetry is made up of particulars. We create poetry by paying attention to particulars in our life. The "particular" could be your ride in your cobalt blue sports car with the top down; or kissing your boyfriend; or smelling fresh roasted coffee in a corner café. It could be the touch of a friend's hand on your shoulder when you felt sorrow, or the sight of a horse in an open field as you drove past. It might be the story of how that empathic person first became your friend or the geological history of the land upon which that horse grazed.

I wanted, if I was to write in a larger way than of the birds and
flowers, to write about people close about me: to know in detail,
minutely what I was talking about. . . . That is the poet's business.
—William Carlos Williams, describing the
genesis of his poem, "Paterson"

As William Carlos Williams suggests, you can write in your journal all the particulars of your life. You don't have to think about anything else but telling your story—how you feel, what you think, what you dream, what you see around you. You can name and describe in extensive detail:

- People, places, things
- Feelings, thoughts, intuitions
- Events, experiences, circumstances
- Facts, imaginings, dreams
- Your inner world, outer world, and the bridge between them

As a poet, you can also use the journal to experiment with different aspects of language:

- Dynamic word combinations
- Sounds and rhythms
- Images
- Metaphor and other poetic devices
- Idioms, slang, everyday speech

These experiments are important. Much more than is generally realized, the sounds and images of your poem, its rhythms and resonances, the small but significant details of speech, are the key to following the thread of deepest meaning. Use your journal for this exploration of language.

Rather than the wide-ranging and sometimes uneven sea of journal writing, where you may shift from insight to insight, poem-making allows you to enter into a more condensed and focused experience. You thus become a pearl-diver when you look for poems or the beginning of poems in your journal entries.

There is no doubt that complete poems will occasionally occur within the flow of your journal writing without any effort. But it is also likely that you will discover fragments from your journal that can later be developed into a poem.

I returned to the car and jotted down some notes. The notes were meant to remind me later of the feeling I had experienced. Dates, names, a brochure, a phrase or line, or sometimes an impression worked in a relaxed atmosphere to revive experiences and permit a chance for understanding and expression.

—Jerome Mazzaro

Almost always my poems begin with a small scrap of language—
a few words or an image.

—William Matthews

There is a specific advantage to using your journal as a springboard for creating poetry. Journaling gives you the chance to experiment with a broad range of subjects and styles. It allows you to:

- Write about anything, unburdened by the need for an overall theme
- Explore disparate subjects and make connections between them
- Be spontaneous, expansive, and fluid
- Focus on a subject that encompasses thousands of years . . . or sixty seconds
- Write vivid, detailed descriptions of any aspect of your life—or of anything that interests you
- Experiment with a broad range of attitudes, voices, writing techniques, and language styles
- Take outrageous dips into your imagination
- Examine your relationship to yourself and to the world outside yourself
- Record a treasure of particulars from your everyday life
- Align with your spiritual values and aspirations

There are exercises for exploring each of these facets of journal writing at the end of this chapter. Experimenting with each of them will give you a tremendous sense of freedom.

If you want wildness and surprise in your poetry, your journal can provide these qualities. The journal is the diverse, broad, organic, and creative landscape wherein you can catch and gather the condensed language of poetry.

The key for beginning to write in a journal is the same as for tapping into your inner poet and writing a poem. It all comes down to the simple act of giving yourself permission. It's giving your "permission voices" more and more room in your mind. It's saying *"yes"* to yourself when it comes to writing. It's writing with the *enjoyment* of becoming and being more fully yourself. Kathleen Adams suggests we keep our perspective of the writing process focused on enjoyment:

> *If you've told yourself for years you can't write, give yourself one more chance to. When you replace a "performance" expectation with an "enjoyment" expectation, you're likely to surprise yourself at how much better you like what you write!*

"Luminous Word Patches": Discovering the Poem-in-the-Journal

Linda Tuthill is a fifty-three-year-old poet and journal writer living in northern Ohio. She worked as a psychiatric nurse for many years, but recently left that profession. Linda explains:

> *Nursing had so many rules and regulations, and I began to realize and admit to myself that I am not a "rules and regulations" person. I felt I needed to give myself permission to find out what I really wanted to do.*
>
> *I was never encouraged to ask the question: What do I hunger for? In my mid-forties, I went through a process of therapy where I began to experiment with reflective writing. At first, writing was just another assignment in my therapy, but I soon saw how valuable that reflection was and the powerful part my own words played in that process of self-discovery. Meditation also helped me tune into the essence of what I hunger for and showed me how journal writing could feed me.*

Creativity is the urge to wholeness, the urge to individuation or to the becoming of what one truly is. And in that becoming we bring the cosmos into form.

—*Jean Houston*

The following series of entries from Linda's journal, poems-in-rough, and personal comments eventually unfolded into a finished poem, called "Reappraisal." The poem is about her relationship with words, her relationship to her mother, and how her mother's use of words deeply affected Linda.

There are at least a few ways to approach an understanding of how this process worked for Linda. Although none of these ways is the "last word," it is possible to name a step-by-step process by pinpointing transition points in Linda's writing as it moved toward becoming a poem.

Another route to understanding how her journal piece transformed into a poem involves a more intuitive approach. This requires a certain willingness to "not know" answers but to attentively follow the prompts and feelings of the pieces when reading them. It is rewarding because there is so much sheer enjoyment in language and surprise in sensing the flow of the creative process. What Linda writes comes about because it "feels" right in her heart, and she follows that feeling.

The following step-by-step analysis can provide wonderful guidance for "doing it yourself." The caveat is that in any creative process, the steps *you* may need to take to get to where you are going may come in a different order or may be altogether different steps. Don't get hung up trying to follow each of these steps precisely. Pay attention to the transitions suggested, and let them nudge you forward. Far more important than following any model or method is that you get a sense for fluid movement in your own creative experience of journal and poetry writing.

With this in mind, I have outlined a nine-step process in which each of Linda's transitions is noted. (My thanks to Kathleen Adams of the Center for Journal Therapy in Denver, Colorado, for helping to formulate these steps.)

Before exploring Linda's journal entries, it would be useful first to read her final poem. After that, we can follow the trail in her journal and see where the poem began to emerge and how its meaning took shape.

Read Linda's poem silently to yourself and then read it out loud. *Catch* the images in your mind as you say each line. *Feel* how the condensation of language communicates the dynamic intensity of Linda's relationship to her mother and to language. *Listen* to her word choices and the life they give to the poem.

REAPPRAISAL

Years too late
a note of thanks Mama
for your potent tongue

Freedom is being aware of all the possible choices and choosing that which you truly want.

—Aadil Palkhivala

piercing needle
rude ripper of seams
shrill shears gashing
my cloth to scrap

Yet your serpent fork's
ferocious tactile prowess
taught me textures
how to discriminate
with index fingers
of imagination
how to tell
gingham from gabardine
dotted swiss from seersucker
georgette from satin
though you did not sew
and lived in a drawer
lined with oilcloth
not imported silk

Yes it was you, Mama
who gave me a quilt frame
wide as the horizon
bolts of fabric
bottomless as the ocean
and a work basket exploding
with luminous word patches

The genesis of Linda's poem was not a straight line of evolution. Understanding the process requires listening closely and allowing for a certain sense of the unexpected.

The first journal entry is a dialogue between Linda's journal and herself, describing the relationship between journal writing and poem-making. In the beginning of her entry, the dialogue focuses on the value of keeping a journal:

Step 1. Dialogue with your journal, establishing a relationship of equals.

ME: *Journal, every morning I come here to play with you and you always welcome me. Now I wonder what is it we do together?*

JOURNAL: *Oh, we play. We do play! I make play legitimate. We dance with words, juggle them, sometimes do a little sword play. Invent new words or discover the hidden meanings in old ones. Remember last week when you looked at the word "restore" and saw it in terms of putting a fresh store of energy back into yourself à la the 23rd Psalm's "restoreth my soul."*

ME: *Yes, that's what you do—renew me, restore, reinvigorate, make me fresh each morning. But how does that happen?*

JOURNAL: *You come to me in the quiet hours of morning and consider writing in me, a spiritual practice that you do faithfully. I have become a pathway to your own interior. I help you know who you are. You have hundreds of entries now asking for help in seeking to be yourself, to follow the deep-down agenda of your soul instead of judging your self-worth by how well you please others. Or by how successful you appear to the outer world.*

ME: *It's like I come and we play together, but the games we play don't have set rules imposed from the outside. We are free to invent without fear of judgment. Inside you, anything goes!*

JOURNAL: *Yes, I'm blank sheets of paper that offer you freedom to do whatever your hands are open to conveying through your pen.*

ME: *How do we get poems, though?*

Linda's journal responds creatively to this question, as a poet might, by suggesting a metaphor for how to get poems—*by playing.* Notice how the journal suggests that the process of forming a poem from the journal is natural, even unexpected and surprising:

JOURNAL: *Well, you're like a child playing with boats, just sitting on the bank of a stream and launching them as the spirit moves you. Your boats are words. And every now and then some of those boats come together and start forming a pattern that attracts your attention. Sometimes you let them form into an unfinished shape and they just remain on my pages. Other times you proceed with them and play some more, work too. And finally you have to call in the editor for consultation. When a poem is "finished" enough, you have the joy of sharing it with others.*

In contemporary America, people are again discovering how to drink from their own wells.

—Lynn R. Laurence

The journal uses the important phrase, "attracts your attention." That is a key phrase for making poetry! What attracts you? At any given moment, where is your attention drawn? Attraction will give you the energy to dive for the pearl of the poem. This sense of compelling attraction and curiosity is how the initial pattern of a poem begins to emerge and form in a vital way:

ME: *How come I finish some and leave others?*
JOURNAL: *I think you work on the ones that seem the most urgent or "hot"—ones that help you understand yourself, pull you by their beauty, and are tools of healing. But the others aren't lost. You may come back to them later and find rich resources. Or more likely, they will nourish other poems without your even realizing it.*

Linda's journal reminds her that nothing is lost. The journal continues to hold hopeful seeds for future insights and, perhaps, future poems.

Journaling *and* writing poetry allow for a tremendous amount of creative interplay among all aspects of yourself and the world in which you live. Linda, in her journaling dialogue, recognizes how she is connected to much deeper currents of creativity than she might "reasonably" think possible. What can't be explicitly "known" can be *experienced* by allowing this interplay to occur:

ME: *There's a lot of mystery in the process, isn't there?*
JOURNAL: *Yes, it gets you in touch with deep places inside you, helps you feel connected to an underground stream that is your source and is part of a much larger flow. Then when poems come they aren't just poems about your little local self and its struggles. They reach out and embrace others whose stories aren't so different from yours. They help people feel less lonely and more like they're part of a whole.*
ME: *Thank you, journal. You helped a lot. You always do. I can't imagine life without you.*

Linda's brief dialogue contains many key insights that support the use of journal writing for enhancing creativity. The daily practice of writing in a journal:

ᴟ Offers moment-by-moment encouragement
ᴟ Allows complete self-expression, which in turn fosters a deeper connection with self
ᴟ Encourages unexpected and experimental language
ᴟ Allows you to notice the ways in which language attracts the reader and listener
ᴟ Involves an element of mystery
ᴟ Preserves your thoughts and feelings, which otherwise might be forgotten
ᴟ Helps connect your personal life to a broader reality

Let's continue with Linda's journal entries that begin to hint at her eventual poem, "Reappraisal."

Linda begins her journal entries with an "entrance meditation." An entrance meditation is a request for guidance and inspiration, a welcome to oneself, a call to adventure. An entrance meditation also encourages an openness to metaphoric language:

Step 2. Write an "entrance meditation" which can take the form of a letter or prayer sent to God or your Muse.

3/13/94

I'm ready, Lord, to expand into new dimensions, broader, wider ways of being beyond my little local self. To escape narrowness I must love broadly—love myself deeply. I think that's the key. Love myself, identify myself as part of God's created goodness. I am created good and whole—no one can take that from me, wrest it, seize it, trash it, for God is my author. I am Her/His poem—live vital wounded. Wounded yes, but not defaced, defiled, defamed in the deep down parts of me—which stream still flows clear, bubble, burbles, gurgles, murmurs, sings its own true song. The wounds are tributaries, flow points, portholes where pus can drain and healing enter. Give thanks for wounds. Love them, use every opening as a pathway, route, via.

Following Linda's entrance meditation, the deepest roots of what became her poem appeared. She jotted down emotionally charged key words and phrases concerning her relationship to her mother and her own yearning to play with language. Linda then free-wrote the following passage, based on those key words and phrases (which are underlined here):

Step 3. Come up with key words, phrases, or images and "free-write" for ten minutes. Don't lift the pen from the paper.

> *Can I say Mother, you wounded me. You were living in a false self world—had divined that success was what? Receiving acclaim, being thought worthy, coming out on top for the works of one's hands or the productions of one's mind. Perhaps success is doing what you love. Just that with no thought of earning esteem. Like Dave's examples of his children rattling pot lids, putting them on and off, opening and shutting the stove drawer. Writing is like that for me. Play. Word play. Can I give myself permission for free play? Free to use those words, wondrous, magical, malleable, each somehow souled. Yes—words to have essences, entelechies, souls—but are willing to change form, metamorphose under the poet's loving attention.*

Linda's last phrase in her journal was suddenly followed by a poem that deals not with her mother and word play but, surprisingly, with the last time she saw her father before he died. It may seem that a journal/poem piece like this is unrelated to the "subject at hand," however, through writing this poem Linda also explored the conflicting relationship she had with her mother. She writes to me that she never has worked further on her poem about her father (although she says she may at some point) but she feels that it definitely cleared the way for moving forward with her central themes about her mother and language.

In the next entry, Linda continues to follow these threads of her relationship to words and to her mother. Again, listen closely. Notice the glimpses of words or phrases or feelings that might have attracted Linda's attention. Notice how the phrase about rattling "pot lids" reappears. This repetition recalls her journal's earlier remark, comparing her writing to playing with boats: "Your boats are words. And every now and then some of those boats come together and start forming a pattern that attracts your attention."

I was born to a feast of words. My mama had her down side, but when it came to words she was a triumph and a wonder—categorizing fabric like she owned a dry goods store—dotted swiss, shantung, gabardine, tulle, organdy muslin, percale, corduroy. Why do I feel like a bastard, illegitimate in the field of words? It's one playing field, theater of operations, workshop of the soul I came to honestly, reveled in early, although of course, I didn't realize it—or give thanks. I have spent far too much time castigating my mother for who she isn't, wasn't, or couldn't be—not enough giving thanks for her word play riches and my exposure from birth. Thank you Mama for words. Can words save? Yes perhaps for me using them, loving them, playing with them like pot lids is why I am here, have come. For this I come! Yes!

Step 4. Identify and find a phrase that reflects the central "theme" in Step 3. Deepen and expand upon this by seeking out the polarity in that theme. (For instance: Mother as enemy, mother as giver of word gifts.)

Over a week passed between this journal entry and the next one that picks up the theme of the importance of word play. Notice how Linda begins to develop the metaphor of the fountain—from something she happens to spot in her immediate environment. This metaphor becomes a way to tie together all the threads that pertain to her overarching theme, which is the freedom to be self-expressive. Linda wrote a letter to me about where she was at this point in the process: "I was holed up in a hotel room near Washington, D.C., while my husband attended a course. I decided to forego sightseeing, shopping etc. and to give myself over to writing for a few days."

Step 5. Notice something in your environment and allow it to become the metaphor for your whole experience.

3/23/94

Urban ugly spreads before me—McDonald's fountain. Hey, I have my own fountain which once iced over, but now is free to spray joyfully, splash, cascade, cooling, cleansing, dousing, nurturing. Can poems be fountains of words let loose from depth beyond fathoming, over which I don't have entire control? . . . Let the words bubble up without judging, editing, naysaying—that can come later if it needs to. Come come come let the words come joyfully with abandon and don't criticize, query, dam—no don't dam the free flow of them—they are eager, ecstatic to break forth from those

underground channels which have held them aging——improving
in savor during the long gestation.
   Release guard rails. Shoot high.

A note on the margin of Linda's journal entry says, "this poem started forming——it is the first rough draft of 'Reappraisal.' "

Step 6. Go through everything up to this point with a highlighter or pen and create a rough draft of your poem.

> *Thanks, Mama*
> *she said*
> *years too late*
> *for a potent tongue*
> *conveyor of tactile impressions*
> *able to whip, lash, startle, mince to a mash*
> *regrettable by products*
> *still your tongue's*
> *fierce tactile power*
> *taught me*
> *to feel between the*
> *finger of imagination*
> *the difference between for instance*
> *chambray and gabardine*
> *dotted swiss and corduroy*
> *pongee and muslin*
> *silk and organdy*
> *though our world*
> *was one of oilcloth, not damask*
> *feedbags, not cashmere*
> *yes, it was you, Mama*
> *who gave me the fabric of words.*

Linda writes in her letter: "At the bottom of this entry I scribbled more fabric words (or word fabric?): Tear, shred, flay, shear me to ribbons, puncture."

It's clear that something dynamic was starting to happen in the language, in the meaning, in the impulse of the forming poem. The next two entries are cornucopias of material that became integrated into the poem. Again, to quote the comments

Step 7. Working from the draft poem, cluster or free associate to move into your poem more deeply.

made by Linda in her journal about the impulse to continue working on particular fragments that eventually become her poem: "I think you work on the ones that seem the most urgent or 'hot'—ones that help you understand yourself . . . and are tools of healing."

Perhaps a sign that this was indeed hot is the fact that Linda notes on the margin of this entry, "I guess I just plunged in without an entrance meditation this day."

> *3/24/94*
> *Cut cloth, <u>bolt</u>, piece—pattern, form—treadle,*
> *presserfoot, bobbin, swatch, switch, swish—marker, dressmaker's*
> *chalk   hem guide—<u>seam ripper</u>*
> *fabric—material—dry goods—yard goods stuff*
> *stitch—buttonhole—facing—basting—lambasting*
> *Oh, imp (my inner child) help me pick the word that counts,*
> *matters, best expression of my own essence. . . .*
> *Believe in the percolations, upswellings, bubbling from beneath*
> *the surface . . .*

This exploration of the fabric of her life continues.

> *3/25/94*
> *. . . mending basket containing ample abundance <u>faille</u>   French*
> *knot   linen—lisle—lace—<u>crêpe</u>—the question is: common*
> *fabrics or uncommon or a mix she would vote for common. I guess*
> *—never knowing they were uncommon*
> *Nylon—yuk! duck, net, twill, ticking, muslin, chino—or-*
> *gandy—organza*
> *<u>georgette</u>—gauze   <u>crinoline</u>—serge   <u>gingham</u>—calico*
> *linsey woolsey*
> *Where would the end be—future fabrics not yet invented*
> *Was my mother the wolf mother who gave me a hard time un-*
> *witting but taught me somehow. . . . Oh yeah—Remember she*
> *had a laughing side   oh yeah, but it all seemed so treacherous not*
> *knowing which side would occur in response to which stimuli—*
> *Oh it was verbal minefield I walked through, walked to, tried*
> *to circumvent but rarely succeeded. Was I afraid of my mother's*

*wasp tongue—yes, I was afraid of my mother. Why? Because I gave
her power to hurt me. Not believing in myself in self sound-
ness. Oh, I tell you now, Mama. I am sound, stable, solid though
flowing. I would still like your approval but won't be diminished
without it. I have called to my own depths and heard sufficient an-
swer.*

The amalgam of journal entries about Linda's mother, the fab-
ric-related words, and the drafts of the poem "Reappraisal" give
us a sense of the interrelatedness of the journaling process and
the writing of poems.

Having gone on this journey with Linda, let's read her poem
once again:

*Step 8. Rewrite the next draft
of the poem.*

REAPPRAISAL

*Years too late
a note of thanks Mama
for your potent tongue
piercing needle
rude ripper of seams
shrill shears gashing
my cloth to scrap*

*Step 9. Rewrite, revise, and
polish.*

*Yet your serpent fork's
ferocious tactile prowess
taught me textures
how to discriminate
with index fingers
of imagination
how to tell
gingham from gabardine
dotted swiss from seersucker
georgette from satin
though you did not sew
and lived in a drawer
lined with oilcloth
not imported silk*

Yes it was you, Mama
who gave me a quilt frame
wide as the horizon
bolts of fabric
bottomless as the ocean
and a work basket exploding
with luminous word patches

Linda's journal was the fecund field that grew this poem. The material in her journal contributed to her poem, and still offers possibilities for further insight and future poems. The relationship between journal writing and poetry-making does not end with the production of a single poem but continues on in Linda's life and in her journey as a human being, poet, and writer. You, too, can foster this relationship.

JOURNAL EXERCISES: WAYS TO ENTER

Portraits

A character sketch (portrait) is a written description of either yourself or someone else. Create language portraits of anyone in your life, using rich detail. Such detail could include:

- Physical characteristics, body language, facial features and expressions, clothes style, colors you associate with the person you're depicting
- The sound of their voice, manner of talking, frequently used words, tone and rhythm of their speech, how they listen
- Their social style, how they greet others, how they might hold a coffee cup or a basketball, how they move in a crowded room or in a natural setting
- The feelings and qualities they express and exude, the impact they have on others, the feelings and qualities that are hidden from expression
- Where they live, the kinds of furnishings in their home, and how such things reflect their personality
- The kind of animal, musical instrument, weather condition, historical or mythological figures they might be compared to

The Dialogue Relationship

A dialogue is a conversation between two voices. In this exercise, you write both voices. Choose one of the following subjects and write a dialogue:

ᗃ *Resistance.* Something to which you have resistance. It could be writing, speaking in public, getting married, doing the dishes, working on computers, or some aspect of your life.

ᗃ *Symbols.* Something that is symbolic for you. For example, talk with a lion about strength, a base stealer about quickness, a ballet dancer about balance, or to your telephone about communication.

ᗃ *Body.* A part of your body. What does it have to say to you? What do you want to tell it?

ᗃ *Feeling.* A feeling, such as anger or sadness. What can you learn from this feeling? What would you like to tell this feeling?

ᗃ *People.* Someone you feel close to, someone you feel distant from, someone whom you have met for the first time. Take the best from each of these and weave a new dialogue.

ᗃ *Material objects.* Talk with a favorite chair, a pillow, a coffee pot, a watch, a house, a pair of shoes, a car, a kitchen table. What kind of personality does that object have? What does it know about you?

ᗃ *Inner wisdom.* Discuss with your higher self or God the most important, essential questions of your life. Also talk about your everyday thoughts and activities—and receive a response. (See Linda's first journal entries earlier in this chapter.)

Perspectives

Perspective is a distinct point of view. This exercise allows you to explore points of view different from those you usually hold. Write from the perspective and voice of:

ᗃ The wind and rain
ᗃ A streetlight in your neighborhood
ᗃ Someone who is aging
ᗃ Someone at midlife
ᗃ A teenager
ᗃ A newborn
ᗃ Someone in an old photograph
ᗃ Your favorite coat, hat, or pair of shoes
ᗃ A particular memory
ᗃ A homeless person you've seen a number of times
ᗃ A foreigner who has just moved to this country
ᗃ An old friend who has not seen you in a long time
ᗃ A place in nature you love: a path you've walked, a place you go to sit

Free-writing

Free-write journal pieces that experiment with the following:

- *Unedited flow.* Begin absolutely anywhere and keep going! Do not edit yourself or stop yourself from saying anything. Write about whatever comes up. Jack Kerouac once wrote pages of material about a scouring pad!
- *Multidimensional realities . . . connectivity.* Consider the theory of physics called the "Butterfly Effect," which says that since everything in creation is interrelated, a butterfly's wings flapping in China can affect hurricanes in Miami, Florida. Write about seemingly disparate things in your life and find connections. What instances of synchronicity have happened to you this month?
- *Expansive, fluid movement in time and space.* Like the novel *One Hundred Years of Solitude* by Gabriel García Márquez, tell a story about yourself that covers hundreds, even thousands of years.
- *Clear documentation of your story.* Tell a mini-biographical story of your life by recording the events of one minute, one hour, a day, or a week. Tell your story in such clear, mindful, step-by-step, specific detail that every significant aspect of who you are is represented.
- *A broad range of writing styles.* Try writing as if you were: president of a large corporation, a trapeze performer, a shamanic elder, a man or woman who has led a social or spiritual revolution, a flower pedlar. Write in the language each would use to best communicate who they are.
- *Spontaneous dips into the imagination, into surprise, into the original.* Make up words and give your own definitions to them. Make up an imaginative story about how some common, everyday object was invented, such as a doorknob, a spoon, popcorn, a tennis racket, a paper clip, a pillow case.
- *Your relationship to life and the world.* Write about something you love to do that puts you in contact with the world.

Exploring Your Daily Life

The philosopher's kind of mind desires the general and the abstract; the poet's mind desires the specific and concrete: "to see the world in a grain of sand."

—*May Sarton*

Use the journal to explore your daily life experience, especially the place where you live. Get to know in detail what is within you and around you.

ᴡ Make a list of the people in your life who are significant, who capture your interest, or who have in some way crossed your path and made a difference.

ᴡ Write about people who are co-workers or who live in your community.

ᴡ Make a list of the places in your community where you regularly spend time or visit: your workplace, your home, where you go to be entertained, where you shop, eat, etc. Next time you go to one of these places, notice as much as you can about the physical surroundings and the people there. Add those observations to your journal.

ᴡ Make a list of the objects in your life that interest you. Pay attention to these objects, whether an old antique mirror, a wall of graffiti, or your favorite flannel shirt. How are they made? Who made them? What journey did they take on their way to you?

A true poet is a friendly man. He takes to his arms even cold and inanimate things, and rejoices in his heart.

—*William Wordsworth*

FEELINGS, THOUGHTS, INTUITIONS

ᴡ Free-write on particular feelings, thoughts, and intuitions you are having at the moment. Describe where in your body you feel these feelings, thoughts, and intuitions. Make note of the expressed feelings, thoughts, and intuitions of others with whom you come in contact on a daily basis.

FACTS, IMAGININGS, DREAMS

ᴡ Write down facts that interest you or seem important to you. What is the larger story behind these facts? Why are you interested in them?

ᴡ Write down your daydreams and your night dreams. Write about where your daydreams take you and what your night dreams say to you. Become the voice of one of the people or objects in your dream and speak your mind.

INNER WORLD, OUTER WORLD, AND THE BRIDGE BETWEEN THEM

ᴡ Describe your inner world. What is of value in there? What frightens you about it? Intrigues you? Delights you? Describe your day-to-day "outer world." What is of value there? What frightens, intrigues, delights, angers you? How are the two worlds related? Tell a story about how you travel between your inner and outer worlds.

Your Poetic Workshop

Use your journal to play with words. Note in your journal the poetic ideas that come to you during the day, including:

- ⩗ Dynamic word combinations
- ⩗ Metaphor and other poetic devices
- ⩗ Images
- ⩗ Sounds and rhythms

Finding a Poem, with Help from Master Journal Writers

Read the following journal entries by well-known poets and writers. What do you find particularly interesting in each one? Notice how something can attract you in a journal entry, demanding further exploration.

Read an entry a second time, but this time underline, circle, or highlight the phrases or words that attract your interest. Don't "think" about your choices—allow your instinct to guide you. It is all right to take fragments or single words. Let your creative decisions happen naturally.

Next, write down those fragments you marked to the right of the journal entry. As you do this, add more to your choices. Let your thoughts flow. You can use Gabriele Rico's clustering technique to develop what you have chosen. Rico describes clustering in Writing the Natural Way:

> *To create a cluster, you begin with a nucleus word, circled, on a fresh page. Now you simply let go and begin to flow with any current of connections that come into your head. Write these down rapidly, each in its own circle, radiating outward from the center in any direction they want to go. Connect each new word or phrase with a line to the preceding circle. When something new and different strikes you, begin again at the nucleus and radiate outward until those associations are exhausted.*

Or, you can use your choices as you did in the "Play on Words" section in Chapter Three. Fit unusual phrases together. Add words. Find a phrase to start with and follow the trail of that fragment. Build upon what interests you. Put groups of words or phrases from different entries together. Experiment! Make a poem!

> {*December 1941*}
> *Everything is flowing, love, writing, talking. I talk with George Barker. He is so quick, so sharp, focused, vital, electric. A taut mind and body, throwing off sparks. Turbulent. His wet Irish eyes, mocking, with that caressing slant towards the cheeks which indicate voluptuousness. At first I did not like his flippancy, his disguises.*

But when he said: "What can one do when one is removed not once, not twice, but a hundred times from one's real self?" at that moment I liked him, understood him.

—Anaïs Nin

Country Days and Nights.—Sept. 30, '82. 4:30 a.m. I am down in Camden County, New Jersey, at the farm-house of the Staffords—have been looking for a long while at the comet— have in my time seen longer-tail'd ones, but never one so pro-nounc'd in cometary character, and so spectral-fierce—so like some great pale, living monster of the air or sea. The atmosphere and sky, an hour or so before sunrise, so cool, still, translucent, give the whole apparition to great advantage. Impress'd with the silent, inexplicably emotional sight, I linger and look till all begins to weaken in the break of day.

—Walt Whitman

Every morning we must love what is lost in us and begin again.

—Beth Ferris

7 February
Thoughts while shaving. A thing I am very ashamed of: that I find suggested confirmation of my "identity" by reading my name in the newspapers. My heart really does do something journalistic—stop a beat, give a jump—if my eye hooks on to the printed word "Spender" or even—now I am getting a bit astigmatic—a confor-mation of letters like it. (Spring for example.) I really admire peo-ple who regard any publicity attached to them as vulgar and odious. I think of them in their cottage gardens with old-fashioned claustral red and white roses, enclosed by hedges, no act of theirs in the slightest degree influenced by any wish for publicity.

—Stephen Spender

Think of yourself as an incandescent power, illumined, perhaps, and forever talked to by God and his messengers.

—Brenda Ueland

June 7
Coming through Pleasant Hill without stopping, I saw new aspects of the wonderful old Shaker houses. The inexhaustible variety and dignity in sameness! The old Shaker colony at Pleasant Hill, just this side of the Kentucky River gorge, is a place that always im-presses me with awe and creates in me a sense of quiet joy. I love

those old buildings and I love the way the road swings up to them. They stand there in an inexpressible dignity, simplicity, and peace under the big trees. They are completely empty now. There have been no more Shakers there for a long time.

—Thomas Merton

My friend Roseanne Coggeshall, the poet, says that "sycamore" is the most intrinsically beautiful word in English. This sycamore is old; its lower bark is always dusty from years of floodwaters lapping up its trunk. Like many sycamores, too, it is quirky, given to flights and excursions. Its trunk lists over the creek at a dizzying angle, and from that trunk extends a long, skinny limb that spurts high over the opposite bank without branching. The creek reflects the speckled surface of this limb, pale even against the highest clouds, and that image pales whiter and thins as it crosses the creek, shatters in the riffles and melds together, quivering and mottled, like some enormous primeval reptile under the water.

—Annie Dillard

July 20, Marrakech—
The roof of the house—lying on mats drinking tea with portable radio & rug & air mattress & candle lamp—lying back after majoun & cigarettes & pipes uncounted—the stars forming huge geometrical patterns, meteorites, and a land of roofs all around, some lighted & some dark, all stretching & jutting flat in every direction, broken by silhouettes of Koutoubia Mosque and others.

—Allen Ginsberg

Blois June 24th 1870
Travelling gets more expensive as we come onto the great routes, for we have to stop at good hotels being women, and sometimes we must go first class when the trains are express. I hate to spend money, but I'm getting better so fast and enjoying so much that I shall go on till my year is out, and then if the expense is very great, come home and go to work. I have May's washing and sundry little expenses for her which I didn't expect, but her passage and dress

A poem, a sentence, causes us to be ourselves. I be and I see my being at the same time.

—Ralph Waldo Emerson

A writer needs three things, experience, observation, and imagination, any two of which, at times any one of which, can supply the lack of the others.

—William Faulkner

*W*hen I am in touch with my process, I am in touch with the process of the universe.

—Anne Wilson Schaef

*took about all her money and she must be taken care of. I hope July
will put a nice little plum "in the crib" for us all. Let me know how
it is, and what Loring's $12 was for.*

—Louisa May Alcott

STARTING WITH A LINE OF POETRY: FAMOUS FIRST LINES

Write a journal entry using as a springboard the following first lines of famous poems. After writing everything you would like to say on a particular line, cull from your journal entry a poem that begins with the famous first line you have chosen:

I will arise and go now, and go to . . .

Come to the orchard in spring . . .

I've known rivers . . .

*Come, warm your hands
From the cold wind of time . . .*

All that matters is to be at one with the living God . . .

White fog lifting & falling on mountain-brow . . .

whatever you have to say, leave . . .

I dwell in Possibility . . .

A REVIEW OF THE NINE-STEP JOURNAL-TO-POEM PROCESS

1. Dialogue with your journal, establishing a relationship of equals.
2. Write an "entrance meditation" which can take the form of a letter or prayer sent to God or your Muse.
3. Come up with key words, phrases, or images and "free-write" for ten minutes. Don't lift the pen from the paper.
4. Identify and find a phrase that reflects the central "theme" in Step 3. Deepen and expand

upon this by seeking out the polarity in that theme (for instance: Mother as enemy, mother as giver of word gifts).

5. Notice something in your environment and allow it to become the metaphor for your whole experience.

6. Go through everything up to this point with a highlighter or pen and create a rough draft of your poem.

7. Working from the draft poem, cluster or free associate to move into your poem more deeply.

8. Rewrite the next draft of the poem.

9. Rewrite, revise, and polish.

> *Creativity once begun goes on. Nothing is so satisfying to the human soul as creating something new. . . . We all long to see our works in print, I know, but this is not the point. It is the act of creation which counts. Every act of creation adds to the creativity in the world, and who knows if it has not some similar effect as the ritual breathing towards the East at dawn.*
>
> *—Irene Claremont de Castillejo*

Seven

The Poetry Writing Circle

Creating a Community of Poem-Makers

There is nothing so wise as a circle.

—*Rainer Maria Rilke*

When you discover something new, I guess it's just natural to want to share it with others. But "the other" becomes, for me, anyone who is curious, who wants to listen, who is willing to grope around and question his existence, who might possibly feel what I felt.

—*Judith Minty*

Sweet are the pleasures that to verse belong,
And doubly sweet a brotherhood in song

—*John Keats*

Circles

After I finish teaching a course in creative writing or poetry therapy, often some of the participants will form writing circles or seek out opportunities in their community that enable them to continue to share their writing with others. In the writing circle, poetry is the centerpiece for people to discover what is best in themselves. This chapter will cover:

- ⋓ An exploration of the benefit of writing circles
- ⋓ Experiences of other people in writing circles
- ⋓ Advice regarding how to start your own writing circle
- ⋓ Exercises to do within the writing circle
- ⋓ Stories of two ongoing poetry writing circles

I believe the greatest gift I can conceive of having from anyone is to be seen by them, to be understood and touched by them. The greatest gift I can give is to see, hear, understand, and touch another person. When this is done I feel a contact has been made.

—Virginia Satir

A circle expresses wholeness. When we sit in a circle with others, not everything is healed nor are all problems solved. However, we are reminded of our oneness in a circle. If a circle is a joining together of equals, it should not impose upon you or limit you. There is freedom in the circle to express yourself creatively. There is respect for others in the circle. Within the circle, we can share the truth of our lives.

If each of the birds in the forest waited until the bird with the most beautiful song could sing, the forest would be silent.

—Unknown

Writing on the page is much like talking into the open space inside a circle. You can write upon the page and the page will give your words room and contain them. Both circle and page will listen to you speak. And as a part of the circle, you become a listener as well.

It is natural then to bring writing and circles together. In our busy and complex lives, it is nurturing to have a place where others welcome the poet in you. It is inspiring to have somewhere to go to share your creative process, a place where your writing can receive constructive and encouraging attention. As part of a writing circle, you are part of a dynamic, creative community. The following comments are by members of the same writing circle:

I feel we may be in different stages of our becoming, but there is a lot of forward movement. There is no need for us all to get anywhere at the same time. We are all moving at our own speed. I love the poetry group because we are all searching. I am drawn to it because we are all on our way somewhere.

—Ginny

For the past four years, I have had the good fortune to participate in a poetry writing and reading circle. It serves as a stimulus for producing poems, a forum for the exchange of ideas and viewpoints, and a gathering of kindred spirits.

—Bruce

I now believe that we are all poets, it's just that most people don't realize it. My hope is that others might one day stumble into a group that shares their poetry. It continuously amazes me what I am capable of learning about others through their honesty and self-revelation in poetry. But it amazes me even more what I am capable of learning about myself.

—Ted

It is natural for a poet to value what he can least explain in his work; what is odd is that readers seem to be able to respond to and identify the same qualities.

—Robert Wallace

Creating a Circle That Nourishes You and Your Writing

You may have at times felt shut out of some circles. You may have joined a circle thinking it was going to support a spirit of wholeness but after a time discovered the people in the circle were closed to creative expression. They may have been more concerned that you follow a certain mind-set rather than be authentic and true to your inner voice.

What appears as a circle may in fact be a clique. No surprise that we might not feel an affinity with such a circle! Rather than having a permeable, breathing membrane like living cells do, cliques discount who we really are in order to foster their own image.

Poets, like any other group of people, are by no means immune to creating such closed circles. Given their lack of acceptance in our culture, it is not surprising that poets, in order to survive, are often very adept at creating what appear to be cliques.

An open circle, however, nourishes its participants and their originality. It allows for each person's full expression. Our joy and sorrow, our delights and struggles will all be heard in the open circle. In the process of speaking, listening, and hearing, the circle breathes life into creative community.

> *We weep with those who weep, laugh with those who laugh and suffer with those in pain.*
>
> —*Leon Battista Alberti*

Circles formed with this intention are sacred. Native American traditions honor the circle of the Great Spirit. Black Elk, the Oglala Sioux holy man, speaks of this:

> *And I saw that the sacred hoop of my people was one of many hoops that made one circle, wide as daylight and as starlight, and in the center grew one mighty flowering tree to shelter all the children of one mother and one father. And I saw that it was holy.*

As poets, it is possible to form a similar kind of sacred circle that will increase our capacity to speak, listen, hear, feel, write, and understand. Such a circle will make for better people and better poems. Marge Piercy describes this kind of sacred circle in these lines from her poem "Councils":

> ☞ *Perhaps we should talk in groups*
> *small enough for everyone to speak.*

We are here to witness the creation and to abet it. . . . We are here to bring to consciousness the beauty and power that are around us and to praise the people who are here with us.

—*Annie Dillard*

We are like spokes on a wheel, all radiating out from the same center. If you define us according to our position on the rim, we seem separate and distinct from one another. But if you define us according to our starting point, our source—the center of the wheel—we're a shared identity.

—*Marianne Williamson*

♀   *Perhaps we should start by speaking softly.*
       The women must learn to dare to speak.

♂   *The men must bother to listen.*

♀   *The women must learn to say, I think this is so.*

♂   *The men must learn to stop dancing solos on the ceiling.*
       After each speaks, she or he
       will repeat a ritual phrase:

♀ & ♂   *It is not I who speaks but the wind.*
       Wind blows through me.
       Long after, is the wind.

EXERCISES

What does a circle represent to you in general? What does it symbolize? What are your experiences of circles?

The Wisdom of Circles

What *images* of circles attract you? When Rilke says "There is nothing so wise as a circle," what does this mean to you? Why is a circle wise? What do we learn from circles? Think of circles—something in nature, something that is man-made. A starfish. Wheel. Eye. Drum. Cookie. Spider web. Living cell. Sun. Name your circle images and then make a quick notation of what they symbolize for you.

Circle Image	What It Says to Me
Wheel	Life has many spokes but one center.
Spider web	Creation is finely made and interrelated.
Drum	The round drum makes the sound of the earth's heart.

_____

_____

_____

_____

_____

_____

Consider how a writing circle could function similarly to some of the circles you have named and described here. Is there one image that might be a particularly good model for your circle? Write a story about one of these circle symbols as if it embodied your vision of a writing circle.

Sentence Stem Warm-Ups

Use these in a beginning writing circle:

I feel safe in a group when _____

My worst fear about my writing is _____

Poetry is a delight to me because _____

Poetry is difficult for me because _____

I don't want this writing circle to be about _____

One of my favorite words in the English language is_____

My worst school experience of poetry and writing was _____

_____

My best school experience with poetry and writing was _____

_____

Some of my favorite poets are _____

_____

Some of my favorite poems are _____

_____

The story of how the first poem I ever wrote came to be is _____

_____

_____

My intention for joining a writing circle is to _____

_____

Writing and Sharing Poetry: A Journey of Solitude and Relatedness

I like the sense of privacy and solitude in writing poems, of being in intimate touch with my own selves.

—*Peter Everwine*

There is something deeply personal and private about poetry-making. It is a journey into your depths. To offer to let others join you on this journey is not something you do lightly. The intimacy that is shared when another person hears what journal writing teacher Andrea Peck calls "intimate conversations with oneself" is worth protecting until you're certain you trust that person.

Yet there is value in sharing your poems and the process of writing with others. After breathing in, it is natural to have an out-breath. Poem-making is the in-breath. The writing circle is out-breath: bringing your poetry out to the world.

Your willingness to share your writing will be influenced by how generally relaxed or reticent you are about revealing your inner life. Here again we are likely to meet up with our own unique censor and permission voices. What would your censor and permission voices have to say about sharing your writing with others?

There is a difference between a censor voice that holds back your growth and a wise voice that cautions you to wait to share your poetry until you find the kind of sensitive listeners you deserve. Regardless of your personal style, selecting a writing circle deserves the kind of attention that you would give to considering a committed relationship or taking a new job. Just as you are doing in those circumstances, when you become part of a writing group you are offering something essential about yourself.

On the other hand, we cannot know for sure how things will go. An element of risk is always involved in revealing yourself.

The creative process must be explored not as the product of sickness, but as representing the highest degree of emotional health, as the expression of normal people in the act of actualizing themselves.

—*Rollo May*

Each friend is present, a world in us, a world possibly not born until they arrive, and it is only by this meeting a new world is born.

—*Anaïs Nin*

Risk is part of what makes the process of self-revelation authentic. Taking such a risk can give you an opportunity to connect with other creative people and improve and explore both your writing and listening skills.

In general, I think it is important to share your writing with people whose values and styles of communicating feel comfortable to you. The people in your writing circle should express a caring and attentive attitude toward you and your work. And of course it's important that you show the same respect to them. From this foundation of trust and support, honesty can flourish—and so can your writing. Finding such a group of fellow writers and friends may be the most important thing you can do as a poet.

At first, you might feel hesitant about sharing your written work. The fears "What will they think?" and "Can I trust sharing my feelings with these people?" are understandable. Again, you are wise to be somewhat cautious. The reason to *consciously* create a writing circle comprising people who will honor each person's unique form of expression is so that you can feel safe about revealing yourself to others and receiving their comments.

Gaining confidence to move ahead comes at different rates for different people. It's not that everyone is reluctant! Some folks are so eager to share that they are always paging busily through their papers (while someone else is reading) to find yet another poem to read. That's not going to help the work of a writing circle. The Tibetan poet-sage Milarepa offers advice that is pertinent here. Milarepa said: "Hasten slowly." One benefit of hastening slowly is that we can listen more closely as we go. Another part of "hastening slowly" is taking the risk a step at a time when our heart calls us to speak.

Knowing that almost everyone experiences a feeling of hesitation in reading out loud, you should feel free to test the waters before plunging in. Allow yourself some time to decide if a particular writing circle is right for you.

Over time, a wonderful intimacy occurs among members of the circle that can feel safe and affirming. Linda writes about her first experience sharing a poem in her group:

The purpose of art is to heal. I believe that every person is a special kind of artist, rather than the common belief that artists are special kinds of people.

—Samuel Avital

> *I remember reading my own first attempt at a poem in a faltering voice four years ago. When a deafening silence greeted the poem, I wished the floor would swallow me up. Why had I ever thought I could write poetry? But eventually the group began to respond. I still remember our teacher Al's comments; he praised the title of the poem as being apt and said I had carried the theme through the poem consistently. After that I was willing to try again the next week.*

Jeanie speaks about how the potent comments of group members inspire new work:

> *There is a kind of creative intimacy that occurs in the circle. Someone says something that resonates with someone else and they let what was said become something new for them. They take off on it and share it back in the group at a later time as a poem-in-progress. That kind of intimacy is really creative—to listen to what someone is saying so that the phrase or image inspires you to go off and make it meaningful to you in your own unique way.*

Whether you share your writing with close friends, with loved ones, or in a more formal writing circle, you have an opportunity to enrich your own life and the lives of those around you.

> *There is only one real deprivation, I decided this morning, and that is not to be able to give one's gift to those one loves most.*
> —May Sarton

The Writing Circle: A Healing Temple and Sacred Theater Space

There are many possibilities for how a "writing circle" might form and conduct itself. This sense of *possibility* is exciting. It allows for the writing circle to express itself in the way that works best for its members. It allows for the unexpected, which is poetry. It makes sense to emphasize this sense of possibility when we are talking about poetry. As Emily Dickinson said about her life as a poet:

> I dwell in Possibility—
> A fairer House than Prose—
> More numerous of Windows—
> Superior—for Doors—

What doors might be possible to open in your writing circle? A writing circle can be a spiritual oasis. It can offer worthwhile psychological support. A sense of aesthetics can be nurtured. Friendships of rare quality can be developed over time. Fine poems can be written, hammered out, and polished. A writing circle can offer a place to blend healing and poetry into the journey that is our life.

It's helpful to listen to the comments of people who are excited about their participation in writing circles to gain a sense of why such a group can be an important and useful part of their lives:

> *The group is essential to keep growing in this craft. I think without it I would still write, but I would stay at the same place. People's poetry changes. It's so exciting! It's really all about personal growth. It's like a lifeline to me.*
>
> —*Ginny*

> *I've learned how to shape poetry. How to explore its deeper meanings and use it as a powerful tool for expression and growth . . . and how to truly listen.*
>
> —*Barbara*

These poets feel that a writing circle both strengthens the quality of their writing and serves as a place of catharsis to encourage their creativity and wholeness.

A writing circle gives members the opportunity to share themselves in a unique way that goes beyond social conventions. The opportunity for self-discovery in a writing circle is also intrinsic to poetry itself:

We are so product oriented, focusing on criticizing texts, so that they become "better poems" and "better stories." And we pay so little attention to the human beings who sit in class, their personal reasons for coming, their pain, their difficulties, what blocks them from creating, what makes them flow.

— *Burghild Nina Holzer*

Dr. Kenneth Gorelick, a pioneer in the field of poetry therapy, and chief of continuing medical education at St. Elizabeths Hospital in Washington, D.C., suggests that the use of a writing circle is to make space for participants to share those "special moments" of "excruciating pain or joy" and is comparable to aspects of fifth century B.C. Greek theater. Dr. Gorelick writes:

If the experience of Greek tragic theater was personally and deeply felt, it would carry over to personal life beyond the theater space. The Athenians knowingly or intuitively linked the healing of tragic poetry with healing per se. The theater festival, dedicated to the spirit of Dionysus, followed immediately upon the festival of Asclepius, whose healing temple stood beside the theater of Dionysus.

Asclepius was the son of Apollo and the healer of disease and preserver of health. Apollo was god of light, patron of mathematics, music, healing, and poetry. Naturally there is a link between health, healing, and poetry. The structural layout and intent of the Asclepian healing temple provided for a physical descent to a special place in the depths of the building and, psychologically and spiritually, into the inner experience of the person coming to the temple. This psychic descent was for the purpose of invoking a healing dream. Dr. Gorelick continues:

After the healing dream, the healed person would mark the occasion by recording the dream. Often the person would compose a poem to close, ceremonialize, and concretize the experience.

The poem shared in the writing circle, the concretization of "special moments," becomes the door to the theater space and "healing temple in miniature" that other members can walk through to access their own healing dream. Dr. Gorelick writes:

> As group members examine the poem and are drawn into its depths, they are like the sufferers seeking their healing dream in the depths of the Asclepian temples. The poem creates a frame in which each person's dream for himself/herself can arise. Drawn into the depths of the poem, the group members are simultaneously drawn into the depths of their lives to find an open space in which they can transform themselves, shape new lives, and create new destinies.

Ted reflects on this aspect of the collective healing process that occurs in his writing group:

> To an outsider, the subject of poetry and its style, form, and function seem to be the purpose of our meetings, but after having spent four years with this group, I believe that our purpose is quite different. My not so secret view is that each one of us is presenting the same poem over and over again. They're the poems of our life's struggles, and they come disguised with new words and new structure each time we meet. We spend quality time discussing the poetic merits of our contributions, but on a subliminal level something much more important is taking place. We're a support group. We meet regularly to emotionally and spiritually uphold one another and to establish life bonds that can carry us further along our interior journey.

Poetry can provide the stage, the special place that allows those who enter that theater an opportunity to find a deeper part of themselves and to experience renewal. The poem read within the writing circle is the part of us connected with our dream. Hearing the dreams of others can help to nourish our own.

The interaction with a particular poem, or the performance of it, becomes a rite of passage from one stage of awareness of self to another, with the poem as the facilitator or guide during the process.

—Janet Rice

Getting Started

Starting a poetry writing circle may be one of the most satisfying things you do to enrich your life. The steps are simple. Your willingness to do some initial planning to get the group started will be more than rewarded by the inspiration the group will give you. All that is required is a handful of people who have an interest in sharing the richness of life and the creative process of using words.

There are a number of ways a writing circle might begin. One of the most frequent and natural is when a creative writing class decides to continue meeting on its own. The class thus becomes a writing circle.

It is usually not difficult to find a creative writing class, especially in cities or large towns. Such a class might be sponsored in your community by:

- Universities, colleges, junior colleges, high school adult programs
- Community centers, YMCAs and YWCAs, Jaycees, senior centers, libraries
- Writing workshops offered by writers and poets

Partway through the workshop or class, announce to people your intention to form a writing group. By doing so, you can elicit interest from one or two other people who are also interested in making a writing circle happen. (Be sure to pass around an address list during class or to obtain one so you can contact people at a later date.)

Find someone with whom you can work on the formation of the writing circle; the two of you can do the initial brainstorming about the writing circle you both envision.

You can also create a writing circle from among your friends and acquaintances. It might include people from various areas of your life—perhaps someone from work, a close personal friend, another parent from your child's school. Perhaps a neighbor or

Sad is his lot who, once at least in his life, has not been a poet.

—Alphonse de Lamartine

someone you don't see often but with whom you feel a kinship. What friends or acquaintances do you feel might be interested in forming a writing circle? Contact them. Share your ideas. See if there is interest. Invite friends to coffee to at least discuss the idea.

Another source of potential writing circle members are readers of this book. You might consider using this book as a catalyst to share with people and see if an interest in forming a writing circle naturally develops.

An initial question to ask yourself is whether you want the writing circle to be same sex or coed. There is value in either of these choices. You might begin as an all women's or men's group and eventually decide to open the circle up to the opposite sex.

The benefit of a same-gender group is that you can avoid the tendency some might have to feel inhibited or to maintain a certain image. Once again, the elements of comfort and trust are imperative and must serve as a foundation for any writing circle. For some, this trust and comfort is more accessible with members of the same sex. If the purpose of your writing circle is to encourage and enhance creative expression, an all-women's writing circle may give women an opportunity to share more facets of themselves than if they only met to discuss "women's issues." The same potential is true for a men's group.

For others, gender is not an issue. It is certainly possible to maintain deep respect and trust in a mixed group. The poem by Marge Piercy on page 182 says it beautifully. The essay by Katrina Middleton later in this chapter also speaks about the value of men and women sharing their writing together.

Whether your writing circle is coed or same sex, you and the others who are creating the circle can decide what kind of tone the group will have. You have the right to set your own ground rules about the direction you want the writing circle to take and the qualities you want it to cultivate.

The exercises in this chapter will help you to explore and clarify your vision for the circle. They will assist you in answering questions about what you want and don't want in your writing circle. These exercises, as well as the entire book, can be used as a guide and support as you begin to form and work within your writing circle.

Once you develop some basic ideas for how the writing circle would function and be most nourishing to you, you can begin to invite more people to participate.

You might start by creating a flyer inviting persons to attend a meeting. State clearly in the flyer your intention for starting an ongoing writing group. Set the date for the meeting far enough in advance so that if people are interested, they will be able to fit it into their schedule. Encourage people to come with ideas for an initial brainstorming session. It's a welcoming gesture to offer simple refreshments at that initial meeting.

It's O.K. if only a handful of people show up. You may already have a nucleus from which a lot can develop. If you have a large turnout, that's wonderful too. You can discuss issues of group size at the first meeting.

Friends and creative writing classes are only a few sources of possible writing circle members. You can also post flyers in these places:

- Libraries
- Museums
- Churchs and temples
- Bulletin boards or e-mail
- Local markets and laundromats
- Coffeehouses
- Community centers
- Cultural centers
- Meditation and healing centers
- Creative writing departments
- Professional organizations
- Women's and men's centers

At the initial organizing meeting, express your intention. Bring a large pad of newsprint or a white board with felt-tip pens to write down the ideas that come up. You don't have to decide on any final answers at the first meeting—in fact, it is better to allow for quite a bit of flexibility and change. You just want to start off in the right direction and get a clearer sense of how the passion you have for writing and sharing with others can manifest.

Sharing this book might be useful to set a tone for the direction you want to go. You might read some of the comments by other writing circle members in this chapter to get a sense of the goals and attitudes you want the circle to emulate.

Here is a list of issues you might want to address. You don't need to address all of these at the initial meeting.

Brainstorming Questions

- Where are you going to meet?
- Can someone offer an office space or their home for a regular meeting place?
- How often will you meet?
- What day of the week? Day or night?
- How many people should be in the group?
- Should everyone get a chance to read at each meeting, or should only two or three people read per meeting?
- How long will each meeting last?
- If the group started as a creative writing class, do you want to continue to have the teacher lead the group?
- Does the group want to have a regular leader or rotating leadership?
- Is there a format or a structure you want to follow?
- How do people feel about confidentiality—should poems be shared outside the group?
- What kind of time commitment do circle participants agree to? Is participation on a come-as-you-can, drop-in basis, or are participants asked to miss only if there is illness or if they need to be out of town?
- In addition to writing, what talents, gifts, or special experiences can people bring to the writing circle?
- Will you share poems by well-known poets as well as those read by group members?
- Do people want to give the writing circle a name?

- Is it all right to invite guests to the writing circle? How many times are they allowed to come without making a commitment to be a regular participant?
- Will someone be in charge of sending out notices or taking care of other administrative chores?
- Will you have food or refreshments? Who will be in charge of this?
- Will you have a "kitty" for people to contribute money for various group needs?

People have dealt with their meeting locations in a number of creative ways. Some groups rotate, holding meetings in a different member's home each session. Another group whose members are clustered in two separate geographical areas have two meeting places, alternating between each location. Another group I've heard of meets in a local café. People can eat or not, come or not, and it's always at the same time.

Some groups choose to have food, which serves to develop their sense of community. Some have created a specific format that they follow, while other groups are more free-form. None is better or worse, they are just different. The fun part is that you can create the kind of writing circle that suits the inclinations of your particular members.

Once you have your initial meeting, much will become clear concerning how you will proceed. Keep the process open—allow the creation of your writing circle to be flexible and alive. Many of these questions may not be necessary, while others will come up at the appropriate time. You can work out the details as your writing circle unfolds. The important thing, after all, is to write and share poetry with one another. Once you have the commitment of a handful of people (five to six should be enough), you can begin your writing circle experience.

Making a Commitment

It is important that each member make a commitment to the group that he or she can keep. Such a commitment can be made after testing the waters for a few meetings. Perhaps it's for a pre-set amount of time—say, three months. It's not that everyone has to make every single meeting, but a sense of constancy makes participation in the group more valuable to everyone involved. It's likely that some people will value the group so much, they will remain members as long as the writing circle stays together. It's also perfectly natural for people to leave and then to come back.

Sometimes, there will be difficulty sticking to your commitment when things get very busy at work, during school finals, or holidays, for example. It's how you handle those busy times that is the key. One of my students who helped to form a writing circle gave this description of adhering to her commitment:

Before our last meeting, it was the end of the business quarter at my job, and I had piles of work and piles of stress and I thought, "How can I possibly devote another night to my writing group? It's too much!" And then, I just went. I drove to the meeting that night and I told myself, "How could I not be here?" This is my group. I am a part of it. I am a part of keeping it together. Even though I am going to get home late and I'll be tired tomorrow morning, there is something about forging through and keeping my commitment. The reward is that I feel like I'm floating out of the room after another special and unique session.

—Jeanie

Deep Listening

The writing circle needs to be a safe place of deep listening. There needs to be a style of listening that will encourage both new writers and more experienced writers to risk breaking new ground. The more this need for safety and openness is honored, the more authentic and meaningful the group's experience will become.

The key to deep listening is respect. Respect doesn't only mean holding someone or something in esteem—or in a certain sense, at a distance. There is a more active quality to respect that has to do with giving careful attention. The root of the word "respect" means "to look at" or "to pay attention to." Respecting people doesn't mean you are going to like everything they do, which in the case of your writing circle means every line of a poem they write, their choice of themes, etc. It means that you will do your best to pay attention and listen whenever someone is reading. What could be more honest and nourishing? Paying attention is a way to both appreciate where someone is and to hear their potential for growth. Respect in the writing circle engenders trust, and trust, in a fundamental way, encourages further growth.

Obviously, paying attention means not interrupting while someone is reading a poem. But it is subtler than that. It means allowing an interval of time after a poem is finished before volunteering a comment. It means listening with as much attention to the silence that comes at the end of a poem, or between the lines and stanzas of a poem, as you would listen to the poem itself. I'm not talking about dampening a lively give-and-take discussion that often ensues after a poem has been read. And I'm also not saying that after a poem is read everyone should be so formal in responding "respectfully" that spontaneity or gut feelings are lost—not by any means! In fact, the spontaneous sighs and ah's, the deep feelings that are sometimes drawn out of us in sound as we listen to poems, are wonderful to express. Yet whatever the effect of the poem, an interval of time after a poem is read can give room for feelings to be felt by both reader and listeners before any comments are given.

This respectful interval gives the poet-writer an opportunity to hear the promptings of an inner voice. After "casting on air" a creation in the company of those who respect and listen, this space of time and silence belongs to the poet-reader. This respectful silence can be the best kind of support possible, and of-

Listening is receptivity. The deeper you can listen the better you can write. You take in the way things are without judgment.

—Natalie Goldberg

fer the most incisive guidance which the writer will feel naturally within.

> *Listening is a magnetic and strange thing, a creative force. When people really listen to each other in a quiet, fascinated attention, the creative fountain inside each of us begins to spring and cast up new thoughts and unexpected wisdom.*
>
> —Brenda Ueland

I know a poet who is part of a writing group that practices, as he puts it, "ruthless compassion" as opposed to "grandmother love" when responding to poems. His reasoning is that "ruthless compassion" is what an artist and every true poet needs. The thesis is that if this kind of toughness is not adhered to, the spirit of poetry will depart from the group. I don't agree. It may work for him, but I feel this approach is limited.

Leaving aside the basic questions of what *is* ruthless compassion and *who* is wise enough to be practicing it, I think to suggest that a group has only two choices is a limited way of describing how people might respond to and talk about poetry. I feel the responses available to people for helping one another so that the best poem can emerge are far more creative, surprising, and varied.

In my teaching practice with children and adults of all ages, I see again and again that respect, warmth, acceptance, kindness, patience, silent observation, humor, empathy, curiosity, care, wit, knowledge, not knowing, and especially an ability to focus upon and listen to someone sharing poems, provide a resonant *atmosphere* for the poet to sense *within* what she or he can do to make better poems. It also helps the group to grow.

This doesn't mean that incisive and direct comments aren't appropriate in a writing circle. Clear feedback is extremely helpful and usually quite welcome. Once a foundation of safety has been developed, critical commentary can help make poems better. But if critical comments about a person's writing cross that person's comfort threshold, it is totally appropriate for that individual to say so. When given the chance to make a con-

There has been so much unnecessary suffering in our century. If we are willing to work together, we can all benefit from the mistakes of our time, and . . . we can offer the next century a beautiful garden and a clear path.

—*Thich Nhat Hanh*

nection with their hearts first, listeners can usually talk about what works in a poem and what does not work in a constructive way.

When love is introduced into art, within a supportive creative community, tremendous things are possible.

"It Takes a Long Time of Getting to Know Someone..."

My poetry writing teacher at Boston University, the poet George Starbuck, once wrote to me that "it takes a long time of getting to know someone before you can make truly constructive comments on their poetry." It was a wise statement by a witty and kind man. Getting to know people at an essential level—that is exactly what is happening in the writing circle. The process of writing, like nurturing a friendship, is the work of a lifetime.

Talking about the kind of criticism his group offers, Ted says:

> *The comments are never hostile, negative, or excessively critical. Some people choose to ask the poet to further amplify the point or intention of their poem. Some might comment about word choices. Whatever the comments, they are always given in a nurturing tone. We didn't start out by design not to hurt anybody's feelings; it just evolved that way.*

Each group needs to determine the style of constructive criticism it is comfortable giving. Some people will want to emphasize poetics. Some may want a psychological focus. Some will bring a spiritual approach to the circle. Actually, all of these aspects can be included in a writing circle.

It is clear to me that in any group truly committed to encouraging creativity, there is a silent magic that is far more important than words or opinions. Beyond comments and criticism, listening and patience are the most essential contributions group members can make to their fellow poets.

Poetry and every other art was and is and forever will be a question of individuality. Tom's can be Dick's and Dick's can be Harry's but none of them can ever be you.

——e. e. cummings

I sometimes think that we would do better not to practice so much criticism but rather learn through years of patient observation.
—Burghild Nina Holzer

The following account is by poet and magazine editor, Katrina L. Middleton. I asked Katrina to tell the story of her writing circle, Range of Light, a group that has met to write and discuss poetry for over fifteen years in the area of Sacramento and Sierra Nevada mountains in California. It is a warm story of community, creativity, and the power of poetry to make a difference. There are excellent practical suggestions in her essay for how to create a successful, long-term writing circle.

Our writing circle began as a poetry class taught at a small junior college in the Sierra foothills. The people in the class simply continued to meet long after the semester ended, becoming a combination of monthly poetry workshop and potluck social.

In each other's homes we've shared Donna's homemade bread, Geneva's deviled eggs, Janet's persimmon pudding, and Wendy's Chocolate Decadence fudge brownies. In living rooms, kitchens, and back yards we've critiqued each other's poems and writings. Over coffee and wine we've discussed the whole spectrum of the "creative process," from germinating ideas to finding time to write. We've also talked about politics, ecology, the Super Bowl, carburetor repair, kids, money problems, and back problems—particles of Life. Through this process of fellowship—sharing our food, our poems, and our lives—we have become better poets and better people.

Our group is not the same one that sat in that classroom over fifteen years ago. Some have continued, while others have moved away or become busy with different facets of their lives. The instructor in that class, Bill Hotchkiss, now teaches in Grants Pass, Oregon, and keeps in touch by occasional letter. Last year, Gary moved to Santa Cruz, but he still attends periodically, making the five-hour drive to get here. Geneva is in the process of moving her family to Arkansas, but she will always be a member of the Range of Light poets.

New people have joined. A few drifted away and then returned. Richard Berger, who suggested our name, Range of Light, from a quo-

tation by John Muir about the Sierra Nevadas, died in 1983. Will Jumper, another beloved member, died last year.

Together we've given readings and worked on projects. Three of us developed a poetry workshop at a senior residence care home one summer, printing a small collection of poems written by the residents. And five years ago we produced a *Range of Light* anthology.

In some ways we are a diverse group, in different careers, and at different stages in our lives. Brian is a grammar school teacher; John teaches high school. Robert is a landscape artist. Geneva owned an antique store for a number of years. We have several office workers, a mail carrier, a pianist, and a rock climber. Bob and Marion live in the high country, with scarcely a neighbor in sight, while Lenore's home is in a busy trailer park in town. Monica and her husband are raising their little girl, Emily, together, while Gwen is raising her children alone. At least six of us are grandparents. There is almost a seventy year range in our ages.

Woven through these differences is connectedness. The writing, and the sharing of our writing, is not some exclusive fragment, separate from life, it is continuous and inclusive to the whole of our lives. Marriage, divorce, children, jobs, unemployment, retirement, illness, and death—we share these things by sharing our words and our lives. Donna recently retired from the university library; she also has bone cancer. While she was in the hospital undergoing tests and receiving radiation treatment, there was a constant trail of poets, like busy ants, weaving into her room, carrying flowers, books, and poems. Homes, café, or hospital room—wherever we gather becomes a sharing of words.

Our group is fluid and informal, so it's difficult to describe a typical meeting. In fact the word "meeting" is too formal. Robert's Rules of Order doesn't apply. Generally, on the third Saturday of each month, people start gathering between six and seven. Occasionally we have a small group of only four or five people, because of timing and other commitments. Sometimes it's a group of twenty-five. There's a lot of noise and conversation in the first hour or so as we greet each other, get our coffee or a glass of wine, and catch up on the news of who's been doing what.

Eventually someone says, "It's getting late; we better start." We

*L*ove is a force in you that enables you to give other things.

—Anne Morrow Lindbergh

move to sit on the sofa, in chairs, and on cushions on the floor in a circle that's irregular and unsymmetrical. We don't have any rules (except that smokers have to smoke outside). But we've developed a few traditions. One is that the host or hostess will begin. Sometimes it's a single poem, sometimes several. Another tradition is that we bring photocopies of our poems. The person reading distributes photocopies of the poem, taking this moment to explain that this is a first draft or rewrite, or to give some background about how this poem came into being.

Even the most practiced poets can feel vulnerable about going public with a newborn poem and may preface their reading with "Well . . . I didn't have a lot of time to work on this." We also recognize that every poem is a distillation of experience and, being human, we want to tell about the elements we left out. It helps us as fellow poets to understand how other poets work and how other poems are born. We keep this explanation/disclaimer period to a minute or less so that we don't spend the whole evening talking around a poem without ever getting to the poem; but it is usually a part of the process. Perhaps it's like taking a verbal deep breath before leaping off the high dive.

When the poet reads, we listen. Then we begin discussing the poem. One tradition is that we first tell what we like about the piece, before offering suggestions about changes or cutting. We give our response to the poem, what lines we felt were strong, what was confusing or unclear, what words seemed weak. Having a copy of the poem in front of us helps listeners give more detailed feedback. Every meeting is an animated workshop, and we have a great deal of lively debate and dialogue with a generous amount of teasing and laughter. This is not a test, there is no pass or fail.

Giving constructive responses to the poem and the poet is what our group is about. Not everyone is at the same level of experience or even at the same stage of life. One of our members is now a strong, accomplished poet, but her poems are different from the ones she wrote about flowers and butterflies when she first began coming to the Range of Light gatherings at age seventeen. She has grown as a poet because she has matured as a person.

It is important that we nurture each other. We will not get profound poetry if we trash the poet in the process. And we remember that

we are fellow poets, not self-appointed authorities. This regard for
each other as people and as fellow poets is the most important tradi-
tion. Each voice is authentic.

WRITING CIRCLE: IDEAS AND EXERCISES

The Story / Poem of a Possible Writing Circle

Use as many of the following words as you can (or want to use) in either a poem or prose poem that illustrates your feelings and vision for a writing circle. Feel free to change the words from nouns to verbs, etc. Explore the root meanings of the words you choose and see if you can use the word in a way that closely illustrates the root meaning:

rigidity	clarity	friendship	humor	creativity	warmth
wisdom	honesty	judgment	respect	elitism	harshness
dance	sensitivity	snobbery	listen	dream	courageous
praise	blame	trust	work	play	distrust
joy	sorrow	imagination	originality	tough	family fights
left out	language	boldness	strength	weakness	timidity
vision	mundane	sun	cry	breathe	moon
men	women	threatens	safe	broken	inspire
wild	fire	ritual	cut	nurture	shall

Warm-Up Affirmations for Your Writing Circle and Yourself

Use the following statements of affirmation as simple "warm-ups" when your writing circle meets—or you can use them by yourself! Write the statements down on notecards and put them in a large bowl so each person can pick one out. These can be read silently or out loud at the beginning of the meeting. On some occasions each member of the group might want to write a spontaneous poem about the affirmation they've picked. (A variation: Have everyone write on the same affirmation.) You can also illustrate these affirmations if you like, make collages with magazine photographs, colored marking pens, etc. (Again, you can do this on your own, too!)

Stretch your imagination.
Listen closely to the sounds of words.
Feel the rhythmic pulse of language.
Read your poetry with your whole heart and breath.
Let your feelings flow when you write.

Ask God to inspire your writing.

Allow the morning light to speak to you.

Invite your Muse to stay in your home.

You are pregnant with the new ideas and energies of poems.

Get to know strange words.

Keep what feels right in your poem.

Focus your attention on the voice and the poem.

There's something to discover wherever you are, it all depends on your vantage point.

Observe all the details of the people in your life.

Allow everything you encounter—a cup, a city street, a flower—to reveal its poetry.

Welcome mundane activities as sources of poetry: grocery shopping, taking a shower, ironing, driving to work.

Make sounds with your voice—enjoy the essence of language.

Notice the first clear sound you hear in the morning.

Listen to others when they read. Open your heart to their words.

"Get it" in writing.

Surprise yourself with words.

Feel the changing pulse beneath your assumptions.

Stop and listen to what other people pass by.

Listen for the "person behind the poem."

What interests and attracts you is the pathway to finding your true voice.

Words of power, clarity, and tenderness are yours for the writing.

Practice nonjudgmental openness in writing your first drafts.

Become what you care about in your writing.

Listen with respect: give people the opportunity to hear themselves.

Delight in your imagination.

Your unique writing style will emerge if you allow integrity to guide you.

Allow your voice to carry the sounds of laughter and tears. It will then give lasting truth to your words.

There is more to life than meets the eye—but nothing the heart cannot feel if enough attention is paid.

Listen for the poem within the poem.

The most profound aspects are often the most simple.

Your creative imagination is vital to the health of the earth.

Listen to the spaces that join everything.

Use verbs that vibrate.

It is all right to play with your words.

Invite the unexpected over when you write.

You are a poet!
Be amazed.

More Sentence Stem Warm-Ups

Fill in the following sentence stems to get to know other members of your writing circle, then create a group poem using everyone's answers.

In the past three days, I felt a sense of wonder about _____

_____

The simplest miracle I know is_____

Language is my _____

A poem resonates for me when _____

Silence is _____

My silence yells out for _____

If my words were tears, they would cry for_____

_____

My courage demands that I speak of_____

_____

The common things I treasure in my life are _____

_____

If I were an inanimate object, I would be a(n) _____

I dance and sing for_____

If I could go anywhere, it would be to _____

If I were a symbol, I would be a(n)_____

If I were a sports metaphor, I would be a(n) _____

If I were exploding fireworks, I would look like_____

If I were a baby, my instincts would be to _____

At a masquerade I would wear _____

If I were an animal, my movements would be like a(n)_____

If I were a drum, my sound would be _____

If I were a spice, I would taste like _____

If I were a scent, I would smell like _____

If I were a car, I would look like a(n) _____

If I were a piece of cloth, I would feel like _____

If I were a well-known poet, I would be _____

Warm Up—Free-Association Words for the Circle

ᗐ Choose a word and free associate off it. Speak the word or phrase out loud at the beginning of the meeting and then have each member spontaneously speak another word without thinking. Keep it going for a couple minutes and then introduce a new word.

ᗐ Choose a number of words from the list below (or one you create) and write them down on slips of paper. Pass the slips of paper around to group members and have everyone write a few lines (no more than three or four) using the words they received. Gather the lines up and read them out loud as one poem.

dream	heart	breast	chalice
sword	grass	boulder	wind chime
candle	book	cedar chest	attic
basement	ring	button	wander
feather	ruby	onion	pebble
sailboat	roots	shelter	wound
shadow	gravestone	weather vane	rubber ball
lighthouse	absorb	search	grab
music box	scrapbook	home movies	picnic table
triumph	chicken soup	steal	apple tree
skate key	brass knob	fireplace	campfire
sleeping bag	lunch box	tropical	watermelon
beads	risk	chewing gum	lipstick
fresh grass	wading pool	fragment	whirl
horse	snowflake	maple leaf	Christmas ornament
kite	fishes	damage	thunder
frozen	blanket	knife	solitude

Warm Up—Dream Image and Real Life: A Group Poem

This is another exercise where small poem fragments are written by each person and then gathered together in a pile and read as one poem. Everyone writes a poem fragment comprising two parts:

1. Everyone writes down on a piece of paper a line or two about a strong image remembered from a recent dream.
2. Everyone writes a line or two about one of the following experiences in life (the whole group writes about the same experience from the list):

Eating a favorite meal
An embarrassing moment
Something unexpected but enjoyable
Something you did that took courage
Your favorite place to sit
Something that brought up fear for you
Something you bought by mail order
The place in your house where there are photographs
Your first:

- Kiss
- Car
- Job
- Time winning something
- Campout
- Book
- Pet
- Time playing sports
- Place you lived after leaving home
- Close relationship
- Experience being alone for a period of time
- Time leaving home
- Experience opposing an authority figure (other than parents)
- Public performance: speaking, singing, acting, etc.
- Time getting fired or leaving a job
- Spiritual experience

When each person is finished, she/he should have a short piece recording: a dream fragment/a waking experience. Gather these pieces up and read them all as one complete group poem.

Suggested Projects for Your Writing Circle

W Once a year, twice a year, or every season, create an anthology of the best poems members of the group have written and read. Someone with desktop publishing skills could produce it in booklet form. You could sell the anthology in local bookstores or share it with friends and family.

W Take the group's poetry into the community: give readings at senior centers, children's shelters, schools, hospitals.

W Twice a year have an open house. Ask each member to invite five people. Post announcements on public bulletin boards. This is a good way to start more writing groups.

W Sponsor a well-known guest poet to come and give a public reading. Have them give a writing workshop for a weekend, to which you can invite the general public.

W Every season hold a day-long intensive writing circle, the format for which can be planned with input from the entire group.

W Go to local poetry readings. Participate in open mike readings, where anyone can come to sign up and read.

W Sponsor a public poetry reading featuring the members of your writing circle. Include an open mike segment.

W Sponsor a poetry program with a local school. Have writing circle poets go into the school and make a presentation, and/or sponsor a well-known poet to make a presentation. Support and/or participate in your state's Poet in the Schools program.

With joy we sit we cry
we confess we are sorry
we are anxious we are tongue-
tied we are heart bound we are
safe we are falling off the cliff
of our heart into a pool
of unswum water so blue we think
we are whales we are one
we breach we cry we breathe
we burst forth like a bull
through the gate headfirst
into the cap of our lives
china splinters slivered translucent
under an eclipsed moon oh watch us
jump over mercy leap with
our capes like wings
that leaves us splendid
as never before
we hover on a scarf of air
wafted in from somewhere
we have never been but plan to go
as soon as possible
yes we are speaking untying
our tongues no longer sorry
and then we come down
and go to where we came from
but something is different
we are smiling our minds
are blue and falling
and nothing hurts.   Amen.

—Perie Longo

Once a week
two transcendent hours
a gathering of poets
other voices, other lives.

Thoughts, feelings, emotions revealed
of joys
sorrows
hopes
regrets
longings
dreams
intimacies only poetry can express
minds, souls touching
my existence confirmed.

Once a week
two transcendent hours—

—Peter Hastings

building family
making friends
weaving circles
songs to sing
drawing up from
bottom of well
sounds of laughter
tears of joy
fill the buckets
with this choice
reaching out
taking in

building family
making friends
howling moon
dancing sky
river of sun
flowing by
healing waters
touching stones
reaching out
taking in
building family
making friends

—Debra Hiers

Eight

The Healing Pulse of Poetry

Breaking Through Your Pain with Words

That's the way writing often starts, a disaster or a catastrophe of some sort, as happened to me. . . . And I think that's the basis for my continued interest in writing, because by writing I rescue my-self under all sorts of conditions, whatever it may be that has up-set me, then I can write and it relieves the feeling of distress.

—William Carlos Williams

An Act of Human Magic

The ritual chants and incantations of shamanism, the healing songs and magic of primitive people with their rich core of poetry, illustrate the vital role of art in ancient medicine. Poetry is indeed a force, an act of human magic, that alters the way we see our lives and so changes us.

——*Morris R. Morrison*

Plato said that beautiful language could induce *sophrosyne*, a condition of stability and integration in psychic life. The ancient Greeks named beautiful language *epode* and *theklerian*—

charms and spells that could evoke calm and well-being in the listener.

Writing in Athens, contemporary Greek poet Odysseus Elytis recollects his memories about the medicinal and protective power of poetry and language, the part "charms and spells" play in his culture:

> . . . *until a few years ago our island nurses, with utter seriousness, chased evil spirits from above our cradles by uttering words without meaning, holding a tiny leaf of a modest herb which received God knows what strange powers exclusively from the innocence of its own nature.*
>
> *Poetry is precisely this tiny leaf with the unknown powers of innocence and the strange words which accompany it.*

India's ancient language of Sanskrit is naturally in tune with healing and health-giving properties. Sanskrit resonates in both its meaning and structure with Spirit and Nature. Just as ancient Greeks believed their language capable of inducing psychic integration and stability, the seers and poets of India's Vedic times knew that Sanskrit promoted equanimity. Mantras and other potent phrases vibrate deeply into the body, mind, and spirit for healing and the raising of consciousness.

The healing power of language has deep roots in the native cultures of our own country. Although most school textbooks of American poetry begin with poems in the English language, poetic language was an integral part of the North American continent long before Europeans arrived—when it was called Turtle Island by Native Americans. Poems were made to respond to every possible aspect of human life—including healing. Poetry gave those experiences a broader, more inclusive context. Poetry recognized something essentially spiritual and beautiful about life.

When we speak about the specific value poetry has for responding to pain and trauma, it is important to remember there was a time when it was *natural* for people to consider poem-making and the creative imagination essential for both healing and guidance. The Greek wisdom culture, the enlightened soci-

*A*nthropological evidence bears witness to the surviving place of poetry in medical practice in disparate areas across the globe—in Siberia and the Orient, in Polynesia, Australia, Africa, and among the American Indians and the Eskimos.

—Dr. Jack Leedy

ety of the Vedas, and Native American peoples—all used language and the creative imagination to communicate healing *and* serve as a guide for living. We have lost our compass, as the Australian poet Judith Wright points out:

> *Since poetry has so small an audience, the notion has begun to grow up that it is a kind of survival from more primitive times, a form of communication no longer needed by modern man. The fact is rather that modern man is something like a survival of poetry, which once shaped and interpreted his world through language and the creative imagination. When poetry withers in us, the greater part of experience and reality wither too; and when this happens, we live in a desolate world of facts, not of truth—a world scarcely worth the trouble of living in.*

We seek "cures" and then continue on in our busy lives without making essential changes. In the process, we separate symptom and cause; living and dying. Doing that, our lives become fragmented. Wright suggests that if we want to go to the heart of what creative imagination gives us, we should not let the healing and guiding aspects of poetry become separated. Both are part of a larger process. This way of looking at poetry's essential role in our lives is the overarching vision of this book.

This chapter, however, is specifically about the healing uses of poetry. It addresses how you can use poetry in your own life to heal old and new wounds. Using creative arts like poetry to help us heal will naturally guide us to a greater sense of wholeness. Even western medicine (albeit often grudgingly) has begun to recognize the arts as a valuable tool for healing. What ancient cultures once knew is coming alive again.

We can only approach the gods through poetry, and if the disease is the disguise of the gods, then our medicine will be full of art and image.

—Thomas Moore

Healing is not something we only do when we are sick; it is part of the process and journey of life.

—Ted Kaptchuk

Poetry as Healer

In the mid-seventeenth century, an American physician named Benjamin Rush introduced poetry as a form of therapy at Pennsylvania Hospital. We don't know what form poetry therapy took at that time and history tells us that the treatment of individuals in mental hospitals was frequently ignorant and brutal; but the use of poetry is an indication that from a very early time doctors have recognized the power of words to heal. Over two hundred fifty years later, poetry therapy is still employed at Pennsylvania Hospital.

Walt Whitman tended wounded soldiers during the Civil War, reading poetry to them on hospital wards and in the field. He wrote and read poems about the brutality of war, about courage, and about the human aspects of military life. The use of libraries in hospitals grew immensely during World War I, as wounded veterans sought out words for solace and healing.

In the late 1920s, a Brooklyn pharmacist named Eli Greifer offered "poetic prescriptions" to people filling their prescriptions. Greifer was a pharmacist, lawyer, and poet. In 1928, he opened the "Remedy Rhyme Gallery" in Greenwich Village in New York City. Greifer believed that memorization of poems was useful for a process of healing he called "psychosurgery." He felt it was possible to "psychograft" the thoughts and feelings of great people into one's own psyche. Methods of poetry therapy have developed and expanded since Greifer's time but in discussing his "psychografting" memorization technique, Greifer sounds more like a shaman than pharmacist:

> We have here no less than a psychograft by memorization in the inmost reaches of the brain, where the soul can allow the soul-stuff of stalwart poet-prophets to "take" and to become one with the spirit of the patient. Here is insight. Here is introjection. Here is ennoblement of the spirit of man . . . by blood transfusing the personality with the greatest insights of all the greatest souled poets of all ages . . . beautiful figures of speech, the melody of rhythm and meter and assonance . . . painted scenes . . . dramatic episodes, love's pervasiveness—all are consecrated by the master poets to gently enter and transfuse the ailing subconscious, the abraded and suffering personality.

In 1958, Greifer met Dr. Jack Leedy, who was the directing psychiatrist at Cumberland Hospital in Brooklyn, New York. It was an auspicious meeting for the future of poetry therapy.

My feeling is that poetry is also a healing process, and then when a person tries to write poetry with depth or beauty, he will find himself guided along paths which will heal him, and this is more important, actually, than any of the poetry he writes.

—Robert Bly

Leedy, ignoring the disdain of many colleagues, became an ardent advocate for the use of poetry in therapy. He was, through his compassion, charm, and drive, a major force in bringing the use of poetry to the attention of the mental health profession. Dr. Leedy founded the Association for Poetry Therapy in 1969.

Sherry Reiter, a clinical social worker and registered poetry therapist in Brooklyn, New York, was a colleague of Dr. Leedy's in the mid-1970s. She recalls with some amusement her first meeting with him: "Jack encouraged me to go to the United Nations and invite each embassy to the next National Poetry Therapy Conference, feeling that in fact the conference was meant to be a World Poetry Therapy Conference. He was so convincing that I *almost* did it! I have, however, become deeply involved in this work since that time."

Many others besides Leedy and Greifer have done important pioneering work in this healing art since the mid-1950s. Sherry Reiter recalls an historic milestone of the poetry therapy movement: "By 1980 poetry therapy as a healing tool was flourishing in different parts of the country. In order to unite everybody and share our collective wisdom, I called a gathering at the New School for Social Research, the place I had earlier taught courses with Dr. Leedy. It was incredible to call together such a diverse group of people."

In 1981, the association further developed professional standards for ethics, training, and credentialing. It is now a nonprofit organization called The National Association for Poetry Therapy. Members comprise a wide range of professional experience, schools of therapy, educational affiliations, artistic disciplines, and other fields of training in both mental and physical health.

But the psychological community is not discovering something new. It is actually returning to its true home.

Poets have always known of poetry's healing power. D. H. Lawrence said that writing was therapeutic and that the process of writing could lead to self-understanding. He called writing a way to "shed one's sicknesses." William Carlos Williams, like Lawrence, stressed that writing "relieves the feeling of distress."

Such noted contemporary poets as Robert Bly, Sharon Olds, Galway Kinnell, and Lucille Clifton gathered with Jungian psy-

We use the evocativeness of poetry, its ability to call forth feeling, to provide words for what is known only in images, and images for what is not known yet.

—Peggy Osna Heller

In order to heal themselves, people must recognize, first, that they have an inner guidance deep within and, second, that they can trust it.

—Shakti Gawain

chologist James Hillman for a symposium called *Poems Aloud* held in San Francisco in 1993. Hillman said in his keynote speech that the symposium was an opportunity "to look to the perennial art of poetry as we now look to good psychotherapy" and to see how "psychotherapy has its roots in poetry."

It is not just "great" poets who can make use of writing to rescue themselves "under all sorts of conditions." You can use poetry for this purpose as well. The poetry you write will help you to explore your life experience. Reading poetry is important too. The capacity of poetry to reconnect us with our feelings is the key to its healing power: Reawakened feeling—*in whatever form those feelings come*—becomes a catalyst for understanding our emotional pain. Poetry therapy is using the writing and reading of poetry as tools for accessing feelings, working with them, and integrating them into a healthy sense of self and soul.

EXERCISE: WORDS THAT CONNECT US TO OUR FEELINGS

Reading (or listening to) and writing poetry—the two wings of poetry therapy, evocation and expression—support one another. The evocative aspect is anything in poetry that draws feeling out of you. The expressive aspect is when you find the words to put your own experience on paper. Let's explore this two-winged process. Read the poem *To Drink* by Jane Hirshfield silently a few times and then read it out loud. Let your voice say the words with feeling. Let them flow out:

TO DRINK

I want to gather your darkness
in my hands, to cup it like water
and drink.
I want this in the same way
as I want to touch your cheek—
it is the same—
the way a moth will come
to the bedroom window in late September,
beating and beating its wings against cold glass;
the way a horse will lower
his long head to water, and drink,
and pause to lift his head and look,

and drink again,
taking everything in with the water,
everything.

What feelings does this poem awaken in you? What images in the poem break through the mind's rational surface to reveal emotions you may have ignored or suppressed? Free associate with lines in the poem. Do you feel sadness, relief, mystery, loneliness, warmth, respect, beauty, love? Write whatever comes up for you. Write freely. What images arise that are connected with those feelings?

_____

_____

_____

_____

_____

_____

_____

What particular lines resonate? ("Resonate" here means that you can feel them emotionally.) Give yourself time to feel this poem. It may just be a word, or a phrase, or an image that catches your attention. The lines that resonate for you may change over time. You can go back to them again and again. What is not clear at one reading may clarify in another. What was meaningful at one time may reveal something quite different several readings later. As you read the poem, what lines are especially significant to you now?

Write out a specific line or two from Hirshfield's poem that attracts you, then free associate with what those lines bring up for you about your life. For instance, where do you go when you hear the lines "I want to gather your darkness / in my hands, to cup it like water"? Working from the lines you choose, create your own poem, following the impulses and feelings brought up by those particular lines.

_____

_____

_____

_____

_____

_____

Poems are among the best, most natural medicines available to us. Like the homeopathic application of herbs, poems can be used to augment the natural healing abilities of our body and soul.

Fathers and Mothers, Sons and Daughters

Finding the Lost Compass

In every family there are difficulties and, often, pain. There may be abandonment, neglect, illness, misunderstanding, abuse, and violence. There are also times of pride and fulfillment, of satisfaction and joy, of tremendous courage in going through hard times. Family relationships can be both nourishing and distressing. It's no secret: there is great complexity in every family's connectedness. What we feel about our closest relatives is not always one way or the other.

But it is the difficulties and sometimes devastating pain we will be talking about here. Those limiting and destructive patterns can repeat themselves in experiences and relationships throughout our lives.

Writing is one of the most important tools we have to more clearly see our family pattern and how it influences our experience. Poetry in particular affords us the opportunity (when we let it) to *feel* our pattern without making judgments about it. We need a container for those feelings so that we can work with them, and metaphor is that container, allowing a whole complex of feelings to come together in one distinct image. The "lost compass" we mentioned earlier in this chapter enables feeling and metaphor to merge in the form of poetry.

Poetry, in turn, guides our inner compass pointing us in a healing direction.

Onie Kriegler wrote a healing poem about her childhood and her relationship with her mother. Her poem states a wish. Contained within that wish is the longing Onie has for recognition of her creative self—a longing for guidance on how to live in this world with joy. In naming that longing, Onie creates a poem that

A poem is anything said in such a way or put on the page in such a way as to invite from the hearer or reader a certain kind of attention.

—William Stafford

Poetry as a tool, a net or trap to catch the present; a sharp edge; a medicine; or the little awl that unties knots.

—Gary Snyder

is really about the recognition and guidance she now gives to herself:

I wish my mother could have warned me about
the possible pains of being her daughter.

She might have drawn me aside as a child and said,
"Honey, my child,
watch out for being too afraid to try new things.
Just look both ways and then give the crossing a try."

I wish my mother could have stood in all her
imperfection and said:
"Honey, my sweet child, don't forget
sometimes it is best to not take yourself
or anyone else too seriously.
Always take your daily dose of joyful abandon."

I wish my mother could have, when I was about twelve,
taken me on a walk on the ocean shore and
reminded me to honor my body,
the matter of my spirit,
the whole expanding, curving, juicy explosion.
The magnificent process of woman-making.

I wish my mother could have been honest about her pain,
not defended nor denied, but said,
"Girl, child of mine,
here are some of the trouble spots,
the edges I have yet to smooth,
the wounds still to be healed.

"Now your life is your own,
but here are the possible pains of being
a daughter of mine.
Don't tie yourself too tightly to these pains.
These are histories moving through you
not places to stand for the ride."

I wish my mother could have embraced herself
with the transforming energy of her rage,
the sweet kiss of her forgiveness, and
set herself free,
> *maybe she still will.*

Reading Onie's poem, we can reflect on the nature of family. She gathers for herself a wonderful insight about familial legacies:

These are histories moving through you
not places to stand for the ride.

> ～～～～～～～～
> *Y*ou need to claim the events
> *of your life to make yourself*
> *yours. When you truly possess*
> *all you have been and done,*
> *which may take some time, you*
> *are fierce with reality.*
>
> —Flonda Scott Maxwell

EXERCISE: WISH POEM TO YOUR PARENTS

This exercise was developed by Jennifer Bosveld, director of the Ohio Poetry Therapy Center in Johnstown, Ohio. What is your wish poem to your parents? A wish poem is different from blaming. It is a way of reframing your experience and using your own creativity to express to yourself what you wanted to hear from a parent when you were a child but did not. What would your wish be? Use Onie's poem as a guide and then say what was not said to you as a child. Say now what you most wanted to hear then—and still yearn to hear. Use this exercise first to shine a light on your past and then to light a torch enabling you to step forward into a creative present and future.

Begin with the following phrases (or other appropriate phrases that you create):

I wish my mother/father could have _____

_____

_____

_____

I wish my mother/father could have looked at me with love and said: "My child, _____

_____

_____

Now incorporate the phrases, or pieces of the phrases, into a wish poem that takes you from your past to the present and into the future.

～～～～～～～～～～～～～～～～～～～～～～～～～～～

Putting the Pain on Paper

Poems expressing a heartfelt "wish" as described above may feel too gentle for what you need to say. The poem you may want to write may be one of rage and pain. That's O.K. too.

Poems articulating your fury, sorrow, pain are totally acceptable. They are often unavoidable. And we can welcome them.

When writing poems of anger and deep pain, you may find it helpful and sometimes essential to have counseling support. Sharing your poem or series of poems with a therapist or a deeply trusted friend with whom you feel safe helps you to process the emotional material the poem brings out. Their listening can help you gain insight into your life and facilitate the process of healing.

What is especially unique about poetry as a healing force in therapy? The empty page. It may seem intimidating at times, but the blank page is capable of receiving the pain and hidden feelings that you may have kept buried too long and now need to express. The empty page won't strike back at you, and the poem you create will become a partner in the healing process, a tangible means of identifying difficult issues. In a therapeutic relationship, the combination of therapist, client, and creative expression by the client is a triad that allows movement and growth beyond conventional clinical labels and filters. New insights and guidance that might never have come to light during a traditional therapy session are frequently discovered in the act of writing poetry.

Approaching a painful subject is not easy—whether you're talking or writing about it. Don't jump into this kind of poem unless you feel the real need to do so and are willing to handle the emotions which are bound to surface in the process. Not everyone will need to write such wrenching poems. Nor will everyone, at any given moment, feel ready to write poems like this.

Here is a poem that tells of the rage, hurt, shame, and pain that is the legacy of childhood sexual abuse:

If we appreciate and respect the children that we were, the spirit of that child within each of us can emerge.

—*Flora Colao*

Writing is a struggle against silence.

—*Carlos Fuentes*

This Child

this child is about to be touched
touched funny   told to shut up

about the fast lesson down   how
if you rub a nipple   it sticks out

hard   this child is about to hide
her nipples inside her shirt   inside

her undershirt   this child is about
to be forced to do without

a father   hurts too much
this child is about to cry at his touch

about to run and hide
this child is about to be deprived

of childhood   it's all shut up
this child is about to be touched

by the power of a man who lies
who will disregard her cries

call her seductive / beautiful / slut
this child is about to give up

clothes silky to the touch   hide
her nipples inside her shirt   this child

will give her childhood up
her own tentative touch

her imagination playing free and wild
the daydreams of a child   this child

will be gone at his touch
offered up   shut up
                    —*Roseann Lloyd*

Roseann Lloyd's poem holds feeling that is almost unbearable. The simple language in lower-case, the halting line breaks, the repetitive fragments of speech that condense the horror and shock of abuse into a few lines, the empty spaces in the lines— all of these show the violent abuse of a terrified, innocent child.

Roseann talks about her process of writing:

One way I discovered I could write about painful subjects was by writing in the third person. I discovered that it was easier for me and gave me some distance. The other thing was that I really wanted to imagine myself as a little girl. So I looked at children who were in sixth grade to see how little they are. Doing that helped me to let go of my childhood feeling that I should have been able to avoid the abuse I experienced. Seeing those children was a way to acknowledge that I was really powerless. Feeling my helplessness is harder to stay with than anger, but it is powerful because feeling it is the beginning of being able to let go of being helpless.

I was also working with rhyme in this poem. Originally, I had thought the poem might become a villanelle; it didn't, but it naturally ended up with a rhyming scheme. The rhyme reminds us of childhood. I think rhyme holds the wildness of the feeling and is a way to contain the subject. Perhaps the most important thing to say is that when I started writing about sexual abuse, I wrote lots and lots of poems. The idea of having total permission to keep writing these poems was powerful and transformative. The process itself was a very healing one.

Perhaps everything terrible is in its deepest being something that wants help from us.
                    —*Rainer Maria Rilke*

EXERCISE: RELEASING PAIN IN A POEM

You can write angry words down and let go of them. Writing "taboo" words and letting them go can allow your heart to become lighter. At the top of a blank page write one raw, charged word or very short phrase. Or choose a word that has heavy personal significance, a word that might hold the key to unlocking some of your pain. Choose a fifteen-pound weight rather than a sixty-pound weight at first. Stay as close to your feeling as you can and allow this word to lead you in writing your pain poem. Free associate and write down the words, sounds, images, metaphors that come to you. Use these to picture and express the feelings behind your chosen word. You can write in the third person if you like, as Roseann Lloyd suggests, to create distance when writing about your pain.

You may want to proceed further after writing this first poem by selecting one line from your poem and continuing to explore that issue. Take that one line and write more. Follow the image thread of that line and allow your images to build, one upon another.

You may want to write this poem of release, this "dumping" poem, read it, acknowledge your courage to write it, and then let it go. You can burn it up, throw it away, or bury it. Writing one poem or even a series of poems is not going to heal all your pain at once. But writing can lead you closer to your own heart, allowing more room for your life, helping you to find your healing path.

Mixed Emotions

Poetry is the clear expression of mixed feelings.

—W. H. Auden

Healing is not only a process of releasing hurt; it also involves accepting things the way they are, while at the same time reclaiming your vitality and well-being. It means gradually replacing rage with acceptance. Poems which express this acceptance are almost always hard-won. You may need to write many poems in which you struggle with core issues in your life before you write with a greater sense of acceptance.

It may never feel appropriate to write a poem of acceptance. This is all right too. Your poem of acceptance may be written *to yourself* for the strength you've shown, for example, for coming through a horrendous family situation.

The next two stories and poems are about acceptance written after much work had been done on releasing old hurts.

I need to concede a considerable area to what I don't know and can't know, and perhaps don't wish to know. Only to understand in a way I do not quite understand.

—John Haines

BOB

My father was a remarkable man, kind and intelligent, but strong-willed and with an iron-bound set of ethics. Though I loved him (and now realize how much he loved me), I had mixed emotions toward him, in life and after his death. I wrote many poems about him, especially in the period one to three years after he died. It became obvious to me that I had many unresolved issues around my relationship to him. I began to write poems that expressed these feel-

ings, using images supplied by dreams, and by memories of him and our life together.

In making the effort to make these father-son outpourings into better poems, I needed to look deeply into who this man actually was and how I truly felt about that. This led me to discover more about the man and about myself than I'd bargained for. At a couple of points the whole thing seemed frustrating and hopeless. The resolution came with a poem called "Driving the Car" where I take our family Hudson after gently informing my father, "you are dead now, you can rest."

"The Real Names of Coal" was written later, at a point where I was reconciled to his quirky personality, when I could see his insistence on learning, knowledge, intellectual rigor, as a great gift to me, rather than just an obsession of his. The incident that prompted the poem was only one of the times when I saw my father's intense curiosity about the world in operation.

THE REAL NAMES OF COAL

Dusk, late winter of forty-six, the old,
worn snow under its layer of soot
sucked at by the wind off the lake,
the smudgy air heavy with the smoke
of a million coal fires, as every Detroiter
stokes his furnace for the below-zero night ahead.

I hold the bag with the milk,
along with my father's White Owl cigars
and the latest issue of **Captain Marvel Comics**
as we pick our way along over the sidewalk
paved with frozen footprints—in ice
that was slush a half hour before.

At our neighbor's a new load is tipped
from a red dump truck—with "Pocahontas Coal"
and a painting of a beautiful Indian girl.
The noise it makes going down the chute
exactly like Tyrannosaurus rex

clearing his throat, my father says, and even
at eight I am dubious—though interested,
wondering how that really did sound.

My galoshes are wet inside and my feet
are alternately burning, or scaring me
by going numb. I ask my father to
please hurry so we can get home
but he stops and picks up two lumps
of something from the gutter.

Wait, he says, See these? putting them
in my hands Some coal, I reply.
No, not just coal. He says, look at them,
look closely. They're different, I say.
Two kinds of coal? That's right, he says,
smiling. These are hard coal
and soft coal—and their real names are
anthracite and bituminous!
He has me hold them and stand there,
saying the long words
until I get them right. I know
he'll ask me again
so I look at these black lumps
and turn them over and over
in my hands, until my mittens are black,
repeating the words until I won them,
the real names of these things,
adding them to my arsenal, my
armor against stupid kids
and bullies, and teachers
who embarrass me in front of the class for
being a daydreamer, wasting my time,
wasting her time, and even wasting
the whole third grade—when I'm usually
staring out the window just to concentrate,
trying very hard to understand why
there should have been both

Triceratops and Stegosaurus—and where they'd gone
since the Upper Jurassic—and how gravity works,
able to call comets back across millions of miles
of empty space, so they don't just go on forever,
and other important things.

I said anthracite, bituminous, bituminous, anthracite,
to myself all the way home and it wasn't until
we were in the warm house and I'd
taken my galoshes off in front of the fire
that I noticed how frozen my feet were.
As he rubbed my bare feet with his big hands
my father asked if I happened to know that
coal was made of squashed fern and dinosaurs?
                                                    —Bob Evans

Bob's poem says much about the way a father and son communicate with one another. This poem offers images and metaphor, rhythms and names of things that crystalize the relationship between Bob and his father. We hear the word "coal" over and over; the cold, hard *c*'s reinforcing the winter tone of the poem—and perhaps hinting at a certain harshness characterizing the father/son relationship.

Focusing on the "black lumps" and Bob's father's insistence that the boy stop and hold them and repeat their difficult names, even though the child is freezing, is an extremely effective poetic device here. First, the father's insistence comes off as somewhat cruel given the cold weather and the boy's desire to get home: *I ask my father to / please hurry so we can get home.* We can feel the tension in the relationship, a tension that would carry over into Bob's adult life.

A shift in perception occurs in the poem when the cold and discomfort are replaced with a sense of delight and power gained in learning the "real names" of coal. These strange words offer Bob protection from the world of mean kids; they become words that give his "daydreamer" self the value it deserves. Bob, writing at age fifty-seven, begins to appreciate the "intense curiosity" of his father and how it has transferred into his own life.

I propose a new form of courage of the body: the use of the body not for the development of musclemen, but for the cultivation of sensitivity.

                                        —Rollo May

One might think that writing a poem like this, a poem that helps to resolve a painful and complex relationship, would have as a catalyst an obvious, powerful image to act as a central part of the poem. Not necessarily. Fleeting details or seemingly mundane events can be the key to accessing your unconscious mind and creative process. Bob told me it was recalling the smell of burning coal on a winter night in Detroit that started him writing.

In writing the poem, Bob followed this impulse, this initial sensory image, and it led him to make remarkable connections. The burning coal was not only related to that cold Detroit night with his father but to wonderful mysteries concerning dinosaurs and language. The initial image he received from his unconscious might have been the feel of the black coal lumps in his small hands, or perhaps the freezing wet galoshes on his feet. In this case, Bob paid attention to what the smell of burning coal evoked and followed the trail this sensory memory initiated. The result was his beautifully ambivalent poem about his connection to his father.

JEANIE

Jeanie works in investor relations in the financial department of a software company. At thirty-nine, she studies in the evenings to get her degree in psychology. Her poem of acceptance about her father grew out of appreciating the lineage she shares with him. Her father was an authoritarian who demanded perfection and withheld any sense of approval. Growing up in this overbearing and overprotective environment was worsened by her mother's death when Jeanie was seventeen. She says:

> *I was always trying to get away from my dad. I wanted freedom from his oppression. Don't put your conservative ideas on me! But after many years of struggle, feelings of alienation, and fierce independence, I came to realize that what I really wanted was connection not disconnection. It took time of working through my rage, writing, patience, and love of others with similar experiences, but I finally came to the place where I could write about the sweetness of the irreplaceable relationship I have had with the people who brought me into the world; my present is so much a part of their past.*

Hopefully I write what I don't know.

—*Robert Creeley*

Jeanie comments on how her poem originated:

My father's parents were immigrants from the Azores off the coast of Portugal. When they came to this country, his mother lived among Native American people. They taught her how to use plants for medicinal purposes. She had a way of responding to natural phenomenon which might be considered superstitious. Partly because she was an Old World coastal woman and partly because of her Native American influences, instead of viewing strong winds and storms as negative events, she would see them as opportunities to connect with deeper forces of the earth and spirit. She would write messages or wishes about things she wanted to happen on little pieces of paper and throw them into the stormy wind.

My father lost his family when he was six and so his memories are sketchy and painful. When I say "I cannot hear their voices," neither can he. Writing this poem brought us together. I realize that he is my link to the past and to these people, especially his mother, with whom I feel a connection. My poem expressed something about this link that is important for us both. After years of hard work, recognizing our common ground is wonderful.

The human heart does not stay away too long from that which hurt it most. There is a return journey to anguish that few of us are released from making.

—Lillian Smith

MY ROOTS ARE THERE IN THE DARKNESS

My roots are there in the darkness
in the superstition
in the sea-centered people
influenced by Indian traditions
sometimes a bitter medicine for Dad
but always a comfort to me.

I wonder sometimes what it would have been like
to touch his mother's hand
to see her dark eyes and her dark hair—so like mine,
so different from the blond blue-eyed
grandmother I once knew.

I'm connected to them and yet only
through one living human being

I cannot hear their voices except through his
I cannot feel their presence except through his
I cannot know their customs except through his
No pictures to look at and dream
No treasures to make my homes theirs
Only gravestones with names I'll never utter
and dates that came long before it was my time to be here
How do I know where I'm from without them?
My only connection—my Dad.

—Jeanie Lawrence

In a moment of courage, Jeanie sent her poem to her father. In their next phone conversation, her father, suddenly gentle and unguarded, expressed how deeply moved he was by her poem. Jeanie, who is still not comfortable calling herself a poet, was surprised by the power of her own words. He insisted on framing this song from her heart. It was a healing experience for them both.

EXERCISE: ACCEPTANCE POEM

What image from your childhood might serve as a starting place for an acceptance poem? Reach into your memory for a metaphor or concrete image signifying your relationship with a close family member with whom you had difficulty.

Use the metaphor or image you've chosen to anchor yourself in your childhood experience—let your imagination and feelings transform these memories in a focused way so you can write with acceptance.

Completing the Circle: A Poem of Celebration and Gratitude

Writing a poem of celebration and gratitude for family members is a way of recording who they are and what they gave to you. It can also be a way of acknowledging your own uniqueness. Writing poems of this nature allows you to move forward in your life with appreciation rather than anger or denial. But such poems may arise only after working hard to understand difficult or damaging family circumstances. Poems of gratitude or celebration of a certain close relationship may never arise for you, and that's all right.

Alma María Rolfs MSW, is a poetry therapist living in Chicago. Her poem, "Those Hands," is a celebration of her mother and grandmother. Alma reflects on the origins of this poem and the path she took to write it:

> I was able to write "Those Hands" after I had moved beyond conflict with my mother. The poem is a demonstration of the sustained positive connection with both my mother and grandmother. These are deep feelings I have but don't always attend to in daily life—the poem is a gift for me because it holds the feelings and reminds me that that I still miss my mother and grandmother.
>
> But my poem was born out of much healing work, which in itself makes the sense of celebration it holds even more poignant. My grandmother was a person who loved easily and whom I found easy to love. In contrast, my mother and I had a much more conflicted relationship. My mother died when I was only twenty-six and my grandmother and I closed the gap her death left. I think my mother had a strong drive to see us as the same and to merge with me. I resisted this for a long time and especially as I aged and saw how much I look like her. This little poem is about those "sights."

REFLECTIONS

My mother once told me
I was just like her.
What did that mean?
Was it a triumph?
Was it a curse?

She glimmers at me now
from store windows,
unexpected mirrors, sudden
reflections. Always,
she takes me by surprise.

Having learned much about my own resistance, ambivalence, and need to separate, I could begin to appreciate many of my mother's qualities. Also, in the course of my own parenting I have become much more aware of the gifts she gave me before the conflicts began. I know that my mother's love of books, music, and word play was absolutely formative. I grew up in Puerto Rico and she worked very hard to bring English literature into my life. My grandmother brought me a love of beauty—a visual and tactile beauty, such as in her weaving and flower arranging. She had an incredible capacity to make a lovely environment. Together my mother and grandmother gave me an appreciative awareness of the intellectual life and an aesthetic sensibility which informs and deepens the life of the senses, both of which have greatly enriched my own life.

What my poem "Those Hands" does is acknowledge both of these women equally without my having to see one as good and the other as deficient. I am now able to appreciate their unique gifts and see how, touched by them, I have developed and refined my own capacities. The last line is about the essential enduring quality of our emotional bond. I wrote it with a sense of gratitude to each of them encompassed within a larger gratitude for the sustained connection I feel with them. I can turn toward them now with my own strengths that may have begun with them but are now my own talents, and my own hands.

THOSE HANDS

Chopin and Brahms I recall:
my mother at the piano,
lullabies poignant in the night,
her small hands fluid
as the northern rivers she loved.
And Scrabble: her fingers
placing the polished letters
in elegant combination, how
she loved to play with words . . .

Other hands move across
my memory now:

another rhythm, equally old,
a layering not of chords but threads,
as I watch her mother,
my namesake, a weaver,
from untidy handfuls of color
bring order, texture,
a shawl, a patterned blanket, a room.

And mine? Though my own hands
move over the page, releasing words,
and in the earth, bringing forth
blossoms and herbs,
arranging tapestries,
symphonies of touch and color,
singing the songs of the hands
of my mothers, still——

                today,

I would gladly turn from these,
to hold in mine, those hands.

EXERCISE: POEM OF GRATITUDE AND LOVE

Alma's poem names specific things that are part of both her earlier and present experiences, such as: lullabies, Scrabble pieces, a shawl, a blanket, blossoms, herbs, and tapestries. What objects/things can you specifically name that were/are an integral part of a family member's life? What feelings are connected with those things?

    What did this person give to you of him/herself? What in his or her life—and in your own—would you like to celebrate?

Things my family member loved or did well: _____

_____

_____

_____

_____

_____

Objects/things I associate with this person: _____

Things I can name about myself that I do well, and things I love in myself that connect me with

this person: _____

_____

_____

_____

_____

Giving Sorrow Words . . .

Making a Bridge between the Past and Present

One of the most difficult things to write about is loss. Words may feel superfluous when we have been sucked into the black hole of loss. Our faculties of concentration and interest are gone and it often seems impossible to focus our attention on words.

Certainly "ordinary" words—well-intended words, words of bad and good advice, words of distraction—are of little comfort to us. The shattered self may feel that words, as we normally use them, are totally useless in our time of deep sadness and loss.

What sort of words might help? Are there any? What did Shakespeare mean when he wrote: "Give sorrow words. The grief that does not speak whispers the o'er fraught heart and bids it break."

We need to let our sorrow choose the words for us. We cannot express grief in a poem unless we surrender to our truest feelings and inclinations. You may find yourself describing your dark mood, how torn and lost you feel, your sense of paralysis, desolation, or anger. Or your sorrow over the loss of a loved one may take the form of a celebration of that person, a poignant memory of one particular time or moment you shared. If there are unresolved issues between you and the person you've lost, your poetry might explore these areas. As always, it is important

The world is a playground,
and death is the night.

—Rumi

not to be judgmental about what comes to you. Whatever form it takes, your poetic expression of loss can become a healing experience.

William Carlos Williams has a way of raising common language to great beauty. Here, he tells the story of how death changes us and, temporarily at least, renders us unable to appreciate the beauty we once relished:

THE WIDOW'S LAMENT IN SPRINGTIME

Sorrow is my own yard
where the new grass
flames as it has flamed
often before but not
with the cold fire
that closes round me this year.
Thirtyfive years
I lived with my husband.
The plumtree is white today
with masses of flowers.
Masses of flowers
load the cherry branches
and color some bushes
yellow and some red
but the grief in my heart
is stronger than they
for though they were my joy
formerly, today I notice them
and turned away forgetting.
Today my son told me
that in the meadows,
at the edge of the heavy woods
in the distance, he saw
trees of white flowers.
I feel that I would like
to go there
and fall into those flowers
and sink into the marsh near them.

I don't write poems because I want to, but more because I have to.

——Maxine Kumin

It may be months or perhaps years before you're able to let your grief speak. That's all right. You may not write at all. That's all right too. Yet there may be a time when something around you draws out the words of sorrow you need to speak. The need to write may come up immediately in the depths of grief. Trust yourself. Allowing the things around you to be catalysts for your writing is one way to begin. The process may come and go in cycles. Your first small step toward "giving sorrow words" is enough for now.

Remarkably, without knowing the poem by Williams, Connie Smith Siegel also used the image of her yard as the place to explore her grief. Connie writes about a weeping cherry tree that was planted years ago in her back yard, which had first come into bloom during a painful separation and divorce. She says:

> *Since then this tree has been a symbol for loss and I still feel a sadness in its beauty. When it bloomed this April, I was especially vulnerable because of a more recent loss, and found myself crying often, and at unexpected times. I finally wrote a poem about the tree and found both a relief from the relentless sadness, and an amazing shift of consciousness. I not only expressed my feelings of loss but became enamored of the tree, and the words that formed around it. The poem evolved almost by itself, as though the tree were speaking through me, as though it was me. The creative involvement in writing this poem created a bridge from the past to the present; writing about my loss generated something entirely new.*

WEEPING CHERRY

In the small backyard
brimming with new green,
the weeping cherry enters
with soft pink blossoms
perfectly formed, melting
the air with a shy radiance.

We planted the tree in the winter
digging into the dark brown earth

Beauty and pleasure refuse to have a definitive form. With their mysterious, almost ironic dance, they elude us, suddenly confronting us with their opposite, reappearing again where we least expect them.

—*Piero Ferrucci*

slipping in the mud, arguing, he and I
about where it should go.

I wouldn't have chosen it myself—
a strange umbrella of drooping limbs
grafted on a straight, proud trunk
huddling in the winter rains,
waiting for its moment.

but when it appeared that spring
young, in ballet dress
eager to be seen, curtsying for approval,
this dazzling show of rosy lights
as it turned out,
was only for me.

It plays its short dance, eternally young,
teasing the bees with fluttering petals,
weeping in the morning rain
weaving its twilight song.

Connie's prose describes the integration of her experience; however, it is her poem that *embodies* the fullest expression of her sorrow.

Rational explanations don't have the ability to reflect the free-flowing form of our feelings. Logical explanations cannot reveal the organic texture of our experience as it crystallizes and then changes into something else. Poetry can.

If we follow the thread of images in Connie's poem (the weeping cherry, the man and woman slipping in the mud and arguing, the drooping limbs, the cherry tree as it transforms with the turn of the seasons) we arrive in that "yard" of grief, change, and release. Lines like "as it turned out, / was only for me" speak the painful truth about loss. Writing about such moments of profound change enables us to discover more about who we are and what we value.

Formulation in words is essential for clarity of thought, though the most subtle and the most profound truths can only be expressed indirectly in images and symbols, in poetry, in music, or in color.

—Irene Claremont de Castillejo

EXERCISE: EXPRESSING LOSS

Begin by writing about the lesser losses we face every day. These are significant because they allow us to experience the sense that we cannot control change. Once we explore this notion in the context of a relatively minor loss, we'll be better equipped to write about the more significant losses in our lives. What small losses have you endured in your lifetime? Saying goodbye to your parents when you were little, as they were about to leave you with a babysitter? Giving up something you really wanted to do because you came down with the flu? Breaking up with a high school boyfriend? Losing something that you valued? Having a good friend move away? Not receiving a promotion that you wanted? What does such a loss bring up for you?

Give these "lesser losses" and "little goodbyes" your attention by creating a metaphorical image. For example, if the loss you are describing is losing a friend who moved to another city, the images might be a suitcase or birds migrating. If you're relating your break-up with a boyfriend from high school, the image might be his '64 Ford. Don't attempt to reach conclusions or make statements about your images. Just let them guide you in evoking your feelings. Rather than talking *about* your feelings, conjure up distinct words and images that *express* them.

List some images that might be emblematic of your smaller losses:

_____

_____

_____

What is it like to experience these lesser losses? Using the images you've come up with, develop one or two of these into poems.

To Bear the Unbearable

We die. That may be the meaning of life. But we do language. That may be the measure of our lives.

—*Toni Morrison*

Paying attention to life's lesser losses may help us deal with our intense grief with less denial. Treasuring the moments fully as they pass may help us to feel more at peace, even with change and loss. But these things in themselves are not enough preparation for the experience of having someone we love torn away from us. In facing such an unfathomable loss, we face the unknown.

Pain and sorrow often stir the creative imagination, and creativity can provide tremendous solace. The pain may hurt like hell, but it can also lead to a keener sense of who we truly are. It can help us to uncover who we want to be and how we want to be connected to the world. Keeping a journal and writing poetry give us tangible, concrete understanding and guidance on these issues.

Mike Bernhardt experienced a transformation by turning to poetry-writing while grieving over the sudden loss of his wife, Susan. On a Saturday after Easter in 1991 they were enjoying their lives together. The next day, Susan died of a cardiac arrest.

Mike tells of his experience immediately following Susan's death:

Nothing was true anymore but the truths of her death and my continued existence. I was shaken to my foundations, forced to decide what I would keep of myself and what I would throw away. . . . For months afterward, the shock of her death would unexpectedly hit me over the head, even as I slowly began to look forward with hope.

I started keeping a journal. I also started to write poetry. When I was in college, I had written a lot of poetry. I was in a lot of pain at that time, too. But I hadn't really thought about poetry for a very long time—I was quite involved in building up my business and making money.

A week or ten days after Susan died, I went to Tilden Park above Berkeley. After walking for some time, I sat down in a field. I started to write. I just wrote . . . what I was feeling. Writing didn't come easily at all at that time but I felt this strong impulse to write. I couldn't not write. One of the things that made it possible to turn to poetry, to creativity, was that there was nothing left that mattered to me. Expressing myself became the only important thing—trying to find out what and who I was—with Susan's death, I no longer knew.

Sometimes poetry was the only way to give words to the overwhelming emotions I struggled with. In finding that I could express my feeling creatively, I discovered a whole side of myself that had been lying dormant. Writing gave me a new sense of strength and wholeness. When I look back now at my writing, I can see how far I have come and remember what I went through. The remembrance of my grief has a healing quality of its own.

All perishes. Only poetry remains.

—Nguyen Chi Thien

A year after Susan's death, Mike wrote the following poem, "Sunday." He was driving down the highway and had the realization that he wanted to write about the actual details of Susan's death. The revelation was that he could *choose* to write about his experience, in contrast to the time just after his wife's death when he had felt *compelled* to write about it. As he continued down the highway, Mike made a note to himself to write this poem about Susan, knowing that he could write it when he was ready.

Mike says, "I didn't write the poem until a month later. One evening, I just sat down at the typewriter and closed my eyes. It came right out. I worked on it over time but essentially the heart of the poem appeared at that time. How had I known a month earlier that I would be able to write this poem? I just knew."

SUNDAY

Together, we survived the terrifying night
of CPR and defibrillation, too many tubes and wires and doctors,
my kisses on your forehead and your eyes kissing me back
until your EKG exploded again and they told me to leave.
I sat outside in the hallway talking softly with you.

In the morning, though your eyes seemed empty,
I dreamed of your recovery and went home to sleep
only to be greeted by a ringing phone and an urgent voice
and I was out again, stuck in traffic on the Bay Bridge,

praying, screaming at God to get me to you in time.
Hoping that curses and prayers might be enough,
I inched and fought my way through traffic and despair
until finally free, nearly drowning

I plunged into the streets racing
to San Francisco General. Sometimes now
I like to imagine what I would have told the police
if they'd noticed. I like to think that I wouldn't have pulled over

I would've just plummeted on at
70 miles per hour up Potrero Avenue letting

them catch up to me in the parking lot as
I ran inside MY WIFE'S DYING! I would've screamed

but they didn't notice.
I ran inside alone
to find my friends crying
and you, dead.

Out of this stark, even harsh, remembrance of his wife's death gradually came a poignancy that could help Mike's heart to break open and melt in tenderness. Here are two poems he wrote after "Sunday":

SECRET MESSAGE

I hear you in my voice,
now that yours is stilled forever.
I hear you in my voice:
an inflection or choice of words,
shrugging my shoulders in that certain way;
now a secret message between us.
It's all I have left of you.

BUDS AT THE END OF WINTER

My grief lives on in me,
an old moldy stump
rotting soft in the woods.
Or a tree in late winter,
buds appearing
red and green on bare branches.

Is there something unique about poetic language which allows for the realization that loved ones live on—that they are not lost to us? The poem may be the only place where it is possible to hear those eternal whispers. Walt Whitman, in his great poem *Song of Myself,* counsels us with this same, miraculous, simple image of the bud and sprout: "the smallest sprout shows that there really is no death."

The dark, rainy winds that whirl through the rugged season of our grief are an integral part of both life and the creative process. Grief moves across the winter terrain of our experience—the same terrain where, in spring, tender green shoots take root and drink.

> The organic shed and scree of winter,
> the withered leaf, the cracked cone,
> wintered bones, new life emerges wet;
> life alive on the edge of this broken,
> this blessed earth.
> This is who I am.
>
> —John Fox

As we explore the creative process further, and as we explore the dark and light of our lives, is it possible that our small sprout of renewal will generate greater faith? Faith invites us to once again feel the quality of refreshing delight, if just for a moment. The poet Beth Ferris wrote:

> . . . Whoever lives inside us speaks now
> through the cracks in our lives.
> Wants us to gently breaststroke through the shade.
> What we have not forgotten whirring in our ears
> like the wings of blue dragonflies
> says, nothing and no one is ever lost to us,
> not even ourselves.
>
> from Fishing with Floyd

It is a lie that there is no Golden Fleece. Each one of us is our own self's Golden Fleece. And it is a deception that death does not allow us to see it and recognize it. We must empty death from everything with which it has been overstuffed, and reach it in absolute purity in order to begin to distinguish through it the true mountains and the true grass, the avenged world full of cool drops which shine purer than the most precious tears. This is what I await every year with one more wrinkle on my forehead and one less wrinkle in my soul: the complete antistrophe, absolute diapheneity.

—Odysseus Elytis

Poetry as Common Ground

The greatest gift that poetry may offer to us, beyond the possibility of encouraging healing in any circumstance, is the bridge of tolerance it builds between different people and groups. I'll close this chapter with a story where nobody really "got better" or "healed," in the usual sense. What happened is that poetry helped two seemingly different groups of people find out how much more alike they are than different.

Perie Longo, Ph.D., a poetry therapist in Santa Barbara, California, brought together highly stressed but artistically gifted high school students from the Santa Barbara Music and Arts Conservatory with societally marginal but open-hearted Down's syndrome teenagers from St. Vincent's School. As if starting a round song, Dr. Longo inspired them to begin by speaking a simple poem of her own:

> I am gentle as a raindrop
> looking for a tree to feed
> but when I hear thunder
> I am frightened as a waterfall going over the edge.

James, one of the Down's syndrome kids, responded with his own lines of delight:

> I am like a rose in a gold river
> You are like a rainforest in the night
> I am sun growing
> My heart is like a river and quiet
> If you looked inside, you would find happiness
> As the sun rises

Dr. Longo says the response of the "gifted" kids to their new acquaintances at St. Vincent's was extraordinary: "They were so elated that these teenagers did not have masks. They did not pretend. It was tremendously refreshing to them. The stress of being caught in the role of 'over-achievers' was released so they could be more happy and simple." A veteran reporter from the *Santa Barbara News Press* who was there to cover the "story" sat to the side, watching this marvelous interaction, tears streaming down his face. Cecily, one of the girls from the Conservatory wrote the following poem to one of her poetic counterparts at St. Vincent's:

A poet, any real poet, is simply an alchemist who transmutes his cynicism regarding human beings into an optimism regarding the moon, the stars, the heavens, and the flowers, to say nothing of the spring, love, and dogs.

—George Jean Nathan

Your mind holds so many strong, wonderful thoughts
all locked away inside you.
If I could light a fire
I would burn away this wall
that separates you from me.

How to explain this healing action of poetry? The ability of poetry to knock down the walls between us? The capacity it has to ignite the fires of transformation? How is it that creativity in the form of poetry is helpful in almost every situation and available to every kind of person?

One answer is that in moments of extreme emotion, the ordinary is insufficient. One reaches for something exalted. One reaches for those things which comfort, guide, inspire, and sustain us. Rituals fulfill these needs, and poetry is a ritualized use of language.

Another answer lies simply in the ability of the blank page to accept our deepest pain—thus releasing it so that healing can eventually follow. Life and death, sorrow and joy—our human experience is filled with perplexing mysteries that can be uniquely felt and explored through our own making of poems.

Nine

Eternity in an Hour

Expressing the Sacred Through Poetry

i thank You God for most this amazing
day:for the leaping greenly spirits of trees
and a blue true dream of sky; and for everything
which is natural which is infinite which is yes . . .

—*e. e. cummings*

I walk out; I see something, some event that would otherwise have
been utterly missed and lost; or something sees me, some enormous
power brushes me with its clean wing, and I resound like a beaten
bell.

—*Annie Dillard*

I say yes and ever yes whenever the distant, unknown, and beloved
beckon me.

—*Kahlil Gibran*

"There Lives the Dearest Freshness
Deep Down Things . . ."

William Blake wrote, "Everything that lives is holy." The recognition of this sacred essence cannot be accessed by facts or known by outward experience, but only by tapping with intuitive, sensitive feeling directly into the inner source that infuses the roots of our being with life.

We could say our ordinary, exterior experience of daily life is generally equivalent to prose, and our internal experience of feeling is equivalent to poetry. Likewise, the miraculous revelations of DNA, of molecular and atomic structures, vibrate and shimmer invisibly within our bodies, and yet do not manifest on the outer surface of our skin, and eyes, and hair, and other features.

Within every rose there is a miraculous place where the essence of *roseness* lives. It is here that the rose bush drinks from the Spirit, the Tao, God, the Divine Mother (or whatever name you prefer) and where, moment by moment, *roseness* transforms into *roses*.

It is not words *about* roses that make sacred poetry. Sacred poetry is made when the *roseness* that lives within a particular rose speaks to us—and we listen and write. It is by connecting and listening deeply to the particular that we reach into the universal, the roseness, and begin to hear the sacred message available to us. Whether we connect with the essence of a particular black bear, grain of sand, grandmother, cat, or star, it is possible to discover in our encounter with that unique individual being this essence that is able to transfigure the ordinary—including turning ordinary words into blessings.

> *Do you know a word that doesn't refer to something? Have you*
> *ever picked and held a rose from R, O, S, E? You say the NAME.*
> *Now try to find the reality it names.*
>
> —*Rumi*

Things have their within.
—*Pierre Teilhard de Chardin*

Just as a bee hovers vibrantly in midair to sip nectar from the rose, you need to listen and feel your way intuitively into that center place of flow where the voice of life's essence resides, and "hover there." Blake is right. This primal language speaks through every thing that lives.

> *There lives the dearest freshness deep down things . . .*
> —*Gerald Manley Hopkins*

You can develop an ability to recognize the sacred in any place, thing, animal, plant, or person that is dear to you.

One way we can get to know a sense of the sacred is by paying close attention to what we naturally resonate with and find uplifting. A fine cellist may sigh with happiness as his bow makes a perfect note drawing sensuously across a string, or parents may discover a unique kind of joy upon hearing the laughter of their child. For the cellist and the parent, the sacred resides in the everyday experiences of their lives. The same is true for each of us. Notice what touches you, what you have an affinity with in the people and things around you, in the things that you do—for these will be the places where the sacred will be found. Such sacred places will help make you tenderly and poignantly aware of yourself and your world.

> *Listen to your friends with such sensitivity that you are leaching the very air that surrounds you. Listen so that, if it were given to you, you would hear the whirring of Saturn's rings, or the least wind a continent away. When you leave your friend, her presence will emanate from you. Notice this, feel this presence radiating away from you so that you can deepen your awareness of the way in which you dissolve the universe and absorb it. . . . If you develop even the least flicker of sensitivity, the universe will come alive within you.*
> —*Brian Swimme, from* The Universe Is a Green Dragon

EXERCISE: MAKING YOUR SACRED LIST

The word "sacred," according to the Oxford Universal Dictionary, means something "esteemed or held especially dear." What do you hold dear? What do you set aside for yourself and God? You *can* touch and feel what is sacred. You *can* listen to and talk with what is sacred. You can hold it close to your bones.

Is music sacred to you? Is your cat? A particular park bench? Hearing laughter? A pale pink horizon from a special hilltop. Making love. A piece of antique jewelry from your grandmother. A friend. Your husband or wife. Something you treasure from the earth that may sit on a home altar or special windowsill. Being with your child. Some object blessed by the touch of someone dear. Someone you love who is far away. Someone you have grieved for. Cooking a meal. Painting. Making furniture. Helping someone. Doing your job. Is there a spot where you played as a child that still shines in your mind? Can you name that place?

Make a list of everyday things in your life; they do not have to be extraordinary. Who and what blesses your life? Name what is sacred to you. This material may later become a poem. For now, just write down what you care about. The word "list" has roots in the word "listen"! Listen to your list.

Names of people, animals, plants, objects, events, experiences, places that are sacred to you:

1. _____
2. _____
3. _____
4. _____
5. _____
6. _____
7. _____
8. _____
9. _____
10. _____
11. _____
12. _____

After you write them down, let these sacred things live in you awhile. Feel them. Leave your list and then come back to it. Say these words or phrases to yourself. Take the feelings of your sacred things deep inside yourself. You'll find poems. They will come to you. Trust what the unknown offers you.

Where the New Place Arises

Wendell Berry, Kentucky farmer and poet, writes about entering into a sacred relationship with the earth—the earth that is new and dying, and then new once again. Resting between these spaces of ending and beginning, of dying and growth, there is the possibility of finding a language that helps us to feel and understand the sacredness of a place. In *Journey's End*, Berry speaks of walking in the woods and knowing himself afresh by knowing the changing earth:

> *I come around a big rock in the stream and two grouse flush in the open not ten steps away. I walk on more quietly, full of the sense of ending and beginning. At any moment, I think, the forest may reveal itself to you in a new way. Some intimate insight, that all you have known has been secretly adding up to, may suddenly open into the clear—like the grouse, that one moment seemed only a part of the forest floor, the next moment rising in flight. Also it may not. . . .*

> *. . . Since I was here last the leaves have fallen. The forest has been at work, dying to renew itself, covering the tracks of those of us who were here, burying the paths and the old campsites and the refuse. It is showing us what to hope for. And that we can hope. And how to hope. It will always be a new world, if we will let it be.*
>
> *The place as it was is gone, and we are gone as we were. We will never be in that place again. Rejoice that it is dead, for having received that death, the place of next year, a new place, is lying potent in the ground like a deep dream.*

The deep dream of renewal Wendell Berry speaks of, walking his Kentucky farmland and woods, is the same deep dream where *roseness* blossoms into the rosebush—it is the deep dream of the sacred where the poet walks; where the new place and the new day and the new year arise.

EXERCISE: FEEL THE SACREDNESS OF A NATURAL PLACE

Visit or visualize a place you have been that touched your heart. A place that ignited your enthusiasm, serenity, and joy. A place that spoke to you about deeper things in life. A place that allows you to feel new insights about who you are or qualities you may have hidden from yourself. If you can go to that place, do so and take a notebook and pen with you. If you cannot actually go there, imagine it—visualize a spot where you can be still or walk quietly. Listen to the many voices of that place. Notice in detail what is around you. The sight and sound, smell and texture of things. Pay attention to your own presence and the presence of the place, together. Feel the essence of that place in your own heart. Feel that place as a friend listens to a friend, let the presence of that place sink into you, as rain sinks into the earth.

> *The poetry of earth is never dead:*
> *When all the birds are faint with the hot sun,*
> *And hide in the cooling trees, a voice will run*
> *From hedge to hedge about the new-mown mead . . .*
> —*John Keats*

Write some lines about your visit. Catch the images and feelings that come up in your experience. You can do this exercise from imagination or direct experience.

_____

_____

_____

*N*ature is our only reliable and authentic teacher.
—*Luther Burbank*

I wrote this next poem after many walks at dusk around the edges of San Francisco Bay. At that time of day, in that fading light, I could feel a beloved to beloved embrace between earth and sky:

BAYLANDS AT SUNSET

To Susan
The names of every thing in this place
fall away with the day
as birds skim upon the breast
of the marsh and then sail
to loosen the brooch of a moon

fastened on the shoulder
of lovely and invisible air,
to loosen the names
that slip away like the gown
the sunlight has brought home
this evening for the horizon to wear.

"... The Frantic Stew of the Whole Day"

Vietnamese poet and meditation teacher Thich Nhat Hanh writes beautifully about finding the sacred in ordinary experience through mindfulness. The following passage from his book *The Sun My Heart* reflects on the sacredness of many ordinary activities. You can apply his words about washing dishes to any other everyday occurrence or ritual. Having a meditative awareness about our everyday activities helps us not only to feel the sacred but to think poetically as well.

The environmental abuses we perpetuate all over the world are largely the results of poetry starvation.

—Brother David Steindl-Rast

WASHING DISHES

To my mind, the idea that doing dishes is unpleasant can occur only when you aren't doing them. Once you are standing in front of the sink with your sleeves rolled up and your hands in the warm water, it is really quite pleasant. I enjoy taking my time with each dish, being fully aware of the dish, the water, and each movement of my hands. I know that if I hurry in order to eat dessert sooner, the time of washing dishes will be unpleasant and not worth living. That would be a pity, for each minute, each second of life is a miracle. The dishes themselves and the fact that I am here washing them are miracles!

If I am incapable of washing dishes joyfully, if I want to finish them quickly so I can go and have dessert, I will be equally incapable of enjoying my dessert. With fork in my hand, I will be thinking about what to do next, and the texture and the flavor of the dessert, together with the pleasure of eating it, will be lost. I will always be dragged into the future, never able to live in the present moment.

Each thought, each action in the sunlight of awareness becomes sacred. In this light, no boundary exists between the sacred and the profane. I must confess it takes me a bit longer to do the dishes, but I live fully in every moment and I am happy. . . .

You can find the sacred right at home. Within the most mundane tasks there is the possibility of encountering the moment in a fresh and delightful way. Eileen Moeller also experienced this in the act of washing dishes:

DOMESTIC POEM

*nightfall I sink
into dishwash meditation
steaming china prayer wheels
crystalline bells of the lost horizon
crockery mandalas
chanting din and lull of running water
breathing slows
moist heat muscles soften
zen poems drip from silverware
my air humming out
in a cleansing melody
washing the frantic stew of a whole day
down the drain
along with the suds
those transient rainbow things
with the thin skin of
a passing instant.*

It is not what we do or what we know that draws forth words revealing the sacred; it's more a question of *how we are in tune with things.* For Eileen Moeller, dishwashing and attention to "a passing instant" was how she caught a "cleansing melody" of fresh images. We have to practice in our everyday lives *how to feel, how to pay attention, how to notice what moves us*—so we can synthesize our experience and feelings to make poems.

"It Seemed, So Great My Happiness, ..."

There is always the unexpected grace that can burst upon us. The Irish poet William Butler Yeats expressed a spontaneous inner awakening of a sacred fire flaming within him in these words from "Vacillation":

My fiftieth year had come and gone,
I sat, a solitary man,
In a crowded London shop,
An open book and empty cup
On the marble table-top.

While on the shop and street I gazed
My body of a sudden blazed;
And twenty minutes more or less
It seemed, so great my happiness,
That I was blessèd and could bless.

We might think that such experiences are reserved for only a select few. Not so. Yeats, though a great poet, was himself surprised by his sudden ecstasy. It is more likely that such sublime events occurring to "regular" people in plain circumstances are not talked or written about as much as they actually happen. In a recent poll taken by a major news magazine, over 58 percent of the people polled in America said that they have had a mystical experience. Even in a world filled with harsh realities and competing egos, awakening to this sense of blessing is in no way out of our reach.

To know the unknown, to see the invisible, to hear the inaudible, and to feel the ineffable is the essence of mystical experience. To hear the inaudible, for instance, doesn't require an effort of self-will or even arduous, formal spiritual practice; but rather, a subtle and receptive turn of heart and inner ear. This shift can be facilitated by sensitively tuning *to the inside of what-*

Eternity is in love with the productions of time.

—William Blake

I believe we are in such a time when civilization has to be renewed by the discovery of new mysteries, by the undemocratic but sovereign power of the imagination, by the undemocratic power which makes poets the unacknowledged legislators of mankind, the power which makes all things new.

—Norman O. Brown

ever you are listening to. Like the bee going inside the rose and sipping nectar, if you sensitively listen *inside* to something particular, it is possible that the sacred will be revealed to you and words will come to you to describe that experience.

At the beginning of this century, the psychologist William James wrote of the availability of these realms just beyond outward experience in this famous passage from his book, *The Varieties of Religious Experience:*

> *Our normal waking consciousness is but one special type of consciousness, whilst all about it parted from it by the filmiest of screens there lie potential forms of consciousness entirely different. We may go through life without suspecting their existence but apply the requisite stimulus and at a touch they are there in all their completeness."*

Sri Aurobindo, a great saint who lived in India during the first half of this century, agreed with James, and further, anticipated the tremendous changes that are occurring now as people begin to awaken to these other realms. Aurobindo realized that the poet has an important role to play in bringing about spiritual awakening in the world. He saw the awakening of humanity as something that would validate the worldview of poets, whose vision is in truth not naïve, but rather presents a far more accurate and complete picture of reality. He writes, in his amazing book *The Future Poetry:*

> *The material realm (too) cannot for very much longer be our sole or separate world of experience, for the partitions which divide it from psychic and other kingdoms behind it are wearing thin and voices and presences are beginning to break through and reveal their impact on our world. This too must widen our conception of life and make a new world and atmosphere for poetry which may justify as perhaps never before the poet's refusal to regard as unreal what to the normal mind was only romance, illusion or dream. A larger field of being made more real to man's experience will be the realm of future poetry.*

The poet is the priest of the invisible.

—*Wallace Stevens*

There are vast realms of consciousness still undreamed of / vast ranges of experience, like humming of unseen harps, / we know nothing of, within us.

—*D. H. Lawrence*

An experience of these "voices and presences" and "atmosphere for poetry" came to me in the course of writing this chapter. I had finished a late evening of writing and had gone to sleep. I had a dream that I was working on this chapter and intently reading at my monitor. Suddenly, the monitor started to rev up, as if it had become a laser printer. The edges where the monitor glass and computer case come together began to part slightly and sheets of paper started to stream out. Alarmed, I didn't yet know that I was dreaming and felt something had gone wrong!

But I began to notice that these pieces of paper had handwritten passages on them and were illustrated with lovely pen and ink drawings, like illuminated manuscripts. I noticed they were signed with names of poets who wrote often of the sacred. These pages continued to stream out of my monitor and float there, encircling the area where I was working.

At that point I became aware that this was not an error but a blessing! I remember tilting my head back as I sat in my chair, looking upward toward the slat board ceiling of the little cottage where I write. The room seemed to fill with cloudlike light and I began to experience a tremendous sense of bliss and peace. I was able to lean back at this point as if held in enormous, loving arms, and enjoy those feelings.

On one hand, one could say this was just a dream. But I refuse to regard that experience as "just" a dream. It felt real and sacred, as if I were being given support from unseen hands in my writing.

We may not talk of them, but all of us have had experiences that we consider special to us, experiences that have changed us in some essential way. They do not have to be "extraordinary" to be special. The plain and simple may reveal to us our most essential nature.

A new age seems to be seeking birth. Much of the new birth will be rebirth of ancient vision; much will be still the proportions of infancy. We are poems in the making: logos at work.

—*M. C. Richard*

EXERCISE: REMEMBERING SPECIAL EXPERIENCES

Remember and visualize a special experience, one that you would consider to be a "peak" or spiritual experience. Here are some suggestions:

- Being in nature
- Helping someone and feeling especially fulfilled as a result
- A higher, special dream
- A time when you felt especially alive and whole: making love, playing with children, doing something challenging, doing something creative
- Doing something simple or mundane and feeling the presence of Spirit
- Experiencing the death of someone close and sensing the presence of that person

Pick one or more of these and journal-write your experience in a detailed and complete way.

Use the journal process outlined in Chapter Six to create a poem from your journal entry. As a further step, choose one significant word or phrase from your journal writing that crystallizes your experience. For instance, the poet quoted below visited the beach, and as she walked, she felt a profound sense of life's vastness but also its delicacy, which she saw in the image of "lacy foam."

> *Lacy edges of foam scallop the beach*
> *stretch to infinity,*
> *mirroring life's vastness;*
> *tiny bright circlets in the foam*
> *turn to sky blue, lilac, and ash,*
> *reflect delicacy—*
> > *both . . .*
> > > *—Laurie La Berge*

Take your own significant word or phrase and use it as a catalyst for a poem. Take this word, feel that you can actually turn it around in the palm of your hand, study it, and let a poem emerge from listening to it.

Hold Infinity in the Palm of Your Hand: Using Metaphor as a Bridge

> *Hold infinity in the palm of your hand*
> *And eternity in an hour*
> > *—William Blake*

I ask participants who attend my workshops to bring an object from the earth that they treasure, or anything that they hold especially dear or that has spiritual significance for them. People bring things like shells, geodes, driftwood, a grandmother's keepsake bracelet, a teddy bear, a fresh sprig of sage, a photograph of themselves as a child, of a family member or of a spiritual teacher, autumn leaves, crystals, a ring, feathers, a favorite cap, a gardenia plant, a walking stick, baby shoes.

We make an altar for these things during the workshop and then take time to place the objects aesthetically on the altar, giving them love, respect, and appreciation. It is extraordinary to see the variety of these treasured articles as the outward sign, an eloquent expression of the inner poets we have always been. Toward the end of the workshop we each gather up our treasure and do a guided meditation and writing exercise that attunes us to the voice of that treasured thing.

One of my workshop students, Kathy Carlson, had brought a horsehair bird's nest she found. Following the guided meditation (see "Hearing the Voice of Treasured Object" at the end of this section), Kathy wrote as the voice and consciousness of the bird's nest spoke to her in its own metaphoric language:

It seems to me that there is in each of us a capacity to comprehend the impressions and emotions which have been experienced by mankind from the beginning.

—Helen Keller

HORSEHAIR BIRD'S NEST

I am the small birds who gathered my strands
And plaited them.
I am the old horses standing in a row.
I am the small grove of windtwisted trees
On the ocean bluff
Their tops knitted together.
I am treetops sailing through fog
Like a ship.
I am the wind that blew me to the ground
To lie tilted on my side
Amid pine cones and broken branches.

I am all that remains of them all.
I too break and pass on
A small fleeting fragile

Wisp of beauty.
Easy to miss.

But in me is the patience and the
Beating hearts of tiny birds.

I held the promise of life once,
Woven from other creatures' lives.
Who will notice them, when they
Quietly drop from the sky
And are no more?

Fleeting moments,
I their only marker,
Easily passed by.
Storyholder
life after life.

Picked up on a hot day
Sweat down your back
Seeking shelter, footsore
Surrounded by people
In a place you usually go to
In solitude.
I found you as you
Had an argument with your father
And decided not to still your voice.

Be the eye that sees me
Pick me up for a time
To remember
To not forget
Small moments, exquisite unseens
Scattered on your path.
But such fragile things as I
Cannot last.

So go back to the grove
On a high windy day in spring

And sail me off the edge
Into the sunset.

In the very first line of her poem, one can hear the bird's voice—singing in the language of metaphor. The nest found her, just as a poem found her. Kathy's poem uses metaphor as a way to move through a whole range of identities, voices, perceptions, and experiences—all connected with the nest. As we already know, metaphor is a device of language that reveals an underlying sameness in apparently different things. Metaphor makes it possible for intangible qualities to take on direct, tangible form. Metaphor is an especially strong device for naming spiritual relationships between things. Kathy could not have noticed the relationships between the horsehair bird's nest and her own life by having a preconceived idea about what to write. She simply "listened" to the essence of the bird's nest, and the poem unfolded.

Kathy naturally felt the flow of metaphor by holding the nest in her hands with love. It is through this expansive, sensitive, intuitive affinity that sacred voices offer themselves to us.

Kathy has worked for over twenty years as a marriage, family, and child counselor and certainly has learned something about the art of listening. The poet side of her, however, had been held in reserve. But over the last five years the insistence of her poetic voice has grown markedly. She wrote me about hearing the voice of the nest and how compelling it was:

> I had planned to keep this bird's nest on my altar—to remind me of improbable fleeting beauty even in a harsh world, woven out of ordinariness and need, a fragile gem. But as I wrote, and sank into connection with its essence, the nest spoke and told me a deeper truth—that I cannot hold onto and freeze things, and that I honor its reality and beauty more by letting it go, open-handed. Even if I forget the nest, its voice is now woven into my own, as are its insights. In letting it go, I have it, alive, in me. . . . Then it is safe to forget, because it is not lost.
>
> What was most moving about the meditation and poetry writing, however, was that the bird's nest spoke to me and told me what was

Imagine the awareness that a leaf may have of the tree's consciousness of its entire self, including that particular leaf. Likewise, behind our individual consciousness lurks a collective consciousness. It is from this level that data are transmitted to the individual consciousness in what we call intuition.

—Pir Vilayat Khan

needed, and it was not what I would have wanted to do. I learned something deeper in listening to its voice than I would have in only listening to my own.

Kathy chose to explore sacred metaphoric connections through a natural object. You might find such metaphoric connections through a spiritual figure, as did another workshop student, Virginia McKim.

Virginia is a woman in her sixties, with bright, sparkling eyes. She had not written much poetry prior to the workshop, but she had written in autobiographical and more experimental ways, partly to develop her intuitive abilities.

During the guided meditation focusing on the sacred, Virginia used metaphor to connect with the spirit of Kuan Yin, the Taoist Goddess of Compassion.

I wrote this poem from the inspiration of the Star card in a tarot deck created by James Wanless. Kuan Yin is represented on this card. I like this tarot deck because the free-form collage of images on each card gives me the freedom to feel the significance of the symbols intuitively.

I came to the moment of writing with a need for the nourishment of Kuan Yin's compassion in order to speak out and know who I am. Who am I? That question is tremendously important to me. Many years ago, in the early 1960s, I was part of the legal research experiments done with psychedelics. In one of my guided sessions, I had an experience of being part of the stars, of being made of star stuff, of oneness with the stars. I remembered that experience of Oneness when looking at Kuan Yin. It has been a goal of mine in recent years to use my writer's voice more, and when all these things came together in this exercise, I found the courage to speak out. The words just fell out of my mouth. Giving myself permission to speak out in whatever way came to me and to be whoever I am somehow led to writing this poem.

Star Woman

Star woman, Kuan Yin, sacred jewel of
luminous lavender jade and sapphire blue;
Sunlit, gold in obsidian sky.

I am the soft white rabbit,
I am the strong snowy egret in flight,
I am off to Oz in a rainbow balloon.

You are a way-shower, servant of the universe,
Pouring iridescent water into my open mouth
so I may speak up and speak out.

I am your sensuous robes.
I am the stars that enfold my heart.
I am the star that I am.

*Through metaphor we pass
from one state of knowing into
the next, ever experimenting,
ever creating, ever flowing, as
the universe does. It is our
state of seeing that makes roses
bloom—in aprons, on paper,
on frozen life paths. Sometimes
this state comes about through
a willful creative leap,
sometimes it arrives as a gift
of grace.*

—Burghild Nina Holzer

EXERCISES

Spiritual Metaphors

If you could choose metaphors to describe yourself and your connection with the sacred, what would they be? It might be anyone or anything that you feel connects you with the Divine, expands your sense of self, joins you with all of humanity and the natural world.

What metaphor could you learn from, as Kathy learned from her horsehair nest? What inspiring metaphor could you identify with, as Virginia identified with Kuan Yin in her poem? Your choices for metaphor can be anything you might think of or imagine. Choose metaphors that evoke feelings such as delight, awe, enthusiasm, power, light, tenderness, and beauty. You could imagine yourself as a flute, a waterfall, a thunderstorm, an enormous wind, the moon or sun, a yearling, a song, or the pounding surf. Name things that attract you. Don't hold back!

My list of metaphors that help me connect with the sacred are:

_____

_____

_____

_____

_____

Now describe yourself as that metaphor, in a way that puts you even more in touch with what is sacred in life. Become that metaphor. For instance:

I am a black bear filled with the power of midnight.
I am the three-day-old foal, my eyes still wet with infinity.
I am the song of dusk inviting the sky to lie down in love and listen.

Write some of your own poetic lines of metaphor:

_____

_____

_____

_____

Metaphor is, after all, a way to know that we are related to everything. When we let the poet that we are sing about our connectedness to life, poems such as this one by N. Scott Momaday emerge:

THE DELIGHT SONG OF TSOAI-TALEE

I am a feather on the bright sky
I am the blue horse that runs in the plain
I am the fish that rolls, shining, in the water
I am the shadow that follows a child
I am the evening light, lustre of meadows
I am an eagle playing with the wind
I am a cluster of bright beads
I am the farthest star
I am the cold of the dawn
I am the roaring of the rain
I am the glitter on the crust of the snow
I am the long track of the moon in a lake

I am a flame of four colors
I am a deer standing away in the dusk
I am a field of sumac and the pomme blanche
I am an angle of geese in the winter sky
I am the hunger of the young wolf
I am the whole dream of these things

You see, I am alive, I am alive
I stand in good relation to the earth
I stand in good relation to the gods
I stand in good relation to all that is beautiful
I stand in good relation to the daughter of Tsen-tainte.
You see, I am alive, I am alive.

Exercise: Hearing the Voice of a Treasured Object

Choose an object that has special value for you, something from nature or anything else that is important to you. It should be something that you can hold comfortably in your hands. If you like, it could be something that you have found especially for this exercise. Just as Kathy found the horsehair bird's nest lying on its side amidst pine cones and broken branches, so you might find something that calls to you. You could choose a flower from your garden, a photograph, some special gift you have received, a keepsake you treasure.

Give yourself time to reflect on your chosen object before you do this exercise. You might want to put it in a special place for a while, perhaps in your special poetry place. Use the interval of time between placing it in this special place and your writing as a time to connect with the voice of your treasure on a deeper than conscious level. You might offer a silent thought or prayer as you begin this process, asking to receive inspiration in your writing. Take some time to breathe into your heart center the essence of this treasure. Ask the Muses to send you a poem. . . .

When you feel ready to write, gather up your treasure and find a comfortable place to sit. Have a notebook and pen by your side. Hold your treasure in your hands. Take a deep breath and release it, allowing any tension and the activity of your day to flow away. Feel the treasure you hold in your hands. Take another deep breath and allow all worries about doing this exercise "right" to flow away from you. Feel the weight and texture of your treasure. Allow yourself to feel this treasure and its value to you. Continue to breathe easily and tune into the sensations in your hands as you hold your treasured object. As you breathe, allow images and feelings to come to you. Picture your treasure in your mind's eye and gaze at it intently. You needn't think of organizing any words or forming any ideas right now, allow what is happening to flow. Watch as these images and feelings emerge.

Continue to breathe easily, holding your treasured object. As you hold it, deepen your sense of being with it by feeling you are listening to it. Listen closely. Listen to the kind of voice your treasure has. Trust your ability to listen right now. Trust your ability to hear. Consider the treasure you have in your hand and the unique message that it brings, the story that it could tell, the song it could sing, the poem it could write. Listen for the tone of your object's voice, the feelings that voice expresses. Take time to listen, just as you might listen to the surf at the ocean. Just as the surf deposits shells on the beach, let words or phrases arise from the object you treasure.

Now with the love that you bring to this deeply valued object, ask it to give you a poem, something it wants you to know, an image or phrase to start with, so you can discover more. Let yourself be a voice for this treasure. Let your impressions begin to take the form of words. What does the voice of your treasure have to say? Follow the stream of feeling and images that come and watch for the ones that seem especially attractive and accurate to you, ones that ask for your attention.

Take some time to breathe . . . and begin to write.

Prayer Poems

Each individual has a subconscious memory of the green earth and murmuring waters, and blindness and deafness cannot rob him of this gift from past generations. This inherited capacity is a sort of sixth sense—a soul sense which sees, hears, and feels, all in one.

—Helen Keller

Prayer is a way to communicate with the Divine. Prayer is a way to love the spirit of whatever is dear to you. Prayer is a way to let your heart cry out. Prayer is a way to come exactly as you are to the Unknown. Prayer is a way to welcome a wider vision of life for yourself.

By prayer, I am not talking about words that are spoken by rote or words imposed upon you from without. I am not actually talking about external words, so much as the vivid, sometimes turbulent, sometimes quiet silences in you that speak to God.

The prayer I am talking about is a very private, silent language of your own heart, which through the force of your longing, begins to make songs or speak words directed toward the essence of things, toward whatever you call Spirit. As Rumi said, "The best form of prayer: say whatever your pained heart chooses."

Prayer is words strung like beads on the thread of your silence.

Remember, God is creativity. I don't want you to even mimic prayers. Create your own prayers. Don't allow it to become like a parrot speaking. I want you to use your own words and allow this creativity to come through. Nobody has a cornerstone on truth.

—*Paramhansa Yogananda*

When I was starting to meditate many years ago, I wrote a prayer asking God to help me. For a long time I let myself feel just what meditation was for me and how I wanted to grow in that practice. I often bring this poem to mind—and it still invokes help and guidance for my meditation practice:

Pure attention is prayer.

—*Simone Weil*

PRAYER FOR A QUIET MIND AND AN OPEN HEART

> *Teach me to set aside*
> *all thoughts of this and that*
> *to remain centered in my heart,*
> *remember God, and let the rest*
> *flow past. To make a still breath*
> *or holy song the poetry*
> *to fill my day, and leave behind*
> *the chatter, clatter in my heart.*
> *To be open to the smallest pulse*
> *of Light felt there, beginning now*
> *to see God in all and everywhere.*

A woman sent me a little prayer poem that poses essential questions that draw to her an answer:

> *am I flesh*
> *or am I spirit*
> *am I exhaling*
> *or am I inhaling*
> *am I dying*
> *or am I being born anew*

> *Yes.*

> —*Denise Ladwig*

In this next prayer poem, the writer asks the Divine to enter into her daily life—in essence, that she stay in contact with "the dreamer" in herself:

THE DREAMER

Pour my eternity
  into the chalice of today
Let me drink, drink, drink
            my journeys down
and travel the night on three white horses
I with a rose
            dangling from my mouth
a star in each eye
a sun in my heart
and the moon to give my crossroads light.
                    —*Sherry Reiter*

Sometimes, a prayer poem is a reminder of what we honor in life. Rilke says, "To praise is the whole thing!" Prayers of praise allow us to make room for everything in our lives, the suffering and uncertainty as well as beauty and light:

Reverence to the trees and mosses, lichens, flowers
Granite face of mountain calling
Lightning cloud and mist descending
Surging wind and roaring rain . . .
. . . Reverence to you,
To him, to it, to her
To never, ever
To be, to wonder and to see
Reverence to the irreverent
To the sacred, blind, outcast, and misjudged
To the sand, the dust, and the furtive desire
To the denier and the denied
The child and the cloud
And the circle closed in upon the Sun
                    —*David Frawley*

The writers of these prayer poems are asking for divine guidance, asking basic spiritual questions, invoking the presence of the Divine in daily life, and making poems of praise. There are endless ways to compose a prayer poem. You could write a prayer poem about your cat or your home, using them as metaphors to talk about the all-embracing Divine. D. H. Lawrence wrote a beautiful poem about the presence of God that included just these things:

PAX

All that matters is to be at one with the living God
to be a creature in the house of the God of Life.

Like a cat asleep on a chair
at peace, in peace
and at one with the master of the house, with the mistress,
at home, at home in the house of the living,
sleeping on the hearth, and yawning before the fire.

Sleeping on the hearth of the living world
yawning at home before the fire of life
feeling the presence of the living God
like a great reassurance
a deep calm in the heart
a presence
as of the master sitting at the board
in his own and greater being,
in the house of life.

With these prayer poems in mind, try writing one of your own. Read the writings and poems of poet sages like Aurobindo, Rumi, and Yogananda; and poems by William Blake, Emily Dickinson, Gerard Manley Hopkins, D. H. Lawrence, and let their words give you inspiration. What are you in awe of? What kind of divine guidance do you wish to receive? What do you love? What reaches your heart in those times when nothing else can? What would you serve and care for wholeheartedly? What do you want to praise? What awakens you to joy?

_____

_____

_____

_____

_____

_____

_____

_____

Each of us inevitable,
Each of us limitless—each of us with his or her right upon the
     earth,
Each of us allow'd the eternal purports of the earth,
Each of us here as divinely as any is here.
                    —Walt Whitman, from "Salut au Monde!"

Suggested Reading

Anthologies

Bernhardt, Mike, ed., *Voices of the Grieving Heart* (Moraga, CA: Cypress Point Press, 1994). Write: Cypress Point Press, P.O. Box 56, Moraga, CA 94556.

Bly, Robert, James Hillman, and Michael Meade, eds., *The Rag and Bone Shop of the Heart: Poems for Men* (New York: HarperCollins, 1993).

Gendler, J. Ruth, ed., *Changing Light: The Eternal Cycle of Night and Day* (San Francisco: HarperCollins, 1991).

Mitchell, Stephen, ed., trans., *The Enlightened Heart* (New York: Harper & Row, 1989). The finest of sacred poetry.

Sewell, Marilyn, ed., *Cries of the Spirit* (Boston: Beacon Press, 1991). A book of poetry by women.

Craft and Creativity

Cameron, Julia, *The Artist's Way: A Spiritual Path to Higher Creativity* (Los Angeles: Jeremy P. Tarcher, Inc., 1992).

Fadiman, James, *Unlimit Your Life* (Berkeley: Celestial Arts, 1989).

Ferrucci, Piero, *Inevitable Grace* (Los Angeles: Jeremy P. Tarcher, Inc., 1990.

Lewis, Richard, *When Thought Is Young: Reflections on Teaching and the Poetry of the Child* (Minneapolis: New Rivers). Available from The Touchstone Center, 141 East 88th St., New York, NY 10128. $7.95.

Packard, William, ed., *The Poet's Craft: Interviews from The New York Quarterly* (New York: Paragon House, 1987). A book of interviews with the finest poets.

Packard, William, *The Poet's Dictionary: A Handbook of Prosody and Poetic Devices* (New York: Harper & Row, 1989).

Rico, Gabriele Luser, *Pain and Possibility: Writing Your Way Through Personal Crisis* (Los Angeles: Jeremy P. Tarcher, Inc., 1991).

Rilke, Rainer Maria, *Letters to a Young Poet,* trans. Stephen Mitchell, (New York: Random House, 1984).

Stafford, William, *Writing the Australian Crawl: Views on the Writer's Vocation* (Ann Arbor: University of Michigan, 1978).

Journal Writing

Adams, Kathleen, *Journal to the Self* (New York: Warner Books, 1990).

———, *Mightier Than the Sword* (New York: Warner Books, 1994).

Holzer, Burghild Nina, *A Walk Between Heaven and Earth: A Personal Journal on Writing and the Creative Process* (New York: Bell Tower, 1994).

Poetry and Healing

Bosveld, Jennifer, and Sandra J. Feen, contr. ed., *Topics for Getting in Touch* (Johnstown, OH: Pudding House Publications, 1994). A creative sourcebook with hundreds of writing ideas. Write: Pudding House Publications, 60 N. Main St., Johnstown, OH 43031.

Coulehan, Dr. Jack, *First Photographs of Heaven* (Troy, ME: Nightshade Press, 1994). A poet physician writes about patients, family, medical practice, and life. Write: Nightshade Press, P.O. Box 76, Troy, ME 04987.

Dion, Susan, *Write Now: Maintaining a Creative Spirit While Homebound and Ill* (Carney's Point, NJ: Puffin Foundation, 1993). Excellent. Write: Susan Dion, 432 Ives Avenue, Carney's Point, NJ 08069.

Hynes, Arleen McCarty, and Mary Hynes-Berry, *Biblio/Poetry Therapy: The Interactive Process* (Boulder, CO: Westview Press, 1986). An excellent book for mental health professionals. Write: North Star Press, P.O. Box 451, St. Cloud, MN 56302.

Leedy, Jack, *Poetry as Healer: Mending the Troubled Mind* (New York: Vanguard, 1985). A classic in the field of poetry therapy. Write: Dr. Jack Leedy, 1049 E. 26th St., Brooklyn, NY 11210.

Lithwick, Dahlia, and Larry Berger, *I Will Sing Life: Voices from the Hole in the Wall Gang Camp* (Boston: Little, Brown, 1992). The poems and stories of children facing life-threatening illness.

Lloyd, Roseann, *Tap Dancing for Big Mom* (Minneapolis: New Rivers Press, 1985). A beautiful and powerful book of poems that deals especially with childhood sexual abuse.

For a listing of works by some of the poets included this book and others not included, see the bibliography—or visit your local library and bookstore.

Resources

The following groups provide information and offer a variety of programs and services related to poetry and poets. There are many groups throughout the country that make it possible to network with other poets and writers. I've not attempted to create a comprehensive list, but in your city, town, or rural area there are most likely poetry readings, writing groups, and other events where writers gather. Events happen in libraries, bookstores, cafés, and many other places. Check your local newspaper or community bulletin board for information about readings, etc. You can also contact your area arts council for information. My thanks to Jane Preston of Poets House in New York City for help in compiling this list.

The following addresses are literary organizations that meet the needs and interests of poets and writers in various regions of the country:

The National Writer's Voice Project of the YMCA of the USA—National Office
5 W. 63rd St.
New York, NY 10023
(212) 875-4261

National Writer's Voice offers programs through YMCA's in local communities. Their mission is to "give voice to people through a democratic vision of literary arts and humanities. [Their] diverse array of programs and services aims to narrow the distinction between artist and audience, and between cultural institutions and the community, making the arts more accessible and life-enriching to the widest possible audience."

Maine Writers' and Publishers'
Alliance
12 Pleasant St.
Brunswick, ME 04011
(207) 729-6333

Poets House
72 Spring St.
New York, NY 10012
(212) 431-7920

Writers and Books
740 University Ave.
Rochester, NY 14607
(716) 473-2590

Just Buffalo
493 Franklin
Buffalo, NY 14202
(716) 881-3211

The Writer's Center
4508 Walsh St.
Bethesda, MD 20815
(301) 654-8664

The Guild Complex
c/o Arts Bridge
4753 N. Broadway Suite 918
Chicago, IL 60640
(312) 278-2210
(312) 907-2189

Woodland Pattern
720 E. Locust St.
Milwaukee, WI 53212
(414) 263-5001

Thurber House
77 Jefferson Ave.
Columbus, OH 43215
(614) 464-1032

Pudding House
60 N. Main St.
Johnstown, OH 43031
(614) 967-6060

The Writer's Place
3607 Pennsylvania
Kansas City, MO 64111
(816) 753-1090

The Poetry Center
University of Arizona
1216 N. Cherry Ave.
Tucson, AZ 85719
(520) 321-7760

The Loft
Pratt Community Center
66 Malcolm Ave. SE
Minneapolis, MN 55414
(612) 379-8999

North Carolina Writers
Network
P.O. Box 954
Carrboro, NC 27510
(919) 967-9540

Hellgate Writers
P.O. Box 7131
Missoula, MT 59807
(406) 721-3620

Beyond Baroque
681 Venice Blvd.
Venice, CA 90291
(310) 822-3006

Intersection for the Arts
446 Valencia
San Francisco, CA 94103
(415) 626-2787

Poetry Center and American
Poetry Archive
San Francisco State University
San Francisco, CA
(415) 338-2227

Eliot Bay Bookstore
1st S & S Main St.
Seattle, WA
(206) 624-6600

Poets in the Schools Programs and Literature in Education:

Geraldine R. Dodge Foundation
154 Christopher St.
P.O. Box 1239
Morristown, NJ
(212) 206-9000
(201) 540-8422

Teachers and Writers
95 Madison Ave.
New York, NY 10014
(212) 691-6590

The Touchstone Center
141 E. 88th St.
New York, NY
(212) 831-7717

Illinois Arts Council
100 W. Randolph, Ste. 10-500
Chicago, IL 60601
(312) 814-6750

California Poets in the Schools
870 Market St. Ste. 657
San Francisco, CA 94102
(415) 399-1565

For General Information About Writing Events, Publications, and Programs Across the Country:

Poets & Writers
72 Spring St.
New York, New York 10012
212-226-3586
800-666-2268 (for California residents)

Poets & Writers is a nonprofit literary organization that serves poets, fiction writers, and performance writers through its various programs and publications. They publish an excellent magazine called *Poets & Writers*. The Information Center can answer specific questions over the phone regarding publishing and calendar dates for national and regional events such as writing conferences, festivals, workshops, and readings.

The Associated Writing Programs
Tallwood House
Mail Stop 1E3
George Mason University
Fairfax, VA 22030
(703) 993-4301

Writer's Conferences & Festivals
P.O. Box 102396
Denver, CO 80250
(303) 759-0519

There are poetry writing festivals in almost all states, with presentations by master poets.

Western States Arts Federation
236 Montezuma Ave.
Santa Fe, NM 87501
(505) 988-1166

CLMP (Council of Literary Magazines and Presses)
154 Christopher St. Ste. 3C
New York, NY 10014

If you are interested in small press poetry publications or want to start one, you can contact CLMP.

For information about journal writing:

The Center for Journal Therapy
Kathleen Adams
P.O. Box 963
Arvada, CO 80001
(303) 421-2298

Kathleen does amazing work in sharing the potentials of the journal.

For information about poetry as healer:

The National Association for Poetry Therapy
P.O. Box 551
Port Washington, NY 11050
(516) 944-9791

The National Association for Poetry Therapy offers publications, seminars, national conferences, certification training, and networking. Association members include therapists, social workers, psychiatrists, physicians, nurses, teachers, librarians, musicians, performers, storytellers, poets, and *anyone who is interested in the use of language for growth and healing.*

Bibliography

Anthologies

Anderson, Maggie, Raymond Craig, and Alex Gildzen, eds., *A Gathering of Poets* (Kent, OH: Kent State University Press, 1992).

Bass, Ellen, and Florence Howe, eds., *No More Masks! An Anthology of Poems by Women* (New York: Doubleday, 1973).

Berg, Stephen, and Robert Mezey, eds., *Poetry: Recent American Poetry in Open Forms* (New York: Bobbs-Merrill Co., 1969).

Dunning, Stephen, Edward Leuders, and Hugh Smith, eds., *Reflections on a Gift of Watermelon Pickle . . . and Other Modern Verse* (New York: Scholastic, 1966).

Fox, John, ed., *Raven's Ink* (Orinda, CA: John F. Kennedy University, 1993).

Howard, Richard, *Preferences* (New York: Viking Press, 1974).

Longo, Perie, Don Campbell, Karin Faulkner, and Toni Wynn, *Waiting to Move the Mountain* (San Francisco: California Poets in the Schools, 1994).

Martz, Sandra, ed., *When I Am an Old Woman I Shall Wear Purple* (Watsonville, CA: Papier-Maché, 1987).

Perkins, David, ed., *English Romantic Writers* (New York: Harcourt Brace Jovanovich, 1967).

Tuthill, Linda, ed., *Ticket to Morning Time* (Cleveland, OH: Sunday Evening Poets, 1994).

Williams, Oscar, ed., *A Pocketbook of Modern Verse* (New York: Washington Square Press, 1965).

Creativity, Ecology, Poetics, and the Writing Process

Bachelard, Gaston, *The Poetics of Space,* trans. Maria Jolas (Boston: Beacon Press, 1964).

Behn, Robin, and Chase Twitchell, *The Practice of Poetry* (New York: HarperPerennial, 1992).

Berry, Wendell, *Recollected Essays 1965–1980* (New York: North Point Press, 1981).

Bradbury, Ray, *Zen in the Art of Writing* (Santa Barbara, CA: Joshua Dell Editions, 1994).

Fox, John, "The Smallest Sprout: The Restorative Power of Poetry," *The Journal of the Healing Health Care Project,* 2:4 (1994), pp. 22–25.

Heard, Georgia, *For the Good of the Earth and Sun* (Portsmouth, NH: Heinemann, 1989).

Hesse, Hermann, *My Belief: Essays on Life and Art* (New York: Farrar, Straus & Giroux, 1974).

Hyde, Lewis, *The Gift: Imagination and the Erotic Life of Property* (New York: Vintage Books, 1983).

Kriyananda, Swami, *Meaning in the Arts* (Nevada City, CA: Crystal Clarity, 1978).

May, Rollo, *The Courage to Create* (New York: Bantam, 1980).

Mayes, Frances, *The Discovery of Poetry* (New York: Harcourt Brace Jovanovich, 1987).

McKim, Elizabeth, and Judith W. Steinbergh, *Beyond Words: Writing Poems with Children* (Green Harbor, MA: Wampeter Press, 1983).

Rico, Gabriele Luser, *Writing the Natural Way* (Los Angeles: Jeremy P. Tarcher, Inc., 1983).

Snyder, Gary, "The Real Work of Gary Snyder," *New Age Journal* 5:12 (June 1980), pp. 26–30.

Steindl-Rast, Br. David, "Nature and the Poetic Intuition," *Ephiphany Journal,* Spring 1983.

The Poet's Journal: A Personal Notebook with Quotes (Philadelphia: Running Press, 1986).

Turner, Alberta, *50 Contemporary Poets: The Creative Process* (New York: David McKay Co., 1977).

Yeats, W. B., *Essays and Introductions* (New York: Macmillan, 1961).

Healing

Bosveld, Jennifer, "Poetry Therapy: Should We Take It Seriously?", *Peranondon: A Magazine for Poets and Writers* 8 (June 1984).

Claremont de Castillejo, Irene, *Knowing Woman: A Feminine Psychology* (New York: HarperColophon, 1974).

DeMaria, Michael B., "Poetry and the Abused Child: The Forest and the Tinted Plexiglass," *Journal of Poetry Therapy* 5:12 (1992).

Ferris, Beth, "Pilgrim on the Road of Love," *Northern Lights Journal,* 1989.

Gorelick, Kenneth, "Greek Tragedy and Ancient Healing: Poems as Theater and Asclepian Temple in Miniature," *Journal of Poetry Therapy* 1:1 (1987).

Heller, Peggy Osna, "The Three Pillars of Poetry Therapy," *The Arts in Psychotherapy* 11 (1987), pp. 341–344.

Keirsey, David, and Marilyn Bates, *Please Understand Me: Character and Temperament Types* (Buffalo, NY: Prometheus Books, 1978).

Leedy, Jack, and Sherry Reiter, *Poetry in Drama Therapy* (New York: Drama Book, 1981).

Lerner, Arthur, *Poetry and the Therapeutic Experience* (St. Louis, MO: MMB Music, 1994).

McNiff, Shaun, "The Shaman Within," *The Arts in Psychotherapy* 15 (1988), pp. 285–291.

Morrison, Morris R., "The Use of Poetry in the Treatment of Emotional Dysfunction," *The Arts in Psychotherapy* 5 (1978), pp. 93–98.

Parabola Book of Healing (New York: Continuum, 1994).

Reed, M. Ann, "The Bardic Mystery and the Dew Drop in the Rose: The Poet in the Therapeutic Process," *The Journal of Poetry Therapy* 6:1 (1992).

Vaughn, Frances, *The Inward Arc, Healing & Wholeness in Psychotherapy & Spirituality* (Boston: Shambala, 1985).

Journals and Journal Writing

Alcott, Louisa May, *The Journal of Louisa May Alcott,* ed. Joel Meyerson, Daniel Shealy, and Madeline B. Stern (Boston: Little, Brown, 1989).

Carey, Ken, *Flatrock Journal: A Day in the Ozark Mountains* (San Francisco: HarperSanFrancisco, 1994).

Dillard, Annie, *Pilgrim at Tinker Creek* (New York: Harper Magazine Press, 1974).

Ginsberg, Allen, *Journal: Early Fifties, Early Sixties,* ed. Gordon Ball (New York: Grove, 1977).

Levine, Stephen, *Planet Steward: Journal of a Wildlife Sanctuary* (Santa Cruz, CA: Unity Press, 1974).

Lloyd, Roseann, and Richard Solly, *Journey Notes: Writing for Recovery and Spiritual Growth* (New York: Harper/Hazelden, 1989).

Matthiessen, Peter, *Nine-Headed Dragon River: Zen Journals 1969–1985* (Boston: Shambala, 1986).

Merton, Thomas, *A Vow of Conversation 1964–1965,* ed. Naomi Burton Stone (New York: Farrar, Straus, & Giroux, 1988).

Nin, Anaïs, *The Diary of Anaïs Nin 1939–1944,* vol. 3 (New York: Harcourt Brace Jovanovich, 1974).

Spender, Stephen, *Journals: 1939–1983* (London: Faber and Faber, 1986).

Truitt, Anne, *Turn: The Journal of an Artist* (New York: Viking, 1986).

Poetry

Berry, Wendell, *Collected Poems 1957–1982* (New York: North Point Press, 1985).

Blake, William, *The Poetry and Prose of William Blake* (New York: Doubleday, 1970).

Cummings, e. e., *A Selection of Poems* (New York: Harcourt Liveright, 1926).

———, *73 Poems* (New York: Liveright, 1963).

———, *Complete Poems 1904–1962* (New York: Liveright, 1991).

Dickinson, Emily, *Complete Poems* (Boston: Little, Brown, 1960).

Eliot, T. S. *Four Quartets* (New York: Harcourt Brace Jovanovich, 1943).

Elytis, Odysseus, *Axion Esti,* trans. Edmund Keeley and George Savidis (Pittsburgh: University of Pittsburg Press, 1974).

———, *The Sovereign Sun,* trans. Kimon Friar (Philadelphia: Temple University Press, 1974).

———, *Selected Poems,* trans. Edmund Keeley and Philip Sherard (New York: Penguin Books, 1981).

———, *The Little Mariner,* trans. Olga Broumas (Port Townsend, WA: Copper Canyon, 1988).

Fox, John, *My Hand Touches the Sea* (Palo Alto, CA: Open Heart Publications, 1984).

————, *When Jewels Sing* (Palo Alto, CA: Open Heart Publications, 1989).

Francis, Robert, *The Orb Weaver* (Middletown, CT: Wesleyan University Press, 1960).

Gibran, Kahlil, *The Prophet* (New York: Knopf, 1993).

Ginsberg, Allen, *Collected Poems 1947–1980* (San Francisco: Harper-Collins, 1984).

————, *Howl and Other Poems* (San Francisco: City Lights Books, 1993).

Hesse, Hermann, *Journey to the East,* trans. Hilda Rosner (New York: Farrar, Straus & Giroux, 1956).

Hirshfield, Jane, *Of Gravity and Angels* (Middletown, CT: Wesleyan University Press, 1988).

Hughes, Langston, *The Collected Poems of Langston Hughes* (New York: Knopf, 1994).

Jeffers, Robinson, *The Selected Poetry of Robinson Jeffers* (New York: Random House, 1959).

Kabir versions by Robert Bly, The Kabir Book. (Boston: Beacon Press, 1977).

Keats, John, *The Selected Poetry of John Keats* (New York: New American Library, 1966).

Kelly, Robert, *The Loom* (Santa Rosa, CA: Black Sparrow Press, 1975).

Kerouac, Jack, *The Scripture of the Golden Eternity* (New York: Corinth, 1970).

Krysl, Marilyn, *More Palomino, Please, More Fuchsia* (Cleveland, OH: Cleveland State University Poetry Center, 1980).

Lawrence, D. H., *Selected Poems* (New York: Viking, 1959).

Levertov, Denise, *Poems 1960–1967* (New York: New Directions, 1983).

Levine, Philip, *New Selected Poems* (New York: Knopf, 1991).

Lorca, Federico García, and Juan Ramón Jiménez, *Selected Poems,* trans. Robert Bly (Boston: Beacon Press, 1973).

Lorde, Audre, *The Cancer Journals* (San Francisco: Spinsters / Aunt Lute, 1980).

Milne, A. A., *The House at Pooh Corner* (New York: E. P. Dutton, 1961).

Milosz, Czeslaw, *Selected Poems* (Hopewell, NJ: The Ecco Press, 1973).

Momaday, N. Scott, *In the Presence of the Sun: Stories and Poems 1961–1991* (New York: St. Martin's, 1992).

Moore, Marianne, *The Complete Poems of Marianne Moore* (New York: Macmillan, 1967).

Neruda, Pablo, *100 Love Sonnets,* trans. Stephen Tapscott (Austin, TX: University of Texas, 1959).

———, *A New Decade: Poems 1958–1967* (New York: Grove Press, 1969).

Oliver, Mary, *Dream Work* (Boston: Atlantic Monthly Press, 1986).

———, *House of Light* (Boston: Beacon Press, 1990).

Piercy, Marge, *Circles on the Water* (New York: Knopf, 1982).

Pound, Ezra, *Selected Poems of Ezra Pound* (New York: New Directions, 1957).

Rilke, Rainer Maria, *Duino Elegies,* trans. Gary Miranda (Portland, OR: Breitenbush Books, 1981).

———, *Selected Poems of Rainer Maria Rilke,* trans. Robert Bly (New York: Harper & Row, 1981).

Rumi, Jelaluddin, *Open Secret,* trans. Coleman Barks and John Moynes (Putney, VT: Threshold Books, 1984).

———, *Unseen Rain,* trans. John Moyne and Coleman Barks (Putney, VT: Threshold Books, 1986).

———, *We Are Three,* trans. Coleman Barks and John Moynes (Putney, VT: Threshold Books, 1987).

———, *The Longing,* trans. Coleman Barks and John Moynes (Putney, VT: Threshold Books, 1988).

———, *Love Is a Stranger,* trans. Kabir Helminski (Putney, VT: Threshold Books, 1993).

———, *Daylight: A Daybook of Spiritual Guidance,* trans. Camille and Kabir Helminski (Putney, VT: Threshold Books, 1994).

Sandburg, Carl, *The Complete Poems of Carl Sandburg* (New York: Harcourt Brace Jovanovich, 1970).

Snyder, Gary, *Turtle Island* (New York: New Directions, 1974).

Stevens, Wallace, *The Palm at the End of the Mind,* ed. Holly Stevens (New York: Vintage, 1971).

Tagore, Rabindranath, *Collected Poems and Plays* (New York: Macmillan, 1937).

TallMountain, Mary, *Light on the Tent Wall* (Los Angeles: University of California, 1990).

Thomas, Dylan, *Collected Poems of Dylan Thomas 1934–1952* (New York: New Directions, 1957).

Whitman, Walt, *Complete Poetry and Prose of Walt Whitman* (New York: Pellegrini and Cudahy, 1948).

Wiley, David, *Designs for a Utopian Zoo* (Raleigh, NC: The Paper Plant, 1992).

Williams Carlos, William, *Picture from Brueghel and Other Poems* (New York: New Directions, 1962).

————, *Selected Poems* (New York: New Directions, 1968).

Yeats, William Butler, *The Collected Poems* (New York: Macmillan, 1974).

Yogananda, Paramhansa, *Whispers from Eternity* (Los Angeles: Self Realization Fellowship, 1949).

————, *Songs of the Soul* (Los Angeles: Self Realization Fellowship, 1983).

Spirituality

Aurobindo, Sri, *The Future of Poetry* (India: Sri Aurobindo Ashram, 1953).

Berry, Thomas, *The Dream of the Earth* (San Francisco: Sierra Club Books, 1988).

Carey, Ken, *Starseed: The Third Millennium* (San Francisco: HarperSanFrancisco, 1991).

Frawley, David, *From The River of Heaven* (Salt Lake City, UT: Passage Press, 1990).

Hain, Marcia Glaubman, and Sherry Reiter, *Twice Chai: A Jewish Road to Recovery* (New York: Coordinating Council of Bikur Cholim, 1991).

Hirshfield, Jane, ed., *Women in Praise of the Sacred: 43 Centuries of Spiritual Poetry by Women* (New York: HarperCollins, 1994).

Khan, Hazrat Inayat, *The Music of Life* (Santa Fe, NM: Omega Press, 1983).

Kriyananda, Swami, *The Path* (Nevada City, CA: Crystal Clarity, 1977).

Levine, Stephen, *A Gradual Awakening* (New York: Anchor, 1979).

Lewis, Samuel, *In the Garden* (San Cristobal, NM: Lama Foundation, 1975).

Swimme, Brian, *The Universe Is a Green Dragon* (Santa Fe, NM: Bear and Co., 1984).

Tagore, Rabindranath, *Towards Universal Man: A Poet's School* (New York: Asia Publishing House, 1961).

Walsh, Roger, and Frances Vaughn, *Accept This Gift* (Los Angeles: Jeremy P. Tarcher, Inc., 1983).

Yogananda, Paramhansa, *Autobiography of a Yogi* (Los Angeles: Self Realization Fellowship, 1974).

Copyrights and Permissions

The author has made every effort to trace the ownership of all copyrighted materials in this volume, and believes that all necessary permissions have been secured. If any errors or omissions have inadvertently been made, proper corrections will gladly be made in future editions.

Thanks are due to the following authors, publishers, publications, and agents for permission to use the material included:

Introduction

Octavio Paz: *The Collected Poems of Octavio Paz 1957-1987.* Copyright © 1986 by Octavio Paz and Eliot Weinberger. Reprinted by permission of New Directions Publishing Corp., New York.

James Broughton, lines from "For a Gathering of Poets," by James Broughton, with the permission of Kent State University Press. Copyright © 1992. Kent, Ohio. 44242.

Chapter One

Reprinted from *The Universe Is a Green Dragon,* by Brian Swimme. Copyright © 1984 Bear & Co., Inc., P.O. Box 2860, Santa Fe, NM 87504.

Chapter Two

Chapter Three

Chapter Four

Excerpt from *Writing the Australian Crawl,* by William Stafford. Reprinted with permission of University of Michigan Press, Ann Arbor. Copyright © 1977. First published in *Field 2,* © 1970.

"Moonstruck," by Carole Dwinell. Printed by permission of the author.

"e. e. cummings," by Carole Dwinell. Printed by permission of the author.

"Rock Hopping Creek," by Jack Winkle. Printed by permission of the author.

"Pah Tempe, Utah," by Connie Smith Siegel. Printed by permission of the author.

Chapter II, "In Which Tigger Comes to the Forest," from *The House at Pooh Corner* by A. A. Milne. Illustrations by E. H. Shepard. Copyright © 1928 by E. P. Dutton, renewed © 1956 by A. A. Milne. Used by permission of Dutton Children's Books, a division of Penguin Books USA, Inc.

"You," by Ian Begg. Printed by permission of the author.

Dylan Thomas: *Early Prose Writings.* Copyright © 1972 by The Trustees for the Copyrights of Dylan Thomas. Reprinted by permission of New Directions Publishing Corp., New York.

Marilyn Krysl, lines from "Saying Things," from *More Palomino, More Fuchsia,* by Marilyn Krysl. Reprinted by permission of Cleveland State University Poetry Center and the author.

"Spidery Grandmother," by Jamie Pearlstein. Printed by permission of the author.

"Remember the fertile trees from where you . . ." by Eric Kallman. Printed by permission of the author.

"Slavery takes away his right to choose . . ." by Matt Moore. Printed by permission of the author.

"Above that ocean . . ." by Judy Davidson. Printed by permission of the author.

Chapter Five

"I am a pomegranate . . ." by Christine Stiegelmeyer. Printed by permission of the author.

"I am purple . . ." by Christine Stiegelmeyer. Printed by permission of the author.

"To a Piece of Paper," by David Wiley, from *Designs for a Utopian Zoo.*

"1939," by Phyllis Williams. Printed by permission of the author.

"Clydie," by Phyllis Williams. Printed by permission of the author.

"Cousin Clydie," by Phyllis Williams. Printed by permission of the author.

Chapter Six

"Razored words pour fourth like jagged rain . . ." by "Anne." Printed by permission of the author.

"A single star, like a beauty mark . . ." by Phyllis Williams. Printed by permission of the author.

"Reappraisal," by Linda Tuthill. Printed by permission of the author.

Excerpt from *The Diary of Anaïs Nin 1939–1944,* Volume III. Copyright © 1969 by Anaïs Nin, reprinted with permission of Harcourt Brace & Company, Orlando, FL.

From *Journals 1939–1983,* by Stephen Spender, ed. by John Goldsmith. Copyright © 1986 by Stepehn Spender. Reprinted by permission of Faber and Faber Ltd., London.

Excerpt from journal entry dated June 6, Pentacost, 1965, from *A Vow of Conversation,* by Thomas Merton. Copyright © 1988 by the Merton Legacy Trust. Reprinted by permission of Farrar, Straus & Giroux, Inc., New York.

"One Paragraph from Page 86," from *Pilgrim at Tinker Creek,* by Annie Dillard. Copyright © 1974 by Annie Dillard. Reprinted by permission of HarperCollins Publishers, Inc., New York.

From *Journals, Early Fifties, Early Sixties,* by Allen Ginsberg, edited by Gordon Ball. Copyright © 1977 by Allen Ginsberg. Reprinted by permission of Grove/Atlantic, Inc., New York.

Kathleen Norris, lines from "Mrs. Schneider in Church," by Kathleen Norris. Reprinted from *The Year of Common Things,* Wayland Press (Denver), 1989. Reprinted by permission of the author.

Lines from *Selected Poems,* by Witter Bynner. Copyright © 1978 by The Witter Bynner Foundation. Reprinted by permission of Farrar, Straus & Giroux, Inc., New York.

From *Collected Poems 1947–1980,* by Allen Ginsberg. Published by HarperCollins, 1984. Copyright © 1984 by Allen Ginsberg. Reprinted by permission of the author.

Chapter Seven

From *Circles on the Water,* by Marge Piercy. Copyright © 1982 by Marge Piercy. Reprinted by permission of Alfred A. Knopf, Inc., New York.

"Range of Light: The Story of a Writing Circle," by Katrina L. Middleton. Printed by permission of the author.

"The Writing Circle," by Perie Longo. Previously published in the California State Poetry Quarterly, Winter '93. Reprinted by permission of the author.

"building family," by Debra Hiers. Printed by permission of the author.

"The Poetry Writing Workshop," by Peter Hastings. Printed by permission of the author.

Chapter Eight

Jane Hirshfield, "To Drink," from *Of Gravity & Angels.* Copyright © 1988 by Jane Hirshfield, Wesleyan University Press, by permission of University Press of New England, Hanover, NH.

"I wish my mother could have warned me about . . ." by Onie Kriegler. Printed by permission of the author.

"this child" by Roseann Lloyd was originally published in *Tap Dancing for Big Mom,* New Rivers Press, 1985. Reprinted by permission of the author.

"The Real Names of Coal," by Bob Evans. Printed by permission of the author.

"My Roots Are There in the Darkness," by Jeanie Lawrence. Printed by permission of the author.

"Reflections," by Alma María Rolfs. Printed by permission of the author.

"Those Hands," by Alma María Rolfs. Printed by permission of the author.

William Carlos Williams: *Collected Poems: 1909–1939,* Volume I. Copyright © 1938 by New Directions Publishing Corp. Reprinted by permission of New Directions Publishing Corp., New York.

"Weeping Cherry," by Connie Smith Siegel. Printed by permission of the author.

"Sunday," by Mike Bernhardt, from *Voices of the Grieving Heart.* Copyright © 1994 by Cypress Point Press, P.O. Box 56, Moraga, CA 94556. Reprinted by permission of the author.

"Secret Message," by Mike Bernhardt, from *Voices of the Grieving Heart.* Copyright © 1994 by Cypress Point Press, P.O. Box 56, Moraga, CA 94556. Reprinted by permission of the author.

"Buds at the End of Winter," by Mike Bernhardt, from *Voices of the Grieving Heart.* Copyright © 1994 by Cypress Point Press, P.O. Box 56, Moraga, CA 94556. Reprinted by permission of the author.

Beth Ferris, lines from "Fishing with Floyd," by Beth Ferris. Printed with permission of the author.

"I am gentle as a raindrop . . ." by Perie Longo. Printed by permission of the author.

"Your mind holds so many strong, wonderful thoughts . . ." by Cecily Longo. Printed by permission of the author.

Chapter Nine

The lines from "I thank You God for most this amazing . . ." are reprinted from *Complete Poems, 1904–1962,* by e. e. Cummings, edited by George J. Firmage, by permission of Liveright Publishing Corp., New York. Copyright © 1950, 1978, 1991 by the Trustees for the e. e. Cummings Trust. Copyright © 1979 by George James Firmage.

Reprinted from *The Universe Is a Green Dragon,* by Brian Swimme. Copyright © 1984 Bear & Co., Inc., P.O. Box 2860, Santa Fe, NM 87504.

"Baylands at Sunset," by John Fox, from *When Jewels Sing.* Copyright © 1989 by John Fox. Published by Open Heart Publications, P.O. Box 60189, Palo Alto, CA 94306.

Excerpts from "The Journey's End" from *Recollected Essays 1965–1980,* by Wendell Berry. Copyright © 1981 by Wendell Berry. Reprinted by permission of North Point Press, a division of Farrar, Straus & Giroux, Inc.

Reprinted from *The Sun My Heart,* by Thich Nhat Hanh (1988) with permission of Parallax Press, Berkeley, California.

"domestic poem," by Eileen Moeller. Reprinted by permission of the author.

Lines from "Terra Incognita" by D. H. Lawrence, from *The Complete Poems of D. H. Lawrence,* edited by V. de Sola Pinto and F. W. Roberts. Copyright © 1964, 1971 by Angelo Ravagli and C. M. Weekley, Executors of the Estate of Frieda Lawrence Ravagli.

Index

Children
    creative freshness of, 85–89, 91
    playfulness of, 94
    poems by, 84–85, 89, 91
    sensibilities of, 89–90
    sexual abuse, 221–23
Circles, images of, 183–84
Circles, writing. *See* Writing circles
Clifton, Lucille, 215
Clustering technique, 174
"Clydie," 143–44
Cohen, Leonard, 43
Colao, Flora, 221
Coleridge, Samuel Taylor, 145
Communication, 118–19
Completeness, 67
"Complications," 73–74
Conformity, 65
Connection, with life, 68
Constructive criticism, 199
Coulehan, Jack, 72–74
"Councils," 182–83
"Cousin Clydie," 144
Creativity, 178
    reconnecting with natural, 57–82
Creeley, Robert, 228
Criticism, 199
cummings, e.e., 43, 65, 96, 125,
    199, 245
Curtis, Edward F., 139

D

Dass, Ram, 17–18
Davidson, Judy, 115
Dead Poets Society (movie), 24
"Delight Song of Tsoai-talee, The,"
    262–63
Details, 156–59
Dialogue, 171
Dickinson, Emily, xi, 117, 126, 188
Dickinson, Ken, 85
Dillard, Annie, 176, 182, 245

"Domestic Poem," 252
Down's syndrome, 243
"Dreamer, The," 266
Dreams, 145–46, 173, 206–7
Dwinell, Carole, 13, 94

E

Eberhardt, Richard, 49
Eckhart, Meister, 136
Eddy, Jeremy, xi-xii, 34–36, 43
Einstein, Albert, 87
Eliot, George, xiii
Elytis, Odysseus, 146, 212, 242
Emerson, Ralph Waldo, 3, 176, 202
Emotions. *See* Feelings; Mixed
    emotions
Enright, John, 40–43
Entrance meditations, 17, 164
Evans, Bob, 227
Everson, William, 57
Everwine, Peter, 185
Everyday life, 5–9, 172–73
Experiences
    first with poetry writing, 58–64
    words resulting from, 33–42

F

Fadiman, James, 81, 93, 151
Faith, 242
Family relationships, 218–33
Faulkner, William, 176
Feedback, 198, 202
Feelings, 32, 141, 152, 173, 216–17
    See also Mixed emotions
Ferguson, Marilyn, 202
Ferris, Beth, 4, 152, 175, 242
Ferrucci, Piero, 8, 40, 133, 236
First Photographs of Heaven (Coulehan),
    72
Fleming, Ginny, 127

Forché, Carolyn, 49
Fox, John, 58, 81, 114, 242
Fox, Matthew, 132
Francis, Robert, 61
Frawley, David, 266
Free-writing, 172
Frost, Robert, 48
Fry, Christopher, 135
Fuentes, Carlos, 221
Future Poetry, The (Aurobindo), 254

G

Gawain, Shakti, 215
Gender, 192
Gibran, Kahlil, 63, 245
Ginsberg, Allen, 9, 18, 36, 129,
    176
Goethe, 90
Goldberg, Natalie, 153, 197
"Goodbye," 40–42
Gorelick, Kenneth, 189–90
Gratitude, 230–33
Graves, Robert, 37, 43
Green, Paul, 91, 102
Greifer, Eli, 214
Grief. *See* Sorrow
Griffin, Adrian, 48

H

Haiku, 6
Haines, John, 224
Hastings, Peter, 209
Healing
    exercises, 223–24, 230, 233–34,
        238
    and poetry, 211–44
    and writing circles, 187–90
Heller, Peggy Osna, 215
Henry, Ted, 76–78, 86
Hesse, Hermann, 14

Hiers, Debra, 209
Hillman, James, 216
Hirshfield, Jane, 216
Holzer, Burghild Nina, 17, 20, 70, 147, 189, 261
Homer, 102
Hopkins, Gerard Manley, 247
"Horsehair Bird's Nest," 257–59
House at Pooh Corner (Milne), 101–2
Houston, Jean, 159
Hughes, Langston, 22, 26–27
Hugo, Victor, 23
Hyperbole, 92–93

I

Illness as Metaphor (Sontag), 72
Images, 130–38
    catching, 137
    of circles, 183–84
    dream, 206–7
    entering, 136–7
    exercises, 91, 127, 131, 135–46, 206–7
Imagination, 110
Impulse writing, 103–4
"In Praise of Ironing," 124
"Inside," 71–72
Intimacy, 13, 33, 34, 186

J

James, William, 91, 254
Jeffers, Robinson, 31
Johnson, Don Hanlon, 77
Jones, Mary, 62
Jong, Erica, 132
Jonson, Ben, xv
Joubert, Joseph, 196
Journal to the Self (Adams), 154
Journal writing, 147–78
    exercises, 149, 170–78

Journey to the East (Hesse), 14
Jung, Carl, 145

K

Kallman, Eric, 114
Kaptchuk, Ted, 213
Keats, John, 126, 179, 250
Keen, Sam, 24
Keller, Helen, 257, 264
Kelly, Mary, 28
Kennedy, John F., 5
Kenyon, Jane, 125
Khan, Hazrat Inayat, 24, 73, 107
Khan, Pir Vilayat, 259
King, Martin Luther, Jr., 5, 48
Kinnell, Galway, xi, 69, 215
Kircher-Allen, Noah, 89
Klappert, Peter, 139
Kriegler, Onie, 25, 218–20
Krysl, Marilyn, 107
Kuan Yin (goddess), 260–61
Kumin, Maxine, 235
Kunitz, Stanley, 99

L

La Berge, Laurie, 256
Ladwig, Denise, 265
Laing, R. D., 32
"Lake Isle of Innisfree, The," 11, 46–47
Lamartine, Alphonse de, 191
Language
    as play, 83–115
    See also Words
"Late Night Cycling," 77–78
Laurence, Lynn R., 162
Lawrence, D. H., 16, 66, 215, 254, 267
Lawrence, Jeanie, 230
Leedy, Jack, 212, 214–15

Le Guin, Ursula K., 57
Levertov, Denise, 31, 59
Levine, Philip, 48, 57
Levine, Stephen, 36
Lieberman, Saundra, 74–76
Lindbergh, Anne Morrow, 152, 201
Line breaks, 97–101
Lipschultz, Marla, 82
"Listen," 13
Listening, 13–16, 34
    and journal writing, 152–56
    to music, 44–46
    and writing circles, 196–99
Lloyd, Roseann, 223
Longo, Perie, 78, 209, 243
Lorde, Audre, 34, 66–67
Loss, 234–42
"Lost Love," 37, 43

M

McDonald, Cynthia, 96
McDonald, Michelle, 11
MacKenzie, Rosemary Sharon, 33–34, 43
McKim, Virginia, 260
McNeal, Mary-Lee, 36–38, 43, 69–72
McNiff, Shaun, 129
McPherson, Sandra, 17
Maslow, Abraham, 202
Matthews, William, 126, 158
Maxwell, Flonda Scott, 220
May, Rollo, xiv, 185, 196, 227
Mazzaro, Jerome, 157
Meditation, 49–50
Memorization, 46–48
Merton, Thomas, 176
Merwin, W. S., 101
Metaphors, 50, 72, 118–25
    as bridges, 256–61
    exercises, 119–20, 124–25, 261–63

multiple, 121–22
organic, 123–24
Middleton, Katrina, 192, 200
Milarepa (Tibetan poet), 186
Miller, Alice, 94
Milne, A. A. 101–3
Milosz, Czeslaw, 12
Minneapolis (Minn.), 7
Minty, Judith, 1, 179
Miró, Joan, 153
Mixed emotions, 224–30
Moeller, Eileen, 252
Momaday, N. Scott, 262
"Moonstruck," 95
Moore, Marianne, 1, 21, 47
Moore, Matt, 114
Moore, Thomas, 213
Morrison, Morris R., 211
Morrison, Toni, 238
Moss, Richard, 2, 40, 230
Mother Teresa, 10
Music, 44–46
"My Roots Are in the Darkness,"
229–30
Mystical experiences, 253–55

N

"Naked Ladies," 39
Nathan, George Jean, 243
National Association for Poetry
Therapy, 215
Native Americans, 212, 229
Nedicine, 72–73
"Negro Speaks of Rivers, The,"
26–27
Nelson, Kimberley, 68, 141
Neruda, Pablo, 123–24
Nguyen Chi Thien, 239
Nin, Anaïs, 147, 175, 185
"1939," 142–43
Northrup, F. S. C., 40

O

O'Keeffe, Georgia, 13
Olds, Sharon, 215
Onomatopoeia, 92
Openness, 93

P

"Pah Tempe, Utah," 100
Pain, 218–24
    See also Sorrow
Palkhivala, Aadil, 160
Parents, 218–20, 224–33
Particulars. See Details
Partners, 141–42
Pascal, Blaise, 123
"Pax," 267
Paz, Octavio, xiv
Pearlstein, Jamie, 108
Perse, St. John, 19, 65, 118
Peck, Andrea, 185
Pennsylvania Hospital, 213–14
Perfectionism, 19, 20
Permission, 18–19, 21–22
Perspective, 171
Philadelphia (Pa.), 6
Photographs, 139
Phrases, 174
Piercy, Marge, 182, 192
Pinker, Steven, 104
Places, 141
Plato, 211
Poems Aloud (symposium), 216
Poetry
    as act of magic, 211–13
    as common ground, 242–44
    in everyday lives, 5–9
    first experiences with, 58–64
    and healing, 7, 211–44
    imagery, 130–46
    and journal writing, 148–78

language as play, 83–115
line breaks, 97–101
memorizing, 46–48
as return to "most human," 2–5,
27–29
sacredness expressed through,
245–68
therapy, 8–9, 213–16
writing circles, 179–209
Poetry Motel (TV program), 7
Poets in the Schools program, 5
"Poet's Voice Is Knocking, The,"
37–38
Point of view, 171
Ponge, Francis, xv
Portrait. See Character sketch
Postcards, 139
Pound, Ezra, 27, 45, 126, 127
Praise, 266
"Prayer for a Quiet Mind and an
Open Heart," 265
Prayer poems, 264–68
"Prayerwheel for William, A,"
130–31
Prose poem, 64, 203

R

Raman, Chip, 137
Range of Light (writing circle),
200–203
"Real Names of Coal, The," 225–27
"Reappraisal," 159, 160–61, 164,
167, 169–70
Receptivity, 16–18
Reclaiming Your Inner Poet
questionnaire, 78–82
Reiss, James, 44
Reiter, Sherry, 215, 266
Relatedness, 185–87
Resistance, 22–23
Respect, 197
Rice, Janet, 190

About the Author

John Fox, CPT, is a poet, certified poetry therapist, and a lecturer in the Graduate School of Psychology at John F. Kennedy University in Orinda, California. He is the author of two volumes of poetry, *My Hand Touches the Sea* and *When Jewels Sing* (audio tape). John also teaches in the California Poets in the Schools Program. He serves as a vice president on the executive board of the National Association for Poetry Therapy. For information about John's public workshops, consultations, conference presentations, and audio tapes of talks and poetry, please contact: John Fox, CPT, P.O. Box 60189, Palo Alto, CA 94306.

Discover more of yourself with Inner Work Books.

The following Inner Work Books are part of a series that explores psyche and spirit through writing, visualization, ritual, and imagination.

The Artist's Way: A Spiritual Path to Higher Creativity   BY JULIA CAMERON

At a Journal Workshop (revised edition): *Writing to Access the Power of the Unconscious and Evoke Creative Ability*   BY IRA PROGOFF, PH.D.

Ending the Struggle Against Yourself: A Workbook for Developing Deep Confidence and Self-Acceptance
BY STAN TAUBMAN, D.S.W.

The Family Patterns Workbook: Breaking Free of Your Past and Creating a Life of Your Own   BY CAROLYN FOSTER

Following Your Path: Using Myths, Symbols, and Images to Explore Your Inner Life
BY ALEXANDRA COLLINS DICKERMAN

The Inner Child Workbook: What to Do with Your Past When It Just Won't Go Away   BY CATHRYN TAYLOR, M.F.C.C.

A Journey Through Your Childhood: A Write-in Guide for Reliving Your Past, Clarifying Your Present, and Charting Your Future   BY CHRISTOPHER BIFFLE

Pain and Possibility: Writing Your Way Through Personal Crisis   BY GABRIELE RICO

The Path of the Everyday Hero: Drawing on the Power of Myth to Meet Life's Most Important Challenges
BY LORNA CATFORD, PH.D., AND MICHAEL RAY, PH.D.

Personal Mythology: Using Ritual, Dreams, and Imagination to Discover Your Inner Story
BY DAVID FEINSTEIN, PH.D., AND STANLEY KRIPPNER, PH.D.

The Possible Human: A Course in Extending Your Physical, Mental, and Creative Abilities   BY JEAN HOUSTON

The Search for the Beloved: Journeys in Mythology and Sacred Psychology   BY JEAN HOUSTON

Smart Love: A Codependence Recovery Program Based on Relationship Addiction Support Groups   BY JODY HAYES

A Time to Heal Workbook: Stepping-stones to Recovery for Adult Children of Alcoholics
BY TIMMEN L. CERMAK, M.D., AND JACQUES RUTZKY, M.F.C.C.

True Partners: A Workbook for Building a Lasting Intimate Relationship
BY TINA B. TESSINA, PH.D., AND RILEY K. SMITH, M.A.

Your Mythic Journey: Finding Meaning in Your Life Through Writing and Storytelling
BY SAM KEEN AND ANNE VALLEY-FOX

To order call 1-800-788-6262 or send your order to:

Jeremy P. Tarcher, Inc.
Mail Order Department
The Putnam Berkley Group, Inc.
P.O. Box 12289
Newark, NJ 07101-5289

For Canadian orders:
P.O. Box 25000
Postal Station "A"
Toronto, Ontario M5W 2X8

_____	The Artist's Way	0-87477-694-5	$12.95
_____	At a Journal Workshop	0-87477-638-4	$15.95
_____	Ending the Struggle Against Yourself	0-87477-763-1	$14.95
_____	The Family Patterns Workbook	0-87477-711-9	$13.95
_____	Following Your Path	0-87477-687-2	$14.95
_____	The Inner Child Workbook	0-87477-635-X	$12.95
_____	A Journey Through Your Childhood	0-87477-499-3	$12.95
_____	Pain and Possibility	0-87477-571-X	$12.95
_____	The Path of the Everyday Hero	0-87477-630-9	$13.95
_____	Personal Mythology	0-87477-484-5	$12.95
_____	The Possible Human	0-87477-218-4	$13.95
_____	The Search for the Beloved	0-87477-476-4	$13.95
_____	Smart Love	0-87477-472-1	$9.95
_____	A Time to Heal Workbook	0-87477-745-3	$14.95
_____	True Partners	0-87477-727-5	$13.95
_____	Your Mythic Journey	0-87477-543-4	$9.95

Subtotal $_____

Shipping and handling* $_____

Sales tax (CA, NJ, NY, PA, VA) $_____

Total amount due $_____

Payable in U.S. funds (no cash orders accepted). $15.00 minimum for credit card orders.
*Shipping and handling: $2.50 for one book, $0.75 for each additional book, not to exceed $6.25.

Enclosed is my ☐ check ☐ money order
Please charge my ☐ Visa ☐ MasterCard ☐ American Express
Card # _____ Expiration date _____
Signature as on credit card _____
Daytime phone number_____
Name _____
Address _____
City _____ State _____ Zip _____

Please allow six weeks for delivery. Prices subject to change without notice.

Source key IWB